Also by Stephen Box

the Way – to achieve success

A Convenient Liaison

PREJUDICE IN LOVE

The Odd
Patients

Blind Ambition

has a Price

Stephen Box

Blind Ambition
has a Price

Stephen Box

Twitter: @theStephenBox
www.thestephenbox.com
www.amazon.com/author/stephenbox
univest@runbox.com

Published 30th August 2023

ISBN: 978-1-7396765-4-4 (sc)
ISBN: 978-1-7396765-5-1 (e)

About this book

This book is intended as a social fable to discuss a number of current aspects of society that challenge relationships and convention.

Ambition is the driver that propels people forward in life, motivating and inspiring them to be successful. But blind ambition can lead to one's demise, infecting anyone and everyone involved. In Shakespeare's 'Macbeth' blind ambition is shown to be the primary cause of the destruction of those around Macbeth and eventually leading him to his own destruction. This problematic characteristic has wedged its way into humanity for many years including our modern society.

When focussed on achieving goals life is full of choices, and you tend to make choices that will bring you closer to your goal. If blind to unintended consequences ambition can prove divisive. To succeed and achieve your dreams on your terms, it's important to maintain a life balance.

An underlying theme throughout this book is the choices we make in life. For example, we cannot choose our 'blood family' but we can choose the people with whom we want to share our lives as family. However, we must be alert to the potential impacts and conflicts with conventional society, and especially when 'blood family' and family collide seeking priority.

About the Author

His life has been filled by one adventure after another having started as a Nuclear Physicist at the Atomic Energy Research Establishment, Harwell, UK. During the 'brain drain' of the mid-1970's he transitioned into the world of international banking using his skills with computers and mathematics and where he ultimately participated in developing the Global financial village post deregulation of capital movement and the breakdown of communism with special emphasis of engaging with developing economies to better the lives of their people. When Stephen's career as a noted International Banker was truncated by health issues, his adventurous spirit turned to writing to fill the downtime, both recording his adventures and using novels to comment on observation of social issues in today's world.

Chapter 1

There is a freshness in the air this beautiful May morning as Richard pulls into the tennis club car park with a mixture of expectation and trepidation. He is about to play with his new partner, Elizabeth, in a round robin, three sets of mixed doubles. Having met her casually at the club several times over the space of a few months he has now committed, at her behest, to be her regular partner for Thursday morning tennis club mixed doubles and other club tournaments. This is his first social commitment for some years, and it feels like a first date where expectations are high. He has shown his prowess as a tennis player at the club for some months, but with no pressure to win matches. He is now expected to support a specific partner, and work as a partnership to achieve results.

As he entered the reception area of the clubhouse, he eyes Elizabeth talking with friends. Little did he know she shared his trepidation and had taken a great deal of subconscious preparation to look her best. She has taken a keen interest in her new partner, feeling unusually warm towards this recent addition to the club. She acknowledged his arrival, made her excuses, and made her way to greet him. 'Hello Richard. Very nice to see you. We're playing Simon and Jennifer for the first set. Do you need to warm up?'

'Good morning, Elizabeth. You look radiant. And yes, it would be useful to hit a few balls before we start.'

Elizabeth blushed but felt comforted with his charm. She wants to know this man both as a player, and as a man. He is very attractive, has an assured presence, but unusually remote. During previous après tennis socialising she had probed but learned little of this man other than he had recently moved to Lincolnshire from London and not married. For a man of his age, she had noticed he is agile on court and has a lethal first serve. She has great expectation of their partnership on court but has fantasised about what might develop off-court.

1

She piled six balls onto her racquet and led the way to the indoor courts. They found an unoccupied court and started to hit a few balls at each other. As he found the timing of his swing, she could feel the increase in power in his shots and reassured by the accuracy of his placement. '*He'll be a good partner*' she thought.

He indicated he would like to practise his serve. She obliged by feeding him balls. He started with a few simple serves to find his range. She observed his unorthodox service action which she had never seen before in her years of playing. But she had also seen the effectiveness of this serve so was not about to pass any comment other than encouragement.

He increased the power of his service, and which were all finding their target. He then stood longer in his preparation before moving his foot to the service line, which was the initial movement in a continuous motion delivering a serve with snap. The ball shot across the net, bounced on the service line, refused to rise above knee height, and passed over the baseline in an instant. This was the shot which had first prompted her to watch his play. Although his success rate with this serve was only around 50% it was unreturnable when accurate and thus a potential key point winner. She loved to watch this service action which resembled a perfectly executed ballet movement – continuous and graceful.

She collected a few balls and practised her own serve noting he was watching her action and placement. He needed to know her serve, so he knew where to best position himself for a return. She felt somewhat lame in her service power compared with his, but she had a high success rate of first service and thus reliable to get the ball into play. After some minutes it was time to start the round-robin, so they gathered their kit and moved towards the play courts. Elizabeth asked him if he had a preferred strategy of play.

'As we have only played together on an ad hoc basis could I suggest a strategy that might work for us and then re-evaluate after a couple of sets?'

'What do you suggest?'

'As you may have noted I do not do orthodox, nor am I conventional. I do what I think maximises our chances of winning. Your shots are not powerful, but you read your opponent well and your placement is mostly accurate. Therefore, I propose, as a general principle, when I serve you play the net and I'll cover the baseline, and anything you miss. When you serve you move towards net cover, and I'll move back as needed. We must be careful not to leave any holes between us therefore if you can imagine a rope connecting us at the waist which length is the distance between us if our racquets are fully extended towards each other then we should never be separated beyond this length. Does this make sense to you?'

She looked at him in amazement. Such precise instructions. No-one had ever been so specific, and certainly not so unconventional. 'Okay, let's try, and see how we do.'

Simon and Jennifer were both in their fifties and had played together for some years. Neither were power players, but they had a tight and proficient game using attrition to beat their opponents into submission. Richard had watched them play and knew the longer the rally the more likely they would win the point.

Simon won the racket spin and elected to serve. Elizabeth preferred to play forehand and thus she would receive the first serve of the game. Richard stood just left of the centre line within the ad service box, so he had full view of the ball toss, the strike, and the travel of the ball. Elizabeth managed a defensive return which was intercepted at the net by Jenifer who skilfully placed it into the tram lines past Richard. The next service to Richard was treated with somewhat more contempt; aimed and placed at the left foot of the server before departing the back of the court without so much as a glancing touch. Richard suggested to Elizabeth she should step half a pace back giving her more time to see the serve and then drive her return wide of the backhand of Jenifer. This worked as Jennifer was not protecting her backhand side.

Simon and Jennifer won the first game, but only after two deuces. Richard won his service game much more convincingly after advising Elizabeth where and how to intercept any return. Richard did not approve of power serves to female opponents, so Jennifer was more likely to return, but mostly defensive.

The set progressed and finally won 6-4 by Richard and Elizabeth. Elizabeth was delighted at both the win, and the way Richard worked with her to maximise their opportunities. Albeit strange to her, his strategy proved very effective. However, the next pair would be a more challenging task. No less than the club champions Andrew and Deborah, with a very feminist lead. Elizabeth had never won a set against this pair and had no illusions about their chances today.

Richard elected to start the set. He could feel Elizabeth's lack of confidence. He took her to the back of the court. 'Elizabeth, this pair are good, but they are conventional players, not champions. They will not expect us to play differently. Please forget who they are and let's test our strategy. If we can hold our own, or even beat them then it will prove our partnership and strategy.'

'Okay Richard, but you need to help me all the way.'

Richard was serving to Andrew so unleashed a full snap serve which hit its mark and passed by the returner unchallenged. Elizabeth looked at Richard with an approving smile 'great serve'.

'I'll put the next serve wide on the backhand of Deborah. I'll cover the centre and you cover the left wing.'

The serve was heavily sliced to her forehand, but she connected, driving the ball directly at Elizabeth who was fast enough to position the ball onto her forehand and drive it through the hole left in the centre of the court. She was clearly very pleased with herself. Perhaps her new partner was about to cause some turmoil with these two.

Richard served another full snap serve to Andrew who only touched the ball with the rim of his racquet.

Again, Richard served a far less vicious serve to Deborah, who returned the ball, starting a rally, which she won. However, she was clearly not happy with Richard. She approached the net to speak with Richard. 'Why are you treating me like some fragile female with your serves? You are perfectly at liberty to serve as you please, and I'm offended you feel it necessary to restrain your serve to me.'

Richard was taken aback with the vitriolic tone of her voice. 'You're right in that I am at liberty to serve as I please, and it does not please me to power serve at any female.'

Elizabeth, as the long-standing club member, thought she should intercede on behalf of Richard. 'Deborah, this is not a tournament and there are no prizes at stake. Richard is relatively new to the club, and we are playing for the first time as partners, feeling our way into a mode of play. Richard knows the power of his snap serve and thus has no desire to cause any pain to anyone. However, if you would like to receive such a serve, then I'm sure Richard will oblige on his next serve on the full understanding that should you get hurt, you have no complaints.'

Deborah responded with a gruff 'understood'.

Richard had witnessed divas like Deborah at other clubs, and he always resented such an attitude. In his 20s he played at the Barnes Tennis Club in London. In the semi-finals of the club championship him and his partner defeated the club champions, who were odds-on favourites to win the tournament. This defeat was achieved by playing a net and baseline strategy rather than conventional side-by-side. The club champions did not accept their defeat gracefully instructing the club secretary to meticulously scan the Lawn Tennis Association Rules to see if they could declare such strategy illegal and thus overturn the result. They were unsuccessful, but he was so outraged he never played there again.

His next serve to Deborah was a fully loaded snap serve swerving to her body. Deborah was standing far too close to the baseline for such a serve and could not move her body fast enough. The ball struck her abdomen with full power. She immediately winced, released her racquet, and dropped to the floor, clearly in much distress. *'Game and set over'* he thought to himself.

Richard took no interest in the ensuing commotion deciding to find a seat at courtside and take a drink from his water flask. Elizabeth engaged in the commotion but the telling smile on her face when she returned to Richard suggested she was not displeased with the result.

'I assume they forfeit the set' was all Richard could muster.

The two remaining sets were only eventful in that Richard and Elizabeth won both. Elizabeth was visibly delighted. Not only had they beaten all opposition, including the club champions, but she could feel Richard had frequently surveyed her approvingly during the morning. This gave her a warm glow not least because she had done much the same with him.

As they were walking back to the reception area, he turned to her 'Would you like to come back to my place for lunch to celebrate our victorious partnership?'

She looked into his eyes 'what a wonderful idea. I have my car, so you lead, and I'll follow.'

Chapter 2

Driving home Richard reflected on the morning, his attraction to Elizabeth, and where he thought this relationship might be going. All he really knew about her was she had lost her husband a little over two years ago to cancer or similar illness. He appears to have left her financially comfortable. She is probably in her early fifties. Beautiful – but not in a glamorous way. Obviously cultured, but very easy and sociable. He had also heard she had a daughter, Jessica, in her early 20's and trying to start her own internet business having graduated from university last year. He found Elizabeth very attractive, and his instinct told him they would be good for each other.

As he approached the gates to his property, he slowed to let her close the gap between them so the electric gates did not close on her. The electronic detection system attached to the gates noted his approach and started their gentle slide open. By the time his Range Rover arrived at the entrance they were fully open allowing both cars to enter with no need to wait. He led her some fifty metres along the main drive past the gatehouse bungalow to an area to the front of the left-hand side of the main house which was laid for visitors, so their vehicles did not need to obscure the beautiful facade of his home.

Elizabeth got out of her car and stood beside him gazing at this magnificent house as he recovered his tennis bag from the rear of his car. 'So, this is your home. I have driven past here a few times during construction, and there has been much local chatter about the size of this property, and who might need such a large house. It's truly beautiful – very large, but beautiful.' She paused for a moment to digest the unusual nature to the facade. 'Your architect clearly does not like sharp corners. All the corners are rounded – must have been hell to build.'

'Do you not think the eye feels a little let down when it follows a wall, and the wall just ends with nowhere for your eye to explore further. A rounded wall encourages your eye to want to follow the curve round to see what is beyond. This is part of the magic of design in the Art Deco period.'

'Is this an Art Deco design?'

'No, not really. I have a passion for Art Deco design philosophy and my dream was to incorporate specific elements into a more contemporary building. Come, let's go inside.'

When they approached the oversized front door, he did not use a key, merely placed his finger on a plate on the wall, cleverly concealed from the casual observer. The door recognised the master of the house, released the latch, and opened to allow entry.

He guided her through the door into the spacious hallway. She took one step inside and gulped at the splendour as she tried to digest the beautiful lines of wide staircases on both sides curvaceously winding their way up the double height void to the first floor. The elegant maple balustrade growing out of the highly glossed burred walnut stair treads reminded her of the incredible sets in glamorous 1940s Hollywood movies. 'Richard, this is magnificent. I feel overwhelmed just looking at it.'

'Thank you. Much love and care went into this house. It's a long-held dream fulfilled. Let's go through to the gym so I can off-load my bag.'

He led her through the hallway, along a corridor and then right, down two steps, through a double door into a spa area. To the right she observed a well-equipped gym, whilst on the left was a changing area. However, her gaze was attracted to the 30m indoor pool flanked on one end with a spa pool, and the other side by a lounging area with large sliding doors onto what looked like a quadrangle garden. Whilst he dropped his tennis bag in the gym, she continued to the edge of the pool next to a low diving board. The lining of the pool was not traditional tiles but glistened like multi-coloured glass making patterns on the water.

He followed her and stood by her side. Without taking her gaze from the water 'What a beautiful pool. How did you get the coloured effect on the pool walls?'

'Instead of conventional tiling I used a coloured glass blasting technique used in grottos. It leaves a perfectly smooth multi-colour glass finish which reflects any light source through the coloured glass crystals. 'Come, have a swim. It will freshen us for lunch.'

He was already sitting on the diving board removing his tennis shoes and socks. 'But I don't have a costume with me.'

He continued to undress himself 'why do you need one. Those windows are only transparent one way, and swimming naked is far more refreshing.'

As she was about to defer this invitation, he dived into the water naked. She looked at him as he glided through the water towards the other end. He turned towards her and waved her in 'come on, don't tell me you're shy.'

She thought for a moment *'he's one strange man, but what the hell.'* She was quickly undressed and slipped into the water not wanting to get her hair wet.

She quickly found the water refreshing, and he was right – swimming naked was a whole new and pleasant experience. She swam towards him. When she reached him, she found she could stand with the water at shoulder height.

'Are you okay?' he asked her.

'Other than wondering how I find myself swimming naked with a man I hardly know, I feel great.' With a twinkle in her eye and a smile 'Now we are here let us swim a little before you fulfil your invitation to feed me.'

They swam a few lengths before he suggested they go shower ready for lunch. He took her hand and guided her up the steps in one corner of the pool and led her to the open showers in the changing area. There were two shower heads, and he turned both on as he directed her to one.

She used the available shower gel to wash her body whilst facing him knowing he was watching her. But his eyes did not display any characteristics of a voyeur or a predator, and he made no attempt to even approach her, let alone touch her. She could not put her finger on what she felt, but she was just as comfortable next to him as she was when showering in the open shower area at her local gym. She had to admit to herself she was also enjoying the view of this man. He was not overtly muscular, but clearly lean and fit. Even at his age there was little sign of tummy sag. And his bottom was lovely.

Richard switched off his shower, brushed off excess water with his hands and left the shower to find towels. He returned with two bath towels just as she was leaving her shower. They each dried off before Richard reached for towelling robes hanging on the wall. She noted there were three robes in a row on hooks – a small, medium, and large size. He helped her into the medium robe which felt very nice on her skin. He used the large robe and then slid his feet into Crocs that were lying on the floor below the robes. 'There will be a size that will fit you' as he pointed to the row of new Crocs.'

'I thought I would retrieve my clothes and get dressed.'

'Why, after such a refreshing swim and shower, would you want to put on clothes in which you have played tennis all morning?'

'Because I don't have any other clothes with me.'

'Why not just stay in your robe for lunch and you can get dressed before you leave? Bring your clothes and let them air in the laundry room just over there', pointing to a door off the corridor leading back to the main house.

She could find no suitable objection, and the robe felt good, so she did as he suggested.

'It's time for lunch so let's scout the kitchen to see what we can find.' As he led the way 'would you prefer champagne or Prosecco. I have both, so whichever you prefer.'

'I think Prosecco would be less intoxicating at this time of day, and I have to drive home later.'

Chapter 3

Upon reaching the kitchen Elizabeth stood in awe at the sheer scale of this room. The length of the main work area was easily 10m and there was a further 2m wide island separating the main work area from the eating area which comprised a round table, easily capable of sitting eight people with 180 degrees of this table surrounded by leather-covered bench seating with four further chairs around the remaining 180 degrees. She noticed the worktops were similar in style to the burred walnut steps on the staircases, but were granite, with maple kitchen base units. 'How many people live here to justify such an enormous kitchen? Do you cook yourself?'

He smiled at her 'I live in this house alone, and I cook. In fact, I enjoy cooking, especially when I have delightful guests to feed.'

'So you do really intend to feed me', she smiled playfully.

'Let us examine the menu possibilities so I can take madam's order.'

Just at that moment Audrey, the housekeeper walked into the kitchen. 'Aaah Richard, it's you'. She looked at Elizabeth 'Aren't you Mrs Sandiman from the village?'

'Yes, I am.'

Richard quickly intervened 'Elizabeth, this is Audrey, my housekeeper. Audrey, this is Elizabeth, my new tennis partner.'

Audrey continued 'so lovely to meet you. And I'm so sorry about your dear husband. My husband, Gerry, knew your husband well as your husband wanted to buy part of our land for a new development. We owned Blythe Farm, but your husband died before a deal could be completed.'

'So you're Audrey Roswell, and you have two sons, Michael and James.'

'That's right.'

'What happened to Blythe Farm?'

'Neither of our sons wanted to continue farming, and both are out in the big wide world seeking their own life. The farm became too much for Gerry and me alone so when we saw this opportunity, and then met this lovely man, we sold the farm and moved here. I take care of the house and Gerry takes care of everything outside. We have the bungalow by the main gate where we're very comfortable, and we just love working here.'

Audrey paused and then continued 'and what about you? Your daughter Jessica was at university so you must live in that big house of yours all alone.'

'Jessica has now finished university and has moved back home with me. She wants to set up an internet business so I'm helping her with it. It was lonely after my husband died, but now she's back I feel much happier.'

'Please give Jess our best wishes.'

Richard was listening intently to this exchange not sure whether to interrupt and get back to lunch or continue to listen as he was gaining valuable information about both women.

Audrey looked at Richard 'what were you looking for in the kitchen?'

'I was investigating what I could prepare as lunch for this dear lady.'

Audrey looked at Elizabeth 'it's late for lunch but I can quickly organise a cold plate, or give me around 15 minutes, and I can prepare some fresh pasta, and bread I made this morning. What would you prefer?'

'If it's really no trouble the fresh pasta and fresh bread sounds delicious.'

'Go sit on the terrace with whatever it is you're drinking, and I'll bring it out to you. It's a shame to be inside on such a lovely day. Off you go.'

With that instruction he grabbed the bottle of Prosecco, two glasses, and directed Elizabeth out to a table on the terrace which was part of the quadrangle surrounded on three sides by the house. To their left was the indoor swimming pool and spa complex, and to the right stylish garaging for his various cars. She could see the pool windows were one way as she could see nothing inside.

Once their glasses were filled, he proposed a toast to the success of the morning tennis, and to their new partnership. She concurred.

'Richard, now we're so intimately introduced, who are you, and what are you doing in this sleepy annex of England?'

He thought for a moment, smiling at this lovely woman who is clearly confused by the events of today. 'I'm prepared to answer your question in two ways dependent upon your answer to a proposal I wish to make.'

'Go on.'

'I appreciate we're not long acquainted, albeit, as you put it, intimately introduced, I instinctively feel I can trust you and, as partners, we can confide in each other. If you are prepared to respect my privacy, and thus not disclose what I would like to share with you I can be open. If you feel such a request is a burden you do not wish to bear, then I can disclose very little.'

'Why all the secrecy?' not understanding the need.

'You may have noticed I'm not a conventional person, nor do I have any ambition to become one. My way of life confuses many people which makes them feel uncomfortable with me. I have no desire to cause anyone any distress as this can lead to ugly misunderstandings. I'm an outsider and which can cause irrational behaviour by conventional thinkers. Therefore, the less people know about me the better. I can generally orchestrate enough to stop people prying into my affairs. Does this make any sense to you?'

She looked intently into his eyes. He was very serious about this issue which, coincidently, made her feel somewhat privileged. 'I'm very flattered you feel such trust in me. I knew from the moment I met you all those weeks ago you were different – not distant, but very private. My feelings are I dearly want to know you and therefore I give my word to you that what you deem to be private and privileged information will go to my grave with me.'

He reached for her hand. She could see his sharp brown eyes welling up. 'Thank you.'

'My name is Richard Lyons. I'm 57 years old. I have dedicated my working life to media strategy which means I develop advertising campaigns and trailers for media such as movies. I have a partner, Jim Spencer, who is a genius at graphic design, and now lives at Totten Place, the large Tudor house close to here – and where I lived for the sixteen months it took to build this house. We have been partners since our mid-twenties, since when we built a formidable global advertising company.'

He became reflective. 'Two years ago, Jim had a serious heart attack. The way we worked inevitably, either or both of us would pay the price. We got ourselves lost in our success and became wedded to our work having little or no social life, or sleep. Jim was worse than me. I would say he averaged about three hours sleep per day, plus occasional power naps, 24/7 for over twenty years. The demand for his genius and my creative skills meant we were flooded with work, and we made a lot of money.'

'I sat with Jim in the hospital after his surgery reflecting on our lives. We agreed we had lost sight of life. Jim's heart attack was a wake-up call. Neither of us had relationships. I divorced over ten years ago, and Jim has never married. Something had to change. We decided then we both had enough wealth for the rest of our lives. But we needed to take serious account of our health so we would live long enough to enjoy the spoils of our success. We agreed to sell the company, my house in London, and to move far enough away to avoid the trappings of easy access to us, but neither of us want to completely stop working. Lincolnshire proved to be the most laid-back county in England, and transport systems are less than convenient. Thus, why we're here.'

At this point Audrey appeared with lunch. She placed a large tray on the table with all the accoutrements needed, even down to olive oil and balsamic vinegar should they choose to soak the wonderful country loaf in it as tradition would dictate in Italy. Elizabeth thanked her for her efforts and she returned to the kitchen.

'Shall I serve while you refresh our glasses?'

He had been so focussed on his speech he had overlooked her empty glass. He decided he would not resume until after they had eaten.

'I'm surprised you're still awake after such a depressing start to my story.'

She placed her hand over his 'On the contrary I sense a lot of pain in this story and thus why you want to share it with someone you can trust. I want to hear all you want to tell me no matter how long it takes.' She returned to her lunch 'this pasta is delicious. You've done well with Audrey.'

'It is perhaps worthwhile explaining how I work with Audrey and Gerry as this is as unconventional as everything else in my life. But they love it, and it works for me. I don't expect Audrey to serve me or any of my guests as in traditional service. Her primary role is to keep the house working. I do as much cooking for her and Gerry as she does for me. We mostly have breakfast and dinner together which also gives us the opportunity to discuss matters domestic. I treat them like family, and they respond well to this idea. If Gerry needs help in the garden, or in the woodland we work together as equals except when he knows far more than I do in which case I'm his assistant taking instruction where necessary. Gerry also acts as my chauffeur on the rare occasions I need him. You have seen Audrey calls me by my Christian name as I do with them. We're a team and I trust them implicitly.'

Elizabeth looked up from her food. 'I realised while we were in the kitchen the relationship was different to a conventional housekeeper so thank you for telling me how it works as I don't want to inadvertently offend Audrey or Gerry.'

As an afterthought 'what do you have against conventional?'

'Nothing at all. It provides a very cosy environment for most people. It's ordered so everyone knows the rules, and how to behave. Most creative people find such a system stifling to creativity and thus why the more gregarious creative types appear odd. They're far from odd. They just cannot live within a rule-based system. If you really think about it, creative people formulate the environment we would deem today, politely, as progressive, or less politely, as extreme. Yet this creativity of today more or less becomes the conventional of tomorrow. As you get to know me, I'll show you how creativity today can offend, yet tomorrow will be deemed as exceptional art. It's easier for me to show you what I mean rather than try to explain it.'

'I have a feeling you will open my mind to a whole new world. I've lived in this quiet countryside for much of my life, but I appreciate there is a different world out there, and now you're telling me there is a further layer to this world where you reside.'

'Does the thought of my world cause you any anxiety?'

She looked him straight in the eyes 'today you encouraged me to strip naked and throw myself into a swimming pool with a near stranger on the premise swimming without clothes would feel great. It did. Then you lead me off to the showers where we casually shower together, and now we have lunch in just our dressing gowns. Conventionally I should feel strange about these activities. But I don't feel any anxiety at all. If anything, I feel very calm and relaxed enjoying a pleasant afternoon with someone very interesting, and dare I say special. I feel privileged, despite your privacy, you're prepared to let me see into your world. For myself I find it incredible I feel comfortable to go with you wherever you take me.'

She paused. 'Now we have finished lunch can we continue with your story.'

'I need some coffee. Can I get you anything?'

'Coffee, white, no sugar would be good.'

He reloaded the tray and took it back to the kitchen. This gave Elizabeth a little time to reflect on the events of today. If someone had told her yesterday she would strip naked and jump into a swimming pool with a stranger she would have laughed at them. Yet she did it. And would readily do it again with this man. She recounts he has not attempted to touch her, and she has no problem with him observing her, even when naked. She certainly felt a thrill to observe him naked. It was rarely she could observe a naked man without having to fend him off. Richard had behaved like a perfect gentleman throughout the day, even in his dealings with Deborah the diva who would unlikely challenge him again.

Richard returned with the coffee. 'I should ask you how long you can stay as I'm being somewhat greedy with your time. For me you can stay for as long as you wish. I have no plans for the rest of the day, and I enjoy your company.'

'I have no plans either other than dinner with Jessica around 7pm. I should phone her to tell her where I am, but my mobile is in my bag, which is in your changing area.'

'Can I suggest rather than vocalise what I do now, I show you my studios and give you a flavour of what we do. Of course, our work is secret. Competitors would pay serious money for confidential work in progress. You can also call Jessica from my study.'

'I would also like to see more of this wonderful house of yours.'

'If you've finished your coffee, let's get started.'

Chapter 4

They took their cups back to the kitchen and then started with the dining room which doubled as a conference room. He opened the double entry doors to reveal a dining room capable of comfortably seating twenty people.

'What a beautiful dining table.'

Audrey's voice piped in from the far end of the room where she was busying herself 'he made that table in his workshop.'

Elizabeth looked at him 'you made this table?'

'I both designed it and made it.'

'When in your busy lifestyle do you have the time to both learn how to make it, and then to put in the hours to make it?'

'Before media dominated my life, I loved working with wood. The building of this house gave me the opportunity to restart this passion and has proven very therapeutic. Both Jim and I agreed to a one-year Garden Leave clause in the company sale agreement, so I had plenty of time to put a workshop together in one of the existing barns.'

The voice of Audrey broke in again 'you wait till you see the bedroom doors. They're so beautiful I'm afraid to touch them.'

'Enough Audrey. You're embarrassing me. Let's move on before Audrey tells you all my secrets.'

'Praise where praise is due boss' came a giggle from Audrey.

They moved back into the corridor. Pointing to the other side of the hallway he told Elizabeth that the various living areas all occupied that section of the house, but she could see these later. He guided her up the circular staircase to the first floor. He explained that the area over the ground floor living space comprised bedrooms and a guest suite. Over the kitchen and dining room end was his workspace and wanted to show her his studios and study.

'Wait, a minute. At least show me the bedroom doors Audrey is afraid to touch.'

He turned back towards the bedroom area and guided her to the first bedroom. She looked at the door. Took a step back to get a better look. And then moved in closer to get a detailed look.

'You made this door yourself?'

'All but the stained glass which I had commissioned for each door.'

The door was a solid beech construction with a typical Art Deco beach relief elegantly curved around the top of the door down past the handle to the bottom of the door. About one third in from the door edge there was a narrow cut-out, approximately one-meter-long into which there was a long stem stained-glass flower in an Art Deco style allowing the light in the room to project the image of this gorgeous flower onto the landing. The door was framed with a three-tiered Art Deco moulding softening the weight of the door.

'Audrey's right. I've never seen a more beautiful door in my life. Your artistic skills are incredible. I can't wait to see what you do in your studios if this is just a hobby. Richard, I'm overwhelmed with the sheer magnificence of this door.'

'We refer to the bedrooms by the flower in the door. This is the iris suite.'

'So, each door has a different flower?'

'That's the general idea.'

She went to the next door, and the next, until she had seen all of them. She then returned to him and reached out to hold both of his hands. 'This is truly an amazing house; and you built it. My husband developed some very nice executive houses, but nothing remotely as beautiful and elegant as you have built here. I'm truly honoured you've let me see this as I'm sure very few people have had the pleasure of viewing this stunning home, built with so much love and creative skill.' Tears were rolling down her cheeks.

He gently wiped away her tears with his thumbs. 'Have you seen enough for one day or shall we move on?'

'I want to see more now I know you're the creative designer of this house. It tells me so much about you.'

'I have three studios on this floor plus my study, sundry storage rooms, a small kitchen and cloakroom for when I work late into the night.' They walked back across the landing, past the staircases towards the first room on the left, being his music editing suite.

This room contained a large screen in the centre of the partition wall with a myriad of electronic equipment on shelves below. About halfway back into the room there was a console desk with one electronic piano keyboard directly in-front of the operator, and another at right angles on the window side. There were also two computer screens, one slightly right of centre above the main electronic keyboard, and the other perched over the corner where the second keyboard met with the primary keyboard. There were two chairs behind the console desk. The walls were lined with cupboards and shelving.

He hit a switch on the desk, and everything sprung into life. 'This is where we compose and edit sound for ads and trailers. This main electronic keyboard can emulate any instrument in a full orchestra and has a 16-track recorder built in albeit we tend to use a specialist computer recorder/mixer which feeds from, and into this keyboard. If we need to compose music ourselves, or we have a rough-cut from an external composer, we feed it into this front computer using the screen in-front of you for completion and edit purposes.' He showed her how he could play music on the keyboard and the resulting score appeared on the screen. 'This keyboard on my left is a synthesiser for creating sound effects which are then added to the edit. Any questions?'

'I wouldn't know where to start. There are more electronic boxes in this room than in your average audio store. How much does it cost for a studio like this?'

'This room cost about a quarter of a million pounds to set up.'

'Wow, and this is just one studio?'

'When Jim and I were in business, such a room worked so hard you could easily afford to completely replace this equipment every year. In addition to the house air conditioning system there is a secondary air cleaning system in this area to deal with the ionisation created by the mass of electronics we use. The carbon filters for this system cost around £4,000 and, when we are really using these facilities, will need changing every three months.'

'Let's move on to the video edit studio next door.'

This studio had multiple screens of different sizes on one wall, with an enormous screen in the centre. One 40" screen was in portrait mode. This time the console desk was computer keyboards and a full video edit console.

'This is where I edit both video and still photographs. There are now so many formats for television, cinema, streaming, etcetera that a single movie trailer can take weeks to format for each media outlet capability required by a client. For example, if we play a trailer on the big screen, we cannot just render it down to say a computer tablet because text that can be read on the tablet will be so over-sized on the big screen. We need to specifically edit for each media type, thus the array of different screen sizes. Add to this voice-overs for different languages, and for which we may have to extend certain sequences to ensure the video does not change before the voice has finished for that sequence. We're talking about time slicing at one twenty-fifth of a second.'

'Why is that screen set into portrait mode?'

'That screen, and the next one to it, are for still photograph editing. If the picture is in landscape mode, then I use the landscape screen. If in portrait mode, I use the portrait screen.' He started the photo edit suite software and displayed photos on each screen. Both were of the same naked lady in different poses. She noted these were not glamour shots – more fine art shots.

'Still pictures are so important to advertisers and movie makers because people collide with them more than motion pictures. Every printed media such as magazines, newspapers, brochures, etcetera use pictures to attract the reader's attention, and most will feature some pretty girl as the initial draw of the eye into the picture. Some are fairly crude, but at the other end of the spectrum some are exceptional art. In every case the objective is the picture speaks to the reader and grabs their attention. Do you remember when you were young there was a nationwide string of shops called Athena?'

'Yes, they sold posters if I remember correctly.'

'You recall well. They made a business of selling posters portraying mostly artistic images people wanted to look at; images that spoke to people. One of their most iconic images was the girl playing tennis, standing at the net with her back to the viewer exposing just enough of her bottom to suggest she was not wearing underwear. That poster sold in the millions. If you have an original print of the first issue of that poster in good condition, it will fetch a small fortune at auction.'

After a brief pause, he continued 'Another obvious example that predates the Athena posters is the movie poster. Again, in our youth there were no computers, mobile phones, and few

TV channels. To sell tickets to watch a new movie, the studios needed to create a poster they would display on billboards, usually outside the cinema. This poster had to be so good psychologically that, with just one glance by a passer-by, would capture their attention to look deeper into the picture, and then to stimulate them into buying a ticket to see the movie. The artistic skills in creating these pictures were fundamental to the initial success of the movie, with word-of-mouth being the follow-up. Today an original print of such a poster for, say Cleopatra, would fetch a six-figure price at auction.'

'Today the big budget campaigns for sectors such as the perfume industry depend on the creative skills of advertisers and the artistic skills of a photographer to create the image that will speak to people and encourage them to buy these products. My role was to plan the best way to capture attention for a product and convey this concept to a genius graphic artist like Jim, or to a brilliant artistic photographer who would translate the concept into a piece of art which will immediately capture the attention of the buying public. From the sometimes many pictures created in this process it was my job to select the image that perfectly achieved my concept. When I look at the images on these screens I know, in detail, what works and what doesn't work.'

'They are beautiful pictures. Who was the photographer?'

'Well actually, it was me in my studio next door. Still art is a new hobby for me. But, over the years, I've worked with, and studied some of the best artistic photographers in the World learning how they compose and light a picture. I want to create stunning artistic shots because I know when I see such a picture. She is the only model I've used to date, but I have some ideas for shoots I want to do for art itself if I can find the right models.'

'*This is the way he looks at me,*' she thought '*like an artist looking for the best way to capture the beauty of the subject. This must be why his observation of me is not offensive.*'

'Would I make a good model', she asked?

'You have some very interesting bone structures, and there is a natural elegance about the way you move. If you're prepared to give me the opportunity to create art with you, I would like to try.'

'I'm too old for such pictures.'

'No-one is too old. If the photographer can see an artistic image, they will capture the art. I can show you stunning pictures of people in their eighties.'

He switched off the photo edit suite and took her to the still studio. This room was as large as the kitchen, was littered with lighting equipment, and various background rolls hanging from the ceiling at varying angles. He lit the studio as if preparing for a shoot. 'Take off your Crocs and stand over there in-front of that background roll.' He picked up his studio camera, switched it on, and ensured the output would display on the mobile screen just to the side of him.

'Okay, I just want you to get used to being in front of a camera.'

'I can keep my robe on?' she smiled with an over-the-shoulder pose.

He smiled at her 'of course you can. I'm not expecting you to pose for me today. I just want to see how photogenic you are, and whether you can relax in front of a camera.'

He asked her to move one pace back. 'The trick is to chat as I shoot. I just want you to chat about anything and everything and use your body and expression to animate the chat. Exaggerate the animation as much as you like. Have some fun with the story and try to change the subject every thirty seconds or so. Are you ready? Go.'

'Help me with a subject to start.'

'Tell me about the incident with Deborah this morning. But try to remember the camera cannot capture your words, so your animation needs to speak for you.'

She started to relate the incident from the beginning. He started to shoot pictures. After about fifteen seconds she switched into the mode he wanted – she was reliving the incident, including animated actions. He kept taking pictures until she exhausted the incident.

'How was that?' she asked.

'Come, look on the screen.' She moved towards the screen as he did a fast forward until the point she dropped into character. He then went through each picture showing her how she reacted naturally to the story she was telling with no sign of being camera shy. She was taken aback at some actions she used to describe her story. She even laughed at some expressions she used.

'Do you see how natural you are once your mind is flowing with your story?'

'Can we try another story?' she asked.

'Sure. Do you have a story in mind?'

'You just shoot when I start.'

She took him by surprise by starting to relate her feelings about today. She got to the incident with Deborah before she settled into free-flow animation. He started to shoot trying to remember where she was for each picture. When she got to the part at the pool this morning, she turned 45 degrees away from him and let her robe drop from her body but gracefully keeping hold of it around her ankles before putting it back on once out of the shower.

'This lady is something else' he thought as he continued to photograph each phase of her story.

When she had finished, she asked how she had performed.

'You were spectacular, gutsy, and I really appreciated your vote of confidence in our relationship when you dropped your robe.

'I never want those pictures shown anywhere except between us.'

'You have my word. Do you want to see them?'

He started to play the sequence trying to recall the part of her story for each animation. Although most were just interesting animation there was the odd shot that was reasonable. When he got to the disrobe part, she was not so sure about the results. Like most women she was highly critical of various parts of her anatomy, but he was happy he could see material he could work with if she agreed to a future shoot.

'They were terrible', she pronounced.

'Can I let you into a secret regarding quality photographs? Even for the professionals they might deem one shot in ten okay. One good shot in a hundred would be a result. For quality art that looks into the soul rather than the visual we are looking at one shot in five hundred to one thousand pictures. These digital cameras allow many pictures to be shot in rapid succession hoping the perfect picture is somewhere in the sequence. The difference between a near miss and the perfect shot can be as small as where the model is in their breathing cycle. If I shoot you properly for artistic purposes, we could take hundreds of pictures to find one quality shot – but that one shot will make the effort worthwhile.'

'So how much for such a camera?'

'This one cost over five thousand pounds.'

She gulped 'and this is a hobby?'

'My aim is one picture that warrants the right to appear in a major gallery.'

'If you are serious about me modelling for you, I'll give it some thought.'

'I'm serious.'

He remembered her need for a telephone 'You still need to call Jessica.'

'Oh, my God. I forgot all about her.'

'My study is next door.'

She picked up his phone and dialled home. Jessica quickly answered. Her mother explained she would be home shortly in time for dinner at seven. It was now after five o'clock, so she decided it was time to finish for today, get dressed, and return home. He escorted her back to the changing room where she quickly dressed, and he escorted her to her car.

'Richard, what a difference a day makes. I have thoroughly enjoyed a wonderful day with you and really look forward to developing our friendship. I would like a few days to absorb all the events of today, but happy to spend another day with you next week if it works for you. And this house of yours – it's magnificent.'

'Thank you so much for spending the day with me. It has been delightful to get to know you. We can either use Tuesday instead of tennis or pick a whole day such as Monday or Wednesday. Call me when you know what you want to do.'

'Bye for now, you intriguing man.' She kissed him on the cheek and got into her car. He opened the gates for her, and she drove away.

As he strolled back to the house, he felt an inner smile. *'What a lovely day with a lovely lady'* he thought. He had sacrificed so much for his work for too many years. This was his first date for nearly ten years with a woman he liked. Thank goodness he had found out in time. He needed to enjoy a good relationship.

Chapter 5

Elizabeth arrived home to find Jessica in the kitchen preparing dinner. They greeted each other before Elizabeth intended to go change out of her tennis clothes. Jess nearly missed the glow in her mother's eyes. 'Wait a minute, mom. What have you been doing today? There is a look in your eyes which tell me my mom has had some fun today and is feeling good about it. Please tell all.'

'Today has been very nice, but I would like to get out of these clothes so you must wait.'

When Elizabeth re-emerged in a house suit Jess was ready to serve dinner. 'So, you have a new tennis partner, and you've spent time at his house. What's he like, and how much more than a tennis partner has he become, or might become?'

'He's a very good tennis player, but unorthodox, which takes some getting used to. He uses a strategy I've never played before, but it works. We won all four sets today, albeit one by default through injury. He's very attentive on court to ensure I can respond to his game tactics, and he's quick on his feet.'

'That all sounds good but does not account for the look in your eyes. You're positively glowing. What happened this afternoon?'

'We went to his house for lunch and a celebration drink. You remember the very large new house on Buntin's Lane that used to be Buntin's Farm – that's his home.'

'Wow. He must have pots of money to build such a large house.'

'Believe me, it's magnificent. I've never encountered a house like it.'

'Who is he?'

'His name is Richard Lyons. He's involved in the media business although now in a semi-retired function. He's a very private person so before you probe too much, I must tell you I'm not prepared to discuss him other than at a superficial level.'

'But what's he like?'

'He's very creative, clever, charming, but with a sadness I couldn't probe. I think there is something in his past that haunts him, and he's struggling to deal with it. But you must not breathe a word of this to anyone. I like this man, and he has trusted me. I must not betray his trust.'

Jess looked hard at her mother. 'You like this man. Hmm. Please, mom, I've never seen that look in your eyes before. I think the word "like" does not begin to describe how you feel about him. What happened this afternoon?'

'Please Jess I'm a little overwhelmed and I need to let several things sink in. I have never thought of involvement with another man since your father died. But this man has taken me by surprise. Feelings have been awakened, but I must walk carefully. At present I feel out of my depth with this man albeit he has not remotely pressurised me, or even made any overt advances. I think he has similar issues as myself, so I'll take my time to know and understand him before attempting any kind of meaningful relationship. Will that suffice your nosey interrogation?'

'Mom, I'm really pleased for you. You need to find happiness, and if this man has aroused feelings in you, I'm so happy for you. You have a life to live, and I can't imagine Daddy wishing you anything less than your complete happiness.'

'What is interesting is his housekeeper and gardener. You remember Michael and James Roswell from Blythe Farm?'

'Of course, I do. I went to school with Michael.'

'Their parents, Audrey, and Gerry have sold Blythe Farm and moved into the gatehouse bungalow as housekeeper and gardener for Richard. And they're very happy there. I had a chat with Audrey who sends her regards to you.'

'Ah, ah Richard has built his mansion, and can afford staff. I like him already.'

'Please Jess, never think this way. Money can be as destructive as it can do good. I don't need Richard's money.'

'Sorry mom. I didn't mean anything like that.' Pause. 'When will you see him again?'

'I'm not sure yet. I need to sleep on the events of today and let him know over the weekend.'

Jess reached over to hold her mother's hand 'I'm so pleased you've at least found a spark that could lead to your future happiness.'

'Thank you, my dear. Today certainly made me look at myself in a different light – and I like how it feels.'

Chapter 6

It was Friday evening. Sebastian was out of money yet again, pleading with his mother to advance him yet more funds to continue partying with his friends. He is now 22 years old, in his final year at university, but spends far too much of his time enjoying a lifestyle he can neither afford, nor ever likely to, unless he can get a grip on his life. His mother is at her wits' end. For the past 12 years since her divorce from Richard Lyons her life has gone from one disastrous relationship to another. And the settlement she received from the divorce is all but spent. She is bitter about this financial situation, especially since she read in the London Evening Standard two years ago Richard had sold his house in Holland Park for £18 million and sold the advertising business he had built with Jim for further £83 million. They had based her divorce settlement on a house valuation of just £1.5 million and his business income of £1 million p.a. She accepted property prices in London had soared over the subsequent 10 years, but she still felt cheated.

As for his business she paid the price to allow him to spend all his waking hours building the reputation of his agency. She was married to him, but he was wedded to his business. This was the reason they did not have a second child – there was never any time for sex. She loved him, and if the truth be known, she still did. This underlying love was probably the constraint to her developing any subsequent lasting relationship. She had remarried, but it only lasted for two years. But vengeance was at the forefront of her thinking now. 'For God's sake I only had the affair for some attention and sex, and now look at me – 48 years old with no prospects of a husband, and a wayward son. Richard is a multimillionaire at my expense and has no interest in his son.'

This last statement was the crux of the matter. Before their divorce Richard made time for his son, and they had a good relationship. However, once Richard discovered the affair between his wife and one of his competitors, and filed for divorce, the jilted lady instinct kicked in with Sarah who then expressed her scorn with Richard by systematically alienating Sebastian against his father. This caused Richard great pain as he lost more and more contact with his son, and then received a letter purported written by him, which could only be described as hate mail. His lawyers, having witnessed the behaviour of Sarah, advised him to agree a one-off settlement with her to minimise the future liability to himself and his business as they saw her returning, and returning for more.

Richard knew that going to Court for access to his son would be futile thus immersed himself in his work for the next ten years, only allowing himself one evening of tennis on a Friday evening to avoid having to attend the never-ending drunken round of interminable receptions every Friday evening – common-place in his profession. He had no contact with his son since receiving the hate mail.

It could be argued Sebastian was too young to understand the parental alienation by his mother, or why he did not see his father anymore. He became withdrawn, lost his enthusiasm for school albeit retaining enough of a standard to make a lesser university, and spent more time with his friends than his mother. His behaviour was a major contributor to the recent short-lived marriage of his mother having physically assaulted his stepfather in a drunken rage. He also became adept at charming others to give him money, or anything else he sought. He certainly had little respect for himself, or the various females with whom he sought his pleasure only to dump them afterwards. His prospects were bleak.

Sarah, sick of this constant call for funds from her son for no gain, but much abuse, stopped thinking about revenge, and start acting upon it. She had no legal right to anything further from Richard, but their son was still in full-time education at university so there was a possibility he could tap into his father's wealth, and maybe get some payback for herself. Unless her son started to focus on his academic work, he would possibly fail his finals and thus need to retake his final year which would add more time for her plan.

'If you need more money, why don't you go see your father and ask him to help fund your waywardness. He's now very rich so he can afford it. He owes you.'

'I haven't seen my father for years. Why would he want to get involved with me now?'

'Because you are still in full-time education, and he has an obligation to help you if I can't afford what you need.'

'So you claim I can go to my father and expect him to help me, and he has a legal obligation to comply?'

'Got it in one. And when you succeed remember how much you owe to me.'

'Where is he?'

'I don't know, but I know someone who will know.'

'Daddy's bank – sounds good to me.'

Chapter 7

It was Sunday afternoon before Elizabeth decided she was ready to arrange for a day with Richard. Although her overall impression of their last encounter gave her pleasant feelings she had wrestled with several frustrating emotional conflicts.

This man was so different to anyone she had ever encountered before she felt insecure about her ability to keep control of the situation. Although the swim and the subsequent shower did not, on reflection, bother her as this would be the norm in other parts of Europe, the impulse to drop her robe during the photoshoot was hers, and hers alone. She questioned where such impulsiveness fitted with her character. On the one hand, she accepted he was a photographer with purely artistic intentions and could demonstrate this, but she was not a model and had not been so blatant for years, not even with her husband.

She concluded her main reservation was the pain he felt when he spoke of his past. '*What is the source of his pain, and how will this affect his behaviour?*' On balance, she felt perfectly safe with him, and the only way she could answer her questions would be to continue the relationship. She picked up her phone and called his number.

'Hello Richard, it's Elizabeth. How are you?'

'All the better from hearing your voice. I was a little concerned I had frightened you away.'

'You are an unusual man, so I needed a little time to explore whether I'm prepared to lift myself out of my conventional, cosy lifestyle, and jump into the water naked and go swimming with you, possibly out of my depth.'

He found her play on events on Thursday amusing but refreshed by the open exposure of her insecurity. 'Will you swim with me?'

'In your beautiful pool I have no reservations. Where we go from there is something I am prepared to explore further. Will that suffice for now?'

'Perfect. When would you like to meet, and would you like to continue to explore here, or shall we go somewhere less intimidating?'

'I still want to explore your magnificent house, and how you live, so definitely at your home. I visit with my parents on

Mondays, and we have tennis on Tuesday afternoon. Would Wednesday work for you?'

'Absolutely. Based on what you've said could I suggest you arrive for breakfast, and plan to stay for supper. In this way you'll have time to explore all you want, and to see how we live here. If you're concerned at all about driving, I will happily collect you, and ensure you're safely returned home after supper. And of course, you will also be at liberty to elect to leave earlier if you so wish.'

'Are you sure you want to entertain me for such a long day?'

'I cannot think of a more pleasant way to spend a day.'

She felt a tingle down her spine at his charm. 'What time would I need to be there for breakfast?'

'I am up at six, and we assemble for breakfast at eight. You are a fifteen-minute drive away. I'm happy to collect you at 7:30.'

'What would I need to bring with me?'

'For just around the house as little as you wish. I'll only wear shorts and a tee shirt. If you were comfortable in your robe on Thursday, could I suggest the same for you.'

'Are you suggesting I don't need underwear' she responded playfully?

'Pure comfort is the rule. If you don't need it, then don't wear it.'

She laughed at a mental picture of her roaming around naked after her experience on Thursday. 'And what about for supper?'

'Whatever you want. Could I also suggest you could bring clothes and shoes for walking if you're interested to know what I plan for the remaining sixty acres that need to be managed.'

'You bought the whole farm?'

'Including the tractors and other farm machinery. Can't have land without lots of boy's toys.'

She laughed loudly 'Do you know how to use them?'

'Oh yes. I grew up in the country and worked on the farms as a kid. I used my tractors a few times during the build.'

Her laughing was now uncontrollable 'I'm picturing you in your wellies driving a tractor. Can't wait to see it for real. Can't resist such an invitation. I would love to join you for breakfast, but I don't want to put you to the inconvenience of collecting me as you'll not be able to have wine with your supper, and prosecco for lunch.'

'Again, not a problem as Gerry rarely drinks alcohol, so my chauffer is at your disposal if need be. I'll happily collect you at 7:30.'

'I'll be ready and look forward to another day of exploration and intrigue.'

'I'll try my best to deliver. See you on Tuesday at the club. Do you think we'll be partnered for at least one set?'

'You can be sure of it. I'm looking forward to us consolidating our partnership. Thank you, and goodbye until Tuesday.'

'Goodbye Elizabeth and enjoy the rest of your day.'

Jess had listened to this conversation with amusement. Her mom was acting like a teenage girl going on a date. *'What a change this man has made to her.'*

They had engaged in conversation about him frequently over the past couple of days and Jess could see her mother lighten in attitude after every such exchange.

She started with a playful taunt 'My mom is going on a date, starting with breakfast no less. And she may not have underwear.'

Elizabeth sat next to her on the sofa. 'Stop it. You're only jealous. I don't wear underwear for breakfast here, so why be different there.' They both laughed.

'So he'll collect you at 7:30 Wednesday morning. Must be sure to be up, and in my jimjams, just to set the mood. Can't wait to meet this beau who has transformed my conservative mom into a spring chicken.'

Elizabeth playfully hit Jess with a cushion as she giggled uncontrollably.

Chapter 8

They met at the tennis club on Tuesday afternoon as arranged. It amused him that Elizabeth had arranged for them to play as partners for all four sets because, as new formal tennis partners, they needed as much practice with as varied an opposition as possible.

She was feeling ever more confident with his unusual strategies, resulting in winning three of their four sets played.

They agreed to participate in the après tennis socialising, sitting next to each other. As usual, he listens more than takes part but keen to observe how she interacted with her friends of many years. Will she exhibit any changes in her behaviour because of the past few days?

Much of the conversation was local gossip, which gave him some insight into the local community. But other than speaking positively about her new partnership on-court, she kept their off-court affair to herself.

After a while, he made his excuses and left, not mentioning their intentions for tomorrow.

Chapter 9

Richard arrived to collect Elizabeth at 7:30am sharp. As he got out of his car, she noted he was as good as his word – just basic pastel blue shorts, a sun-bleached orange tee-shirt, and Crocs. No wristwatch, no jewellery – nothing.

Jess was looking through the window 'Wow mom, he's a dish.'

She felt over-dressed in her slacks and blouse and full underwear. Instinct told her she was too conventional for such an unconventional date. 'Jess, will you please answer the door to Richard and invite him in. Keep him busy for a few minutes while I change.'

Jess smiled at her mom. She couldn't wait to see what she would wear.

She opened the door in her jimjams with an ear-to-ear smile on her face. 'Good morning, you must be Richard. I'm Jess. Pleased to meet you. Please come in. My mother is not quite ready.'

Richard followed her into the house. *'Audrey was right – it is a larger than a normal residence for these parts.'*

'Can I get you anything?' Jess was trying to break the silence.

'You're very kind, but no thank you. And if I may say so you're beautiful, you have your mother's features.' He had quickly scanned Jess. Lovely face, and her hair hung lazily over her shoulders. Under her jimjams, which were her size rather than baggy, his discerning eye detected a lean and fit body she carried as if floating on air. She had long fingers which exuded feminine grace. He noted she would make an excellent model.

Elizabeth reappeared wearing an elegant linen blouse, loosely flowing over fitted shorts. Jess could see she was still wearing a bra, but a soft one, more geared to modesty rather than shape. Overall, she had chosen well, and she looked much younger. Richard noticed her hair was no longer tied back but hung down naturally over her shoulders. This presented a much softer, younger picture. She had restricted makeup to a little eye shadow and lipstick. 'You look lovely Elizabeth. Ready to go exploring?'

Elizabeth picked up a bag she had packed with other clothes, and her handbag. 'Yes, I'm looking forward to an interesting day. Bye-bye dear, don't wait up.'

Jess giggled. 'Have a good time you two.'

Once in the car, Elizabeth still felt overdressed. 'Richard, I thought about a minimalist approach, but I don't feel comfortable sitting at a breakfast table so exposed with Audrey and Gerry – certainly not yet.'

He reached over and put his hand on her knee, 'Comfort is the only rule, and that means mentally as well. You look great so please relax and let's enjoy our day.'

She felt better now. This was her issue throughout her decision what to wear as she had already gone the full-Monty with him, not once, but twice.

A device in the car alerted the gate the master of the house was approaching. It glided open. He drove through the gates, along the drive, and then swept in front of the house, continuing to the far side where he turned left towards the garage area and parked in the allotted space for this car. Already attuned to the constant surprises presented by this man, she realised such a large garage block must contain several cars. She was not disappointed. She could see four cars and a van in total with a Bentley limo at the far end, a Porsche next to it, then the Range Rover in which she had been sitting, then a Jaguar Estate car with a Mercedes van at the end. And there were still spaces for more.

As they strolled out of the garage, 'can I ask why so many cars, or is this a silly question?'

He turned and looked at the cars pointing to the van first 'heavy lifting, shopping, country, fun, formal.' He then turned away, continuing to the house. *'Ask a silly question'* she thought.

He guided her into the house through the front door, 'Would you like to use a bedroom for any changes of clothes, or will the changing area suffice?'

'Will we swim today?'

'If it's on your schedule, most certainly. If not, then possibly. I have no fixed schedule for today as I would prefer to go where our day leads us.'

'Then why don't I use the changing area as my outside clothes are in my bag.'

'Good. Let's go drop off your bags and see what Audrey has for breakfast.'

As they entered the kitchen, all those wonderful aromas of an English breakfast wafting from the stove. 'Good morning, Mrs Sandiman. Lovely to see you again.'

Elizabeth moved over to the side of Audrey at the stove. 'Please call me Elizabeth.'

Looking at the stove, 'What a wonderful breakfast.'

'Richard has proven remiss for not providing a brief regarding your preference for breakfast, so I've covered all possibilities. I assume you take breakfast.'

Elizabeth, amused at the scold aimed at Richard, who was standing looking at the ceiling as though he had not heard her, 'How can I resist? The aromas are making me hungry already.'

At that moment Gerry emerged through the kitchen door. 'Good morning, Mrs Sandiman. You probably don't remember me, but I came to your house a few times to speak with David, God rest his soul.'

'Yes, I remember you. I'm so sorry I didn't make the connection. Please call me Elizabeth.'

Audrey piled an endless supply of food on the table from all the ingredients of a full English breakfast, with fresh bread, warm croissants, toast, honey, coffee, tea, and juice. Gerry slid into the bench part of the table and Elizabeth slid in next to him from the other side. Audrey and Richard formed the flanks sitting next to their respective partners. They all tucked in.

Richard broke the silence as everyone was eating 'Today we have our first guest for breakfast. As such an honour is only extended to family, and very special friends, then we shall continue our normal morning ritual as though Elizabeth is family. So, Gerry, what do we need to know today?'

Audrey turned to Elizabeth 'Don't mind him. He is very excited to have you here today, and both Gerry and me will do whatever we can to make your visit with us as enjoyable as possible. Anything you need, just ask.'

'Thank you for your warm welcome. I just want to fit into your normal routine and not cause any fuss.'

Gerry turned to Richard 'I'm fixing the fences on the bottom field before topping the grass. I may need your help on the couplings later this morning, but other than that I'll be okay.'

'Good, just give me a shout when you're ready. Elizabeth wants a secret scan of the house on her own.' He turned to Elizabeth, 'the only limits I must impose is you cannot scout my work area for as much your safety as anything else.'

Audrey thought he could have phrased this differently 'No-one's allowed in those studios, including me, without him being there. So many cables, papers, and other obstacles. They only get cleaned every other week, and he watches over me so I don't disturb anything.'

'It's okay Audrey, I've already seen them. They're not my interest today – all boy's toys'. They both laughed. 'I want to see the beautiful design and craftsmanship that has been so lovingly built into this magnificent home. I have seen none of the living rooms on the other side of the staircase, and I'd love to see the bedrooms.'

'When Gerry and Richard go play with their other boy's toys, you just let me know if you want me to show you anything, or where things are.'

'Thank you, Audrey. You're very kind.'

After breakfast Richard suggested they tour the grounds to walk off breakfast and for her to see the layout of the formal grounds. As he only moved in just three months ago, there was still much to finish, especially outside, so he had to explain what would be once completed. He had allocated nearly six acres for the house, bungalow, sundry other smaller buildings, a tennis court to be, and formal gardens including the quadrangle which faced south, thus sunshine all day. Beyond that there are two spacious modern barns; one of which was now his workshop, and the other for all the machinery to take care of both the formal gardens, and the remaining land bank, much of which was pasture with some eight acres of woodland. All she could see from the back of the house was beautiful countryside. This property is not overlooked by anyone. *'Part of his privacy requirement'* she thought.

Chapter 10

They spent over an hour touring before Elizabeth felt she had a good understanding of what is already built, and what is still intended. When they got back to the main house, he made coffee, and they went out to the terrace.

'Are you ready to continue with your story as I believe we got as far as why you chose Lincolnshire.'

'I could continue, but on reflection I think a little reciprocity might be in order because I know very little about you, and much of that is third hand.'

'Have you been spying on me?'

'No more than the socialising after tennis, and what I've heard in the past few days.'

'My story is very boring compared with yours. And will only take a few minutes.'

'Can I be the judge of that?'

'You know my name. I am fifty-two years old. I was married to David for twenty-five wonderful years. You've met our lovely daughter, Jess.'

'David was in the property business from his teenage years learning the skills necessary for him to eventually become a significant developer in these parts. Unfortunate one job he did in the 1960s was to dismantle a former military base close to here. Most of the buildings were made from asbestos. A little over two years ago they diagnosed him with asbestosis and died within three months.' Her head dropped as she shed a tear. He put a hand over hers as comfort.

She collected herself. 'For myself, after university I met David. He hated paperwork. As you probably now realise, there is much paperwork attached to property development, so I became his administrator, and we worked very well together.'

'Until a few days ago I just ambled on with my life, not sure what I wanted to do. I am financially secure, so I want to help Jess get her business working.'

She looked at Richard, 'That's it, my life story in just a few minutes.'

'I'm so sorry about your husband. It must have been a terrible shock for you. I only hope the MoD adequately compensated you for your loss.'

'They did, but it can never replace someone so close to you.' Her head dropped.

He was not sure whether to put an arm around her shoulders or just leave her to reflect on her memories for a while. He adopted the 'if in doubt, leave it out' maxim and finished his coffee. Then he reached over and held her hand. 'Thank you for sharing your story with me. I can see there are still some raw emotions, so I don't want to pry further.'

'Richard, you are fast becoming my soul mate, my only soul mate. If you can bear it, I would like to share some of my feelings with you from time to time. I've kept them to myself since David died, but I need to deal with them so I can move on.'

'It would truly honour me to be your soul mate, punch bag, comfort blanket – whatever you need.'

'Thank you. We both appear to have demons from the past which still haunt us.'

Audrey shouted from the kitchen, 'Richard, Gerry is ready for you.'

'Okay, on my way.'

'Are you alright if I leave you for a while? You can see the rest of the house and I will track you down afterwards. Perhaps then a swim to get the dust off me, and to wash away your sorrow.'

'Yes, I would like to look around. The magnificence I know I can expect to experience will certainly lighten my mood. And a swim would be nice afterwards.'

'I'll see you in about twenty minutes.'

Chapter 11

Richard returned to the kitchen to wash his hands. Audrey was busying herself with lunch.

'Have you seen Elizabeth recently?'

'I think she's now upstairs looking at the bedrooms. She loves the living room. Do you know she can play the piano? She played your grand piano so sweetly.'

'Interesting.'

He found her exiting the guest suite. 'Richard, all of it is so lovely. I feel like a little girl in wonderland. And the orchid in your bedroom door is sublime – very fitting for you. I hope you don't mind I went into your bedroom, but I didn't know until I was inside.'

'The only restricted area in this house, without my presence, is along there' pointing to his working area. 'Have you seen everything you want to explore? Do you want to take me anywhere to explain any of the architecture?'

'Your guest suite is better than a 5-star hotel suite. Has anyone used it yet?'

'No. Besides Jim, you're the only guest here so far. Would you like to christen it?'

'I think if I stayed in this house, I wouldn't want to be alone.'

He got this message loud and clear.

She looked at him smiling, knowing he had banked her suggestion 'How about a swim?'

They went to the changing area. She removed her clothes without hesitation and led him to the pool.

After they had been swimming for a while, she swam up to him and put her arms around his neck for support, letting her body float down until she was up against him.

She lifted her head, so she was looking at him, 'Can I ask you a question?'

'Of course.'

'When are you going to kiss me?'

His sure footedness immediately evaporated. He needed to think quickly as he felt paralysed. 'Elizabeth, I haven't been near a woman in over ten years. I've found someone I would like to be with, but I don't want to scare her away. I won't attempt anything with you until I'm sure you'll respond favourably.'

'Close your eyes. Now hold me.' She moved her lips to his and gave them a gentle kiss. Then again, with more connection. He responded, so she kissed him more fully.'

'Was that nice?'

'Very.'

'Enough to add kissing to our relationship?'

'He smiled.'

She pushed away from him. 'Now catch me if you can if you want another kiss' as she swam off.

He chased after her, caught one of her feet, pulled her to him, turned her and claimed his prize.

After they separated, she looked at him with a very satisfied smile. 'Shall we shower ready for lunch?'

He led her to the shower, but this time only started one shower head. 'I would like to add something to our relationship. We shower together. I shower you; you shower me.'

He took the shower gel and gently washed her back and then reached under her arms to wash her front, paying particular attention to her breasts. *'How lovely to be caressed this way'* she thought as she started to have feelings in her loins not experienced for some years. Then he turned her to rinse her off. She said nothing, just looked at him with a big smile on her face.

'Is this okay with you?'

'Give me that gel and turn around.'

Once they had finished showering, he found towels for them. 'Do you want to get dressed or will a robe do for lunch?'

'I like the nakedness, but we must dress for lunch so the robes will be fine.'

Chapter 12

Lunch was outside on the terrace. Gerry had come up from his grass topping, and Audrey was on fine form with lots of funny stories and jokes. Elizabeth felt at home with these people. Her sadness during the morning was now history. And now their relationship was sealed with a kiss, she was totally relaxed.

After lunch Richard suggested they get dressed and take a walk in the woods as he had found some wild orchids, but he would only show her where they are if she promised to tell no one. In theory, he should report such a finding to the local conservation people, but he did not want the interference, as must have been the case with the previous owner. He had no intention to do other than nurture these beautiful plants, so did not need prying eyes on his land.

They dressed and started for the woods. Elizabeth had not really considered just how large an area is 60 acres. They walked the perimeter past the bungalow. She wanted to see inside, but he told her she should speak with Audrey. She did not quite understand this rebuff because it was his property – but he pointed out it is their space. He also showed her where Gerry was about to build a half-acre walled garden so, by this time next year, most of their vegetables and fruit will be homegrown.

At strategic locations in the grounds, he stopped to show her the view, not least towards the house which was the highest point on the farm.

She held his hand most of the way. Her gait was not so much walking but danced her way as would an excited child. He reflected on her initiating kissing in the pool and sensed she has made a decision; crossed a line. She is relaxed, playful, and very chatty. When they got to the woodland, she wanted to run and hide in the trees. He could always see where she had gone but prepared to play along as she was having fun. He took her to the stream running through the woods, and where the wild orchids were growing on the banks. The shards of sunlight beaming through the trees splashed through the well-formed pale white lobes with brown, almost bronze splashes igniting the red-tipped hymen inside the plume.

She was on her knees admiring these beautiful plants, being careful not to damage any of them. He stood and watched this wonderful lady, thinking the Gods were shining their light upon him.

She stood and pointed to a tree from where they could see the full carpet of blooms with the stream running below. 'Come, sit with me and admire this rare beauty.'

He sat against the tree, and she sat next to him, encouraging him to put his arm around her so she could tuck her head into his shoulder. She let him get used to this situation before turning to him 'could I steal another kiss. This is such a romantic setting I want to be kissed.'

He looked at her but saying nothing gave her a long and passionate kiss. Afterwards she snuggled into him, watching the sunlight dancing over the orchids. 'Thank you for bringing me here.'

They could hear Gerry topping the fields. 'He must be down by the river. Let's go see if there is any animal life being disrupted.'

They emerged out of the woods into the field. The aroma of freshly cut grass filled their nostrils. He guided her to the riverbank which was the furthest boundary to his property. He told her he had observed young deer a few months ago in this area, but had not seen them since moving in, but wanted to encourage them to feel safe on his land.

She looked towards the house. It was majestic, almost floating over the surface of the fields. 'David developed some stunning executive properties, but nothing on this scale. I congratulate you on your artistic creativity, and your tenacity to deliver your dream.'

They slowly made their way back to the house, heading for the track that went past the barns before entering the formal boundary of the gardens. 'Can I see your workshop?'

He guided her past the already open barn used for the farm machinery and entered the code into the entry pad of his workshop. The roller doors and window shutters opened. Each barn was some 600m^2 with a 7m beam. She saw several internal buildings and a substantial open plan area with several woodworking machines, and a sizeable makeup table. Just inside the door to the right was a room with a window, the shutters to which opened with the door. He explained this was a clean room for electrical and electronic projects. Behind this was a wet room, kitchenette, and toilet. At the back were storage rooms for wood, hand tools, and other stores.

'I've seen machines like this in professional workshops. They must have cost a small fortune.'

'Most of the woodwork in the house, including all doors, skirting, dado rails, cupboards, and built-in cabinets were made here. These machines pay for themselves. As most of the materials I use are hardwoods, the machines must be robust.'

Resting on the makeup table there was a large white circular object with what looked like a control panel.

'And what's this project?'

'It is a rotating platform for my photo studio. Sometimes I look at a model and can't quite determine the best angle to take the shot. As you have seen in my studio, moving around a model is not so easy as I would need to change the lighting as well, asking the model to move is likely to lose the pose. Therefore, my plan is to stand the model on this platform, and set, say, a 5-degree incremental rotation. The camera will automatically take a picture after each increment. I only need to finish the synchronising electronics with my camera, and it will be ready to install.'

'How do you know about electronics?'

'When Jim and I first built our media business, electronics such as PC's were recent additions. We had to build what we needed ourselves. Much of Jim's specialist graphics capability was designed and built by him. Old habits die hard.'

By the time they returned to the house, it was past five o'clock. They went back to the changing area and removed their walking clothes. She dressed into the clothes she wore when she arrived, and he back to his shorts and tee shirt.

Chapter 13

As the sun was still delivering the warmth that encourages outside living, they made a pot of tea and went to the terrace to sit for a while.

She wanted to explore his background more. 'Could we go back to your story as I feel there is a part of yours I have yet to hear?'

'My story is all around you. This is me and my life.'

'Are you prepared to tell me about your marriage, and why it failed?'

'I see. You want to explore the dark side of the force. Painful territory for me.'

'That's why I would like you to share it with me because I feel the pain is still lurking beneath the surface and thus is part of you.'

'I married Sarah just before Jim and I formed our own business. I was already successful, and I had a nice house in Holland Park in London. We quickly had a son, Sebastian. When we started our own agency, the market was very cutthroat, so winning business was hard-fought, and required long hours to both work on projects and generate new business. We had the advantage we were both in demand for our technical skills, but I don't think either of us realised the amount of other work required to keep a business working. Jim will be the first person to admit he is totally incapable of the business side of a company. All business administration fell onto my shoulder. Thus, even when I found time to go home, there was always some administrative issue needing my attention. I made time for my son, and we had a great relationship but, on reflection, I abandoned Sarah. She clearly felt lonely, so had an affair with a key competitor. I found out, felt so angry and betrayed I filed for divorce. The divorce process was acrimonious, as most are, and the jilted wife took her revenge by alienating my son against me. My lawyers advised a one-off settlement to draw a line under the whole

49

sordid business. Still Sarah was angry with me and my access to Sebastian got less and less until one day I received a letter from him which can only be described as hate mail. I haven't seen or heard from either to this day. I buried myself in the business until Jim had his heart attack two years ago.'

She knew instinctively this was the pain she had detected in his eyes. 'How old will Sebastian be today?'

'He was ten when we got divorced so he'll be twenty-two now.'

'Have you never thought to find out where he is now as he is old enough to take a more circumspect view of what happened when he was younger? If you had a good relationship with him for ten years, this will still be in his memory.'

'To be honest Elizabeth, I've concentrated on Jim, who is like a brother to me. And building this house. Can we leave this subject as it's casting a dark cloud over an otherwise lovely day?'

She knew this discussion was over for today, but just as she must confront her demons with his help, he must also confront this pain with her help. 'Thank you for telling me about Sebastian.'

Chapter 14

After supper Richard took Elizabeth home as she felt exhausted from her long day. When they arrived at her home, Elizabeth told him she did not want to invite him in. 'Your home has no history. This house is full of it. I don't want any part of our relationship in this house. Jess has been telling me for some time I need to move on and away from a house so filled with the past to the point of suffocating the future. You've helped me to realise Jess is right, and I know I must move on.'

She changed the subject 'Will you play tennis tomorrow morning?'

'If you're there, then I'll certainly come.'

'You can be sure of it, my darling.'

'I'm going to see Jim after lunch on Friday. Would you like to join me as I would really like you to meet him?'

'Of course, I'll come. He's such an important part of your life. Shall I come to you, and we go from there?'

'We should meet for lunch as I need to prepare you for the shock that is Jim and then go to see him. Let me think about the logistics and we can speak tomorrow.'

With that, they enjoyed a tender kiss, and she was gone.

Richard spent the entire journey home reflecting on this extraordinary day. Their relationship had progressed in leaps and bounds. When he finally got to his gates, he did not know how he got there.

Chapter 15

Sarah had used her contacts well. They had provided the details she needed regarding the location of her ex-husband.

Sebastian was in his room getting ready for yet another party. She knocked on his door and went in. She handed him a sheet of paper. 'Your father has moved to Lincolnshire with Jim. He is living with Jim while he builds a house for himself. My contact told me they are not very active business-wise, so your father will not be busy.'

'But how do you suggest I approach him, mother dear?'

'Be alive to the fact your father is clever, shrewd, and will not tolerate your general attitude. For him, blood is not thicker than water, so you cannot play the happy family card. You must use your charm. If he gets any idea about the insincerity of your intentions, he will cut your feet from under you.'

'Therefore, what I suggest you do is to write to him in your own handwriting explaining now you are grown up, and about to finish university, you would like to meet with him. Tell him a little about the past twelve years, and what you hope to do in the future. This should be enough to start contact. Once you initiate contact, I'll tell you how I think you can succeed.'

'Cool. Let's go raid Daddy's Bank.'

Chapter 16

Jess was waiting for her mother with the full intention of an interrogation. 'Hi mom, how did your day go? Please come sit with me and tell all.'

She knew what was coming so casually went about dropping her bags and organising a glass of wine for herself. She was feeling tired. It had been an emotionally exhausting day. She had completely surprised herself at how fast she had pushed the boundaries, but she felt good about what she had achieved. 'I'm not sure I want to discuss any of it tonight as I'm very tired.'

'Come, sit with me, and rest a little. I just want someone to talk with for a while as I've been on my own all day.'

'Why didn't you go out? It was such a lovely day, so why stay here?'

'There is the minor issue of my internet business. It will not create itself. Business folk do not get time off just because the sun is shining.'

She had forgotten about the work still needed to get her business started. 'So what did you achieve today? Where are you with the website design?'

'I'm getting there. The poor broadband speeds make progress slow, but I'm happy with progress. But how was your day?'

'My dear, I'm not about to give your chapter and verse about my relationship with Richard. Suffice it to say progress is very encouraging.'

'That sounds great mom, but what does it mean? Your change of clothes this morning took years off you. You went from frumpy mum to up-for-it woman.'

'Don't be silly. What do you mean by up-for-it woman?'

'You transformed from somebody who was not really available, to someone who is looking for some fun and adventure.'

'Then I would say I found it.'

Jess, excitedly, 'Wow mum, come on, tell me what happened.'

Chapter 17

After a very satisfactory four sets of tennis, they sat alone together for a few minutes.

'What have you decided about tomorrow?'

'After describing your house to Jess last night, she wants to come and see for herself. Could I bring her tomorrow morning to see the house, as you need to meet her properly? She can then come home after lunch to get on with her work while we go to Jim. You could drop me back home later.'

'Sounds okay with me. How's she getting on with her internet business?'

'The broadband speeds around here are very poor, so progress is slow. I think it frustrates her after the speeds she enjoyed at university.'

'Tell her to bring everything she needs with her tomorrow. I have a fast broadband so she could work at my house tomorrow afternoon, and then we could all have dinner together later.'

'I'll put this to her and see what she wants to do. What time would be convenient for us to arrive?'

'Whenever you like. You are welcome to come for breakfast so long as Jess comes in her jimjams. Audrey is clearly looking forward to seeing her again.'

She smiled at him, 'You do realise her jimjams yesterday is her cheeky way with you.'

'I got that, and thus why she needs to repeat it tomorrow if she wants breakfast.'

'I'll let you know this evening. I think the interaction with you two will be interesting.'

'By the way, to keep me out of trouble with Audrey, does she have any specific breakfast requirements?'

'I'll call you later.'

Elizabeth spoke with Jess about the proposals for tomorrow. Jess was packed and ready within five minutes. 'Muesli, yoghurt and juice please.'

Other than juice, Elizabeth did not recall any of these items on the table yesterday. 'Darling, I don't think muesli and yoghurt are on the menu, and it's too late for Audrey to go shopping.'

'Then whatever. I'll make do.'

Elizabeth phoned Richard and told him they would be there for breakfast. And it was too late for Audrey to change her menu.

He smiled to himself, '*She's a game lass. I like her already.*'

Chapter 18

They both arrived at the house just before 8am. Audrey opened the gate and then went out to greet them. When she saw Jess flagrantly wearing her jimjams, she laughed and scooped her up in her arms. 'Jess, how lovely to see you. My, how you've grown.' She stepped back to look at her. 'What a beautiful woman you are. If my boys could see you now, they would not be floating off around the world.'

'Thank you, Mrs Roswell. It's so nice to see you again.'

'Jess you're a woman now so you call me Audrey.'

'Good morning, Elizabeth. Lovely to see you again.' as she took the hand of Jess. 'Now you come with me. I have a lovely breakfast ready for you. It's so nice to see you.'

Richard observed all of this as he came out to greet Elizabeth. 'Good morning, my dear. Seems Jess is at home already' as they watched Audrey lead her into the house. He took her hand, and they followed into the kitchen.

Audrey was repeating to Gerry all the chat about how grown she was. Richard found all this so amusing, especially as Jess looked like a teenager in her jimjams and slippers.

Jess approached Richard 'Good morning, Richard, and thank you so much for the invitation.' And then with a cheeky glint in her eye, 'Do I meet you dress code for breakfast?'

He smiled, 'You look wonderful, and you're very welcome.'

They all sat down for breakfast, which was dominated by the fuss made by Audrey towards Jess. He observed Audrey probably missed not having a daughter of her own.

After breakfast Jess retrieved her backpack from the car and Elizabeth guided her to the changing area so she could get out of the jimjams into her daywear. They went back to the kitchen to find Richard and Gerry discussing some issue regarding the workload for the day. When he looked at Jess in her shorty shorts and tee-shirt, without a bra, he smiled to himself. *'Everything about this young woman makes me smile'* he thought.

'Jess before your mother takes you to view the house can you sit with me for a few minutes and describe your internet project.'

'Sure. Let me get my laptop and I'll show you.'

She was back with her backpack in seconds. She explained she wanted to create a business where she would advertise the products of small businesses for them, organise and process sales, and then pass the orders back for shipment. It impressed him with both the idea and her novel approach to both seeking small business producers and finding customers. What she needed was a slick website with punchy graphics, and most of all a fast web-based server system. 'Okay young lady, you go sight-seeing with your mother while I do some necessary chores and give your project some thought.' He turned to Elizabeth who had been very attentive during their discussion 'I'll be in my study when you've both finished.' He turned to Jess 'bring your laptop with you to my study and I'll give you the codes to tap into my broadband. I think you'll be happy with the speeds here.'

It was nearly two hours before they arrived at his study. Elizabeth had done the full tour with Jess, both inside and outside. He moved from his desk to the comfortable seats in his office comprising a sofa and two armchairs.

'This place is a dream' declared Jess. 'Wherever you look you see beautiful images, and the inside is breath-taking. No wonder my mom could only say I had to see it to believe it.'

'This place is a dream fulfilled for me, especially when it's finished. There is still more to do before I complete the dream.'

'Mum tried to describe your bedroom doors. Now I've seen them, I couldn't find the words to adequately describe their elegant beauty. And mum tells me you designed and made them. Makes them even more special.'

'Hopefully, you will spend more time here over the coming months so you will see for yourself the dream fulfilled.'

'Now about your project. Would you mind if I helped you with your presentation and graphic requirements? Media is my business so I might give you some input.'

'Mum told me about your secret studios and all the equipment you have. Can I see them?'

'I'll show you in a few minutes. But first, can I suggest a change of plan for you? I think you should come with us to meet my graphics partner, Jim, and bring your work with you. Whereas I don't think he's ready for us to take on a major commission, he's champing at the bit to do something. If you use those twinkle eyes of yours to win his support for what you want to do, it will give him something to do, and your graphics will be world class.'

'Are you serious? Mum says you consider this man, Jim, a genius. Why would he be interested in a silly minor project like mine, and I couldn't pay for such input?'

'Jim has more money than he knows what to do with, but he has nothing to occupy his time. He's also family to me. Let's be clear. I'm not going to ask him to help you. You must convince him of your project, and your commitment. Your pretty face and cheeky attitude will do the rest.'

'Wow. I don't know what to say. I'm overwhelmed.'

'Then just say 'yes, you would like to come with us.'

'Yes, please.'

'Okay, let me show you my workspace which, no doubt, your mother has told you is off-limits, and any projects are secret, albeit we are not working yet as Jim needs a little more time to recover.'

'He turned to Elizabeth 'do you want the tour again my dear?'

'I'll go help Audrey with lunch. Then you can be more technical with Jess.'

Before taking her to the studios he explained to her what he does, and how this fits with the work in which Jim is so expert.

He then showed her the sound studio and the video studio, including the stills of the model he had shot, before taking her to the photo studio. He explained to her the pictures he shoots and his reason for wanting to capture a perfect artistic image that will merit a place in a major gallery.

'Have you taken pictures of mum in here?'

'Yes, but only fooling around to see if we can eradicate her shyness in front of a camera.'

'Did you succeed?'

'Certainly. She responded to the techniques photographers use to calm their subjects, but it will take more work before I can completely relax her.'

'Do you think I'm photogenic?'

'Go stand over there and I'll show you.' He adjusted the lighting to suit her skin colour before priming his camera. 'Let me see confidence ooze out of you.'

He shot a few pictures, but she had lost some of her outgoing personality. He looked up at her, 'Have the lights caused you to retreat, or the camera?'

'Probably a little of both.'

'Come here and look at where you were standing. Is there anything to fear?'

'No.'

'I want you to be the girl in her jimjams this morning, with all her attitude, to walk back to that space, and when she's ready, to turn and let me see it. Think you can do it, or do you need your jimjams?'

'So, you want attitude, do you? How raw?'

'As raw as you want. Go.'

She walked with a swagger, stopped, whipped her head around with a saucy come-and-get-me-if-you-dare look, and then slowly turned on her heels, rotating around until she faced him head on. He captured all of it.

He lowered his camera. 'That was the girl I saw this morning. Come look at the pictures.'

He had shot some thirty pictures, and he displayed them on his studio monitor one at a time, explaining to her the difference between a snap and a picture, and where he would change her posture to improve the picture.

'You're clearly photogenic, but did you enjoy playing such extraverted attitude to the camera?'

'I felt wild. You gave me permission to unleash, so I did.'

'So, your inhibition before was more to do with what you thought I would think of you. Let me tell you something between you and myself. I really like the sassy side of you, and you have the intellect to project it without it being crude or offensive. With me you can be as wild as you like, so long as you understand my boundaries. And I think you'll quickly and surely find those without my help. And, therefore why Jim will jump at the opportunity to help you if he likes your project.'

She paused whilst considering what she wanted to ask. 'I would like to try a photoshoot. Is this something you're prepared to do with me?'

'Let's sit down and discuss what you have in mind, and for me to explain how it works because there is much more to it than lighting and pictures. But, subject to us both being happy after that discussion, then I would like to try some pictures with you.'

'Must be lunchtime, and then we need to get away to Jim, so bring your project.'

Chapter 19

Totten Place was a mid-sized Tudor house with eight bedrooms and four reception rooms. Jim liked the isolation of this house being at least 400m from his nearest neighbour, and the care of the architect to get the lines of the façade in perfect proportion. Lines were his life, so he always viewed them differently to everyone else. When they both moved there two years ago, they made several cosmetic changes such as changing the expansive dining room into his studio using the same one-way glass as Richard was using at his home to replace all the windowpanes to ensure prying eyes are thwarted. They also fitted blackout rollers to the insides of these windows as, when colour balance needed to be perfect, all other light sources needed to be eliminated.

Richard had employed a couple, the wife of whom was a registered nurse, and her husband was a plumber who, as with all such trades, had expanded his capabilities to general repairs. He had encouraged them to sell their home, as they wanted to downsize and then buy the cottage of their dreams. This cottage needed a full refurbishment which Richard organised and then put it out for corporate let, thus securing their retirement, and providing an income. He wanted them to live with Jim and take care of him, not least restricting his working hours. This has worked well to date. Richard had structured a similar situation with Audrey and Gerry such that when they retired, they had a home to go to which was generating a secure income for them until they retired.

They arrived a little after 2pm. Margaret, the nurse, answered the door and let them in. 'Hi Richard. He's in his studio.'

There was no red light above the door, so Richard opened the door and walked in, followed by Elizabeth and Jess. The room was dimmed with the blackouts in place. The three screens in-front of Jim were the only light source. He turned from his console 'Richard, my friend. So nice to see you.' They hugged each other.

Jim turned to Elizabeth, 'you must be the lovely Elizabeth. I've heard so much about you from this smitten teenager' pointing to Richard. They all laughed.

'And who is this pretty lady?' as he took the hand of Jess.

'She is Jess, the daughter of Elizabeth. I didn't have time to tell you about her as I only decided just before lunch to bring her.'

'Are you married, sweet lady?'

Jess laughed, 'Are you proposing to me already?'

Jim turned to Richard 'I like her already. Can I keep her?'

'Actually, you may be able to help her with a project she has, but I'll leave her to speak with you about what she's trying to achieve.'

'Do you like it?'

'It's novel and has potential.'

'Will she live here while we do it?' They all laughed again.

'Knowing the way you work she would be very lonely.'

Jess liked him already. Unassuming, charming, playful, and self-effacing.

Jim turned to the ladies, 'would you beautiful ladies like to look around while I have a quick word with Richard about an idea I'm working on?' He threw a switch and the blackout rollers rose, letting in the daylight.

As light filled the room, Jess was shocked by the visual of Jim. He was smaller than her, seriously balding with ragged patches of hair scattered across his head, bulging eyes, and resembled an emaciated refugee who had lived in solitary confinement for years.

Once daylight filled the room, the jaws of both women dropped. The walls were covered in iconic images from blockbuster movies such as Star Wars and James Bond, all of which they recognised. Jess noticed a display cabinet in the corner housing trophies. Her eyes immediately noted two BAFTA trophies flanking an Oscar statue.

Jess was so overwhelmed she could only gulp to Jim 'Wow, this is incredible. I'll happily marry you.' Everyone laughed.

Jess held Jim's hand with tears in her eyes. 'Richard told me you're a genius, as understated as everything else he says about your work together. I'm so honoured to meet such a creative superstar. But my project is not worthy of your attention.'

'Has he told you about the nobodies we made into household names by managing their media? Pretty lady, we'll sit together, look at your project, and maybe make you a business goddess.'

Once Elizabeth recovered her composure, she watched all this rapport between Jess and Jim, thinking *'what a smart daughter I have. She'll go far in life.'*

'Come Richard, sit with me and tell me what you think of my idea while these beautiful distractions satisfy their curiosity. Margaret has organised tea in the sitting room for later.'

'Beautiful ladies. When you get bored in here, there is more to amuse you in the sitting room; out of the door and second on the left.'

It took some twenty minutes before the men emerged from their discussion. Elizabeth noted it took just seconds for both men to become totally absorbed in what they were doing. Everything around them, including the presence of herself and Jess, had been blocked out, total focus and concentration. She realised she would need to get used to this when these men start projects again. It was now completely clear to her how Richard had lived for the ten years prior to Jim's heart attack. But she could not deny her admiration for what she sees in this room. She also wondered why Richard did not have their work displayed in his home. She made a mental note to ask him over dinner tonight.

Jess had already departed for the sitting room, not wanting to waste a single moment, studying every picture she could find. She thought some of them were actual photographs until she got close to them, only to realise they were drawings. *'Such talent'*, she thought.

The other three joined her in the sitting room where Margaret had prepared a full English tradition afternoon tea.

Jim asked Jess to join him on the sofa, asking her to describe her project to him. He listened carefully. 'So, you are helping small businesses to have an international platform for their products by providing them a safe portal to allow customers to purchase them.'

He impressed her with his ability to condense her project into a simple statement. 'That's the best description I've heard; simple and concise.'

'That's what we do. Advertising time is expensive, so we condense the message into as few words as possible, with maximum delivery. You're helping the small guys play with the big guys. I love it. Let's go into my studio and look at what you've got.'

He turned to Richard, 'you know your way around here. Why don't you have tea and then take your lovely lady for a tour of my kingdom? Don't need you crowding my pitch with this young lady.'

Richard smiled, *'Jess has totally captivated him. She'll soon have a stunning website, and any other media material she needed.'*

Elizabeth looked at him, 'What are you looking so smug about?'

'You have one hell of a daughter. She's smart and beautiful. She would pay a significant six figure fee for what she is about to receive. And Jim will deliver the very best for her. Let me show you around as there is much to see in this place.'

Eventually they returned to the studio to find Jess totally absorbed in what he was drawing for her.

Richard broke the silence. 'How are we doing here?'

Jess looked up. 'Mum, look at these graphics. They're fantastic.'

Elizabeth looked over her shoulder and could not believe her eyes. The visuals he was developing freehand in such a short time were like a finished product.

Jim looked up. 'I guess you've come to spoil my fun and take this lovely lady away from me.'

'But I'm happy to come back on my own! This is so much fun' exclaimed Jess. 'Can I come back tomorrow?'

'Of course, you can, my dear. 2pm good for you?'

'I'll be here and thank you so much.'

'No problem, my dear. It's been a little boring around here now Richard has moved into his castle. To have both brains and beauty in the same package will be a real pleasure.'

They said their goodbyes, thanked Margaret, and made their way home.

Whilst walking from the garage to the house, Jess needed to say something. 'Richard, thank you so much for helping me. Is it okay if I kiss you?' Without waiting for an answer, she kissed him on the cheek.

'Why, thank you. You can do that any time.'

Elizabeth thought how well these two get on. She knew she need have no fear about causing her any problems if she develops a lasting relationship with this man.

All the way home she could not get the images these men had created out of her head. And why had he not mentioned the Oscar – such an achievement?

Chapter 20

Buntins was quiet. Elizabeth expected Audrey to be preparing dinner. 'Where's Audrey?'

'She and Gerry have gone to visit her mother who is not well. We fend for ourselves tonight. But before I start dinner, let me get Jess set up on my broadband so she can come anytime she likes to continue her work.'

'Why don't I start dinner while you and Jess go do what you have to do. It might take some time to find my way around this kitchen, but we don't have any time constraints. I'll call when I'm close to serving.'

Richard and Jess retreated to his study, where he gave her the access codes for his broadband connection. The speeds she could achieve amazed her.

'What line speeds can you get, and how did you manage this when us ordinary folk only get about 2Mbs download and less than 500k upload?'

'The person who owned this farm before me had a quality copper cable installed directly from the exchange, and the equipment in the exchange to support the speeds. Currently, I get about 40Mbs download, and 11Mbs upload. Later this year they will upgrade me to fibre optic cable when I expect to get 100Mbs download and 20Mbs upload.'

'Do you have your own server?'

'Yes, I do. It's next door, but as I have no need for a website at present, it only operates as a local network to feed my video and music libraries around the house.' He paused. 'You've just given me an idea. Let's go next door.'

He opened the door of the next room to his study. It was intended to be a room for printers and other sundry electronics, but he had opted to put these machines directly into the studios. Now it was just storage whilst he finished organising his workspace. It was about 4m square, with two windows overlooking the rear quadrant.

'Proposition. What about if I clear out this room and install a desk, chair, cupboards, and anything else you need, and you work from here? The server is in that cupboard in the corner so you can use it as your online environment so your business will run 24 hours each day with reasonable bandwidth.'

'Why are you doing this for me, we only met yesterday?'

'Jess, I'm a man of instinct, and my instinct tells me you are going to be spending a lot of time here in the coming months. I have what you need to get your business up and running. Jim will finish your graphics in a few days once he formulates what you need. Your biggest frustration appears to be the poor broadband speeds around here. As things stand, even if your graphics are working next week, you still cannot trade without bandwidth because as soon as you get a few customers on your site at the same time it will grind to a halt, and your customers will go elsewhere. Therefore, my proposition closes the constraint loop, and you can start trading.'

She thought for a moment. 'If it's any consolation, I share your instinct although I haven't discussed this with mum. My second instinct is we're going to get along fine. My mother wanted this meeting to be sure your relationship was not going to adversely affect me, which means she's serious about her relationship with you, and which makes me thrilled for her. Therefore, my answer to your proposal is…….' she reached up to him and gave him another kiss 'and thank you.'

'Two kisses on our first date. A record for me. It's going to be a lot of fun having you around. Let's find out how your mother's doing.'

When they returned to the kitchen, Elizabeth was leaning over the stove watching her creation. 'Hi mom. Need any help?'

'No dear. We're nearly ready.' She looked at Richard 'Once you know your way around this kitchen it works very well. Audrey has everything organised, and there is a logic to it. The stove is lovely to use. Can you please organise whatever it is you propose we drink?'

'I have some lovely Burgundy in the cellar. I'll fetch a bottle.'

'You have a cellar?'

'Of course. Where do you think the pumps and filtration systems are for the swimming pool, and the heating for the house?'

'So why was this not part of my tour?'

'Obviously not nosey enough when you were exploring. There are also two roof voids. You could put a tennis court in each of them.'

'Tell me later. Please get the wine as I'm ready to serve. Jess, can you lay the table, please?'

They centred much of the conversation over dinner around Jim. There was still incredulity about the sheer magnitude of his achievements, and the quality of his work.

After dinner was over, and the kitchen put back into good order, it was past 8pm. Elizabeth decided they should leave for home, not least because she would like to interrogate Jess about her feelings, not that she had any doubt about her response. They agreed both would arrive for lunch tomorrow, Jess would then go to visit Jim, she would then bring Jim back with her for dinner. Jim would stay over and spend Sunday with Richard to give Margaret a day off.

Chapter 21

'What are your overall feelings about Richard, and his home.'

'Great. Can't wait for you two to get married and move in.'

'So, you think you'll come live with us?'

'Where else would I go as you would sell this house. I wouldn't want to live here alone. There's plenty of room for me there.'

'A little presumptuous, don't you think?'

'Mom, when are you going to get on the curve. Both Richard and I know where this is going, so why the hesitation. You're made for each other, and he would be a great father figure for me. He has already offered me an office in his work suite, and all the internet access I need for my business. Where do you think I'll live when you two get together?'

Elizabeth was speechless. 'The two of you appear to have my future mapped out for me.'

'No mom. We're just voicing what you already know, but afraid to say. You two are not spring chickens, so get on with it. Long courtships are for teenagers while they save for their own place. You've both been there before, so you know the rules.' She laughed, 'Come on, mom. I love you and want you to be happy. This man is perfect for you, so go for it with my unconditional blessing.'

'What else have you two been scheming?'

'Nothing. We both realise this is good for all of us, and I'm so happy for the first time since daddy died.'

'When I see you two together you already look like father and daughter after just one day. It's uncanny. You even spar with each other, but both have fun with it.'

'Mom, I like him, and so do you. Audrey and Gerry are great. And Jim is on another planet. What a privilege to have met him.'

Elizabeth retired to bed with her head spinning. But Jess was right, she wanted to be with Richard.

Chapter 22

Jess and Elizabeth arrived at Buntins a little before noon. Richard was busy in the kitchen preparing lunch.

'Where's Audrey?'

'Weekend off.'

'Why didn't you say? We could have arrived earlier to help you.'

'I had shopping to do, so no problem.'

They had lunch, and Jess departed to visit with Jim.

He took Elizabeth to the patio with their coffee.

'Richard, can I ask you for a favour?'

'Off course. Fire away.'

'Last week, whilst at my parents, I mentioned you. They would love to meet this person who has lifted me out of my shell. Would you come with me on Monday, just for lunch with them? I appreciate it will not be the most exciting of dates, but it is important to me they're happy with what I do. They've been so concerned about me since David died.'

'Will Jess be with us?'

'I think she has to be so they can see how you and Jess get along.'

'Then consider it a date.'

'Thank you. I appreciate your understanding. It's all part of conventional life, I'm afraid. But we'll endeavour to make it as painless as possible.'

Changing the subject 'I've another more delicate subject for you to help me with.'

He looked at her, 'Now where are you going?'

'The subject is sex. I would like to know your thoughts regarding sexual relations.'

'Well, that's a pole shift. Are we talking in general, or specific?'

'Richard, I've not had sexual relations with a man for over five years. You tell me it has been over ten years for you. When you touched my breasts in the shower it was lovely, and I want more. But how do we progress, as this is proving to be a genuine dilemma for me?'

She was trembling with nerves speaking of such intimacy, but it was a real issue for her, and she wanted to bring it to his attention. She had initiated kissing. He had touched her intimately. But how do they progress to a loving relationship?

'My goodness lady, you never cease to surprise me. Here I am moving gently from first gear to second because I don't want to spoil anything between us, and you are raring to move to top gear.' They both laughed.

'But you're right. I felt paralysed at your forward approach in the pool, but the result was wonderful, including in the shower. I now know the opportunity is there to progress. My only real suggestion is we be impulsive with each other and go where it takes us. I think we both know how we feel about each other, even after just a short time. I'm confident we'll find our way to a loving relationship.'

'Do you mind if I use terms such as darling when we're together?'

'It will flatter me.'

'Then, my darling, we need to spend the time together to complete our goal.' She kissed him on the cheek.

They both sat back in their chairs, reflecting on the quantum leap they had just expressed to each other. She was shaking at what she had said *'such a tart'* she thought to herself. But she could not control her feelings for this man. They just came pouring out. He was smiling at the prospect of not having to be so careful. He could now pursue the one thing missing in this new home of his – a loving relationship with a lovely woman; something missing from his life for far too many years. And her declaration regarding sex had left him dumbfounded. He could not remember a single relationship in his life where the woman so openly expressed her desire for sex.

They both awoke from their thoughts, looked at each other with loving eyes, and made their way to the kitchen, hand in hand.

'Let's go for a swim.'

He noticed she was more playful in the water. She wanted contact and would engage in any way to get it. He decided to be much more intimate with her. He caught her, pulled her close to him with her back to him. His hands moved from her waist upwards to her breasts, which he gently caressed. She leaned into him, wanting more. 'This is so nice darling. Swimming naked is the only way to feel alive.'

She was so close to him she could feel the movement in his loins as his erection developed. Her mind was now in a pleasant place. *'Relax. Let this go where this takes us'* she thought as her loins were responding. She so wanted him to touch her below so she could display her total submission to his advances.

His thoughts were how nice it is to experience such intimacy after so many years. On previous occasions with her he had fought to suppress an erection. But now he felt unabashed about this most obvious sign of arousal. She had given him consent to progress to sex; there are no more barriers. They were alone in the house. They could do whatever came naturally.

He noted she had made no attempt to move away from his erection. On the contrary, was it the movement of the water causing her bottom to caress him, or was she doing it herself? He slowly moved one hand down her front past her tummy, then across her abdomen continuing in expectation of being halted before reaching that most intimate of regions. She did not stop his progress.

She felt his fingers explore her. *'Thank you, darling'* she thought as she opened her legs relying on him to support her with his other hand. She felt her loins gush with pleasure as he explored deeper. This activity pulled her harder against his now full erection, which added to her pleasure.

He could feel the warmth generated in her loins. *'Is this the time to take her, here and now in the pool?'* He considered.

He turned her to face him. Her smile answered his question. They kissed, a long passionate kiss. She had both arms around his neck. He reached down and lifted her buttocks, spreading her legs on either side of his. He felt the connection of the head of his erection against her vagina. She reached down to guide him in as he lowered her onto him. She returned her hand to his neck, pulling him to an even deeper kiss as he pulled her fully onto him. Her legs instinctively wrapped around his waist. Her mind was a haze of pleasure recalling how much she had missed such intimacy. She heard a voice in her ear 'How is our progress towards sex?'

'Really nice. I want more.'

He started to slowly move his hips to allow him to move in and out of her whilst holding her hips steady. She hummed with pleasure.

'Darling, why don't we go somewhere to finish this.'

He lifted her off him, and they walked towards the showers.

He switched on a shower. They both held each other tight as warm water streamed across them. They applied gel to each other. His erection had not fully deflated. As she gently washed him, he responded again. She was in no hurry to finish her task as she enjoyed touching this now throbbing erection.

He could wait no longer. The shower was stopped. He encouraged her to the now warm floor and thrust deep into her. Her groan told him all was good. He leaned over her, arms fully extended so the only contact was where they were co-joined. When he thrust into her, she held his forearms to stop her slipping around on the wet floor.

She could feel the heat generating in her loins. He felt so good inside her. Oh, how she had missed sex.

He increased the urgency of his movements. She felt herself totally relax as she could feel herself moving towards orgasm. 'Yes, please my darling. More. So nice.'

He felt himself ready to explode into her. She started to spasm. He thrust harder. Her spasms increased. They exploded together.

Once their orgasms had quieted, he dropped onto his elbows, still inside her, to kiss her. This kiss was urgently passionate.

When they parted, she stroked his cheek, 'What are you doing to me, you lovely man? And don't ask me how I feel because I don't know the words to describe how wonderful I feel.'

He smiled at her 'I'll settle for why did I leave this pleasure for so long? You talk of the changes to you over the past days. I can't believe how much you have transformed my life.'

They both laughed at the ridiculous nature of their relationship. Two middle-aged people acting like they were enjoying sex for the first time.

He lifted himself out of her. 'Why don't we finish our shower and go celebrate our progress.'

He lifted her up and restarted the shower. The cleansing process was seductive and passionate. They pampered each other, then dried each other before moving to the kitchen to find a bottle of prosecco, and then to the patio.

Jess came bouncing in with Jim. They were both in good spirit. Whilst greeting her mum, she immediately noticed her mum's pupils were dilated. '*My mom has crossed a frontier this afternoon*' she thought, '*Well done Richard. Won't be long now before this is my new address.*'

Richard went to greet Jim 'Hi, Jim. How did this afternoon go?'

'Good. Jess needs to get me some product info about her existing clients, and then we are good to go.'

'How can you work with her sitting by your side? You are usually insistent no-one can watch you work.'

'She's too pretty to leave outside. And she knows what works for her concept.'

'Come, have a drink as we are way passed the cocktail hour. We are on prosecco, or would you like a G&T?'

'Prosecco sounds good.'

He poured two glasses and handed them to Jess and Jim.

Elizabeth was busy with dinner, so they all sat around the kitchen table.

Jess gave Richard a kiss on the cheek.

'What did I do to deserve that?'

'Progress towards our goal.'

'*What has she noticed?*' he thought.

Chapter 23

Richard arrived to collect Elizabeth and Jess at 10:30. It was a little over an hour's drive to her parents, so they should get there before midday – traffic permitting.

The thought of being paraded in front of her parents to see if he's good enough for their daughter was so alien to him. It was not in his nature to seek approval from anyone for anything. If anything went wrong, he adopted the stance that seeking forgiveness is always easier than seeking approval. Had Jess not been included, he would probably have declined this visit.

Elizabeth spent much of the trip briefing him about her parents. When they got there, he quietly asked Jess to rescue him if necessary. She smiled at him. 'Don't worry, I'll hold your hand throughout this ordeal if it becomes too heavy for you.'

He somehow knew she would. He felt more relaxed knowing she was aware of his dilemma as they introduced him.

The entire visit was stilted and uncomfortable. Her parents were no match for him, but he was polite and only joined into conversation when he could not avoid it. Jess was quick to see this visit was not a good idea. Chalk and cheese. She carefully encouraged this meeting over. She certainly did not want her nan and grandpa impeding her mum's happiness, and her future.

Chapter 24

It was Tuesday. Club tennis. Richard was interested to see how Elizabeth would react to him at the tennis club now he had been formally introduced to her parents. She had, again, organised they stayed as partners for all four sets, and she was much more relaxed during play. Now used to the way he liked to play, knowing it was mostly successful, she did not need as much instruction from him. Their partnership on court was becoming established.

What he did notice is she was still not prepared to exhibit any overt behaviour towards him and referred to him using his Christian name. Was she still so unsure about their relationship she was not yet prepared to share it with her friends? *'I think tomorrow we need to overcome any remaining uncertainty.'*

Chapter 25

He picked her up in time for breakfast. She is in a playful mood with a spring in her step.

Audrey did not miss any of this. *'What a lovely couple they make.'*

Their activities were far more relaxed, no hesitation. They wandered around the grounds, stopping to chat with Gerry about progress and his ambitions for a walled garden. She wanted to understand more about the grand plan for Buntins and even wanted to see all the boy's toys in the land machinery barn jumping on a tractor as if to drive it.

'Will you show me how to drive a tractor? I've lived in the country all my life but have never ridden on a tractor, let alone driven one. I'm very envious of boy's toys. Why should they have all the fun?'

'We'll put it on a wish list for you. Any other equipment interests you?'

'All of it. I want to till the fields, collect the harvest in the summer sunshine, and top the fields to taste the sweet smell of cut grass.'

'I think you need to sit with Gerry whilst romancing about farming. I think you may learn a different perspective. But you shall have your day in the fields.'

'Richard, you have such a heavenly life here. I so want to be part of it.'

'Then you shall have it. Shall we adjourn for a swim before lunch?'

'It's such a lovely day. Can we visit the orchids and save our swim for later?'

'Whatever you wish. Let's go.'

Chapter 26

When Elizabeth returned home, she found a message from her mother asking her to call.

'Hello mother. You rang.'

'Your father and I have been discussing your relationship with Richard. We think he's a very interesting man, but also very assured about what he wants. This concerns us as you will need to be strong to have any influence with this man. Clearly Jess gets on with him very well, but we feel they will leave you in their wake. Are you sure this man is good for you? Life for you was lonely with David in the last years of his life, especially when Jess went off to university. Are you prepared to be lonely again?'

'Mother, if we had this conversation a week ago there may have been some merit in what you say. And when comparing Richard with David, you need to remember David was still very active in his business, whereas Richard is essentially retired. We spent the entire day together today, and it was wonderful. I appreciate your concerns, but I need to get myself a life. Jess won't be with me forever, and I'm not getting any younger. In any event, we're only building our relationship, so I have time to evaluate every step along the way.'

'My dear, you are still a fabulously beautiful woman with no financial worries. Are you trying to tell me you cannot find a man more in keeping with your upbringing?'

'Mother, I know you and Dad have my best interests at heart, but Richard has shown me a different world to that of my upbringing, and I enjoy being part of it. I know my insecurity will give me some problems, but I feel so comfortable with him. Surely, I have nothing to lose by continuing this relationship to see where it goes.'

'We don't want to see you hurt, my dear. Richard is so different to the men you know. We only wanted to express a note of caution.'

'Okay mother. Your message is loud and clear, but I'm tired so need to sleep as we play tennis tomorrow morning. We can talk more when I see you next Monday. Give my love to dad.'

'Goodnight my dear. We don't want to interfere, but we have your best interests at heart.'

'Goodnight.'

Jess had listened to this conversation. 'Is nan trying to spoil your relationship with Richard?'

'She thinks he's too much for me, and you and Richard will leave me in your wake. She has a point. You two are clearly on the same wavelength. Whereas it's good to see you get along so well, it does sometimes leave me feeling I'm not included. I know this is my fault, but I need to be sure I won't become irrelevant.'

'Mom. You're not, or never will be, irrelevant in this relationship. Richard loves you, and you're the one person who brings to him what he has lacked for so many years – a loving relationship. I know you had sex with him on Saturday. It was emblazoned all over your eyes. And you both enjoyed it. How long has it been since you felt this way?'

'How do you know we engaged in sex?'

'Mom, a woman's pupils dilate after good sex. When Jim and I arrived, your pupils were well and truly dilated. Now you go get your beauty sleep and get this show on the road. Oh, and please remember I need the car tomorrow to go see Jim. If Richard can follow you back here after tennis, that'll be great.'

Chapter 27

Tennis on Thursday morning did not go so well. Richard could sense Elizabeth was preoccupied. She was certainly not focussed on her game. After every point she lost, she looked at him with apologetic eyes. It didn't matter to him. He knew her dilemma and was looking forward to helping her through the conflicts confusing her.

After completing the fourth set, he suggested they skip the après tennis social session and leave. She told him Jess needed the car to go to meet with Jim. She followed him to her house and pulled into the drive.

'Why don't you go change out of your tennis clothes. I want to have a quick chat with Jess about her work.' She did not resist. He went to the office where Jess was working.

'Hi Jess. Can I have a word?'

'Sure. Come in.'

'When you've finished with Jim, can you come to the house and tell me what furniture you want in your office. You're welcome to stay for dinner and go home with your mother.'

'That works well for me. And thank you again for everything. I'm so grateful.'

'A kiss will do.'

She laughed, got up from her desk, and gave him his kiss on the cheek. 'Mom is a little confused today so she might need some TLC. Nan tried to turn her against you last night.'

'Interesting. But all will be good by the time you arrive.'

'I have every faith in you. Go make mom happy.'

Elizabeth did not say a word on the way home. He parked in the garage and carried the bag she had brought with her. As it was lunchtime, they went straight to the kitchen where Audrey was busy preparing. Gerry was already seated. Audrey noticed Elizabeth was a little pre-occupied.

'Hello Elizabeth, my dear. How was tennis?'

'Not so good today. I couldn't focus.'

'Not to worry. So much happy confusion around this week. Even I'm confused, but it feels good.'

'How is your mother?' asked Elizabeth.

'She's getting old, but she battles on. Losing my father some months ago was a blow, leaving her lonely.'

'I'm so sorry, Audrey. I know what it's like to lose a husband, and I'm much younger. It must be awful the older you get.'

'We must get on with our lives and enjoy the time we have. My mother depended far too much on my father. His loss has left a big hole in her life. I'll be surprised if she can get over her grief.'

'She has you, and this must be a great comfort to her.'

Richard was listening, but knew he needed to close this conversation. 'Whatever time you need with your mother is alright with me. We can hold the fort.'

'Thank you, Richard, but my place is here. Of course, I'll give my mother what she needs, but our life must continue as well.'

'Does anyone have any preference for what we drink because I feel like a celebration. Champagne or prosecco?'

Elizabeth turned to him, 'what are we celebrating?'

'My dear, I was not being specific; just a celebration of life.' He knew this confounding distraction would change the mood, and wanted to make an announcement, but it needed to be a surprise.

Audrey piped up, 'I've not had champagne for a while. So long as dinner is prepared by whoever is left standing, I'd like champagne.'

'So be it. Elizabeth, can you get the glasses while I get a bottle.'

'She looked at Audrey 'What's he up to now?'

'Beats me, but he has a good heart.'

Lunch was a single course with open house for dessert. Richard filled the glasses. 'I want to say something to the assembled people at this table.' He had their attention. 'Elizabeth my darling, will you marry me?'

Everyone looked at Richard in disbelief. Elizabeth looked at him, 'You seriously want to marry me?'

'I do most earnestly and seriously want you to be my wife if you will have me.'

She tested his brow just in case he had a temperature, but nothing out of the ordinary. She looked at Audrey, who was nodding her head in approval.

'Richard, you are the strangest …. but most wonderful man I have ever met. I would happily be your wife, my darling.'

They moved together for a loving kiss as Audrey clapped her hands in joy.

He looked up holding his glass 'You see; we have a celebration.'

Audrey had tears of joy in her eyes. Gerry looked totally confused. Audrey raised her glass, 'to Richard and Elizabeth, may your life together be full of joy and happiness.'

After they exhausted the toasting Audrey piped in excitedly, 'Does this mean Jess will live here as well?'

Richard responded, 'Jess is very welcome to live here, and I hope she will.'

Elizabeth turned to Richard with a knowing look in her eyes, 'You and my daughter plotted this, don't deny it.'

'I don't accept any plotting of any description, I just know how I feel, and I have the approval of Jess to express my feelings. Anyway, I can't keep taking you home after wonderful days together, so I choose to give you good reason to stay with me.'

Elizabeth had tears in her eyes, 'My darling, I'll happily stay with you. You have made me so happy.'

Chapter 28

Jess arrived around 5pm to find Audrey busy in the kitchen. When Audrey saw her, she rushed to her and hugged her tight.

'What's happening?'

'We're having a special dinner tonight to celebrate.'

'What are we celebrating?'

'Richard and your mother are getting married.'

'What!'

'Richard proposed to her at lunch. It was lovely.'

'Where's mom?'

'I think they're having a swim.'

Jess dropped her backpack and went to the pool.

'Hello my dear. Did you have a pleasant afternoon with Jim?'

'Clearly not as good as yours. Audrey has just told me the news. I'm so happy for you both. I need to come in and hug you both, but I don't have a costume.'

'We don't use costumes in this pool. And it feels great.'

'Mom! what a change in you.' She stripped off her clothes and dived in towards her mother, hugged, and kissed her. She beckoned Richard to join them. They all hugged together. She turned to Richard 'You deserve three kisses today' kissing him three times on his cheek.

Richard turned to her, 'I hope you will live here as well'.

'Will tomorrow be early enough?' They all laughed.

'Why don't you select a bedroom, and we'll get it ready for you, if only periodically initially. I've asked your mother to come live here with me as soon as she can. We will try to arrange a marriage date tomorrow.'

'I'll be happy to move here with my mother, preferably over this weekend. Jim will have my graphics ready on Wednesday and will bring them here.'

'We need to go plan your office so it's ready for you. Let's go shower so we can get organised before dinner.'

Jess walked out of the pool and into the shower with her mum and Richard as though it was the most natural thing in the world. Her life was about to dramatically change, and she felt so good about the future.

Dinner that evening was a very joyous occasion. Audrey was over the moon with the news Jess would live there, and Jess had already chosen the tulip bedroom suite. They drank so much they stayed overnight. Audrey was off the blocks so fast to make up Jess's room and even took the toiletries from the guest suite bathroom for her. She had already prepared Richard's bathroom for such an eventuality.

Later that evening, Elizabeth got into bed next to Richard. 'Well, my darling, we lie together at last.'

He held her close to him. 'And how do you feel about it?'

'It's so nice to feel wanted and loved again. Everything over the past two weeks has been so fast and confusing for me. But your lovely proposal to me has now removed my anxieties. I feel calm, as though a storm has past, and refreshing sunshine beams down on us. I know you will care for me and help me through this transition period, so I feel safe in your arms.' She kissed him and then snuggled into his shoulder. It was late. They were both exhausted as they slipped into peaceful slumber.

Chapter 29

Richard was up bright and early. He went for a swim to clear his head before retreating to his study. He wanted to make a list of everything needing to happen over the next few days to ensure the move would be as smooth as possible. He underlined his priorities: Engagement ring, wedding date, furniture for the office Jess would use.

Armed with his list, he went to the kitchen where Audrey was already at work. Jess came bounding behind him. 'Good morning, Audrey. Good morning, Richard' and a kiss. Do I have time for a swim before breakfast?'

'Of course, my dear, breakfast in about thirty minutes' Audrey responded. She was off to the pool.

Audrey came over to Richard and gave him a hug. 'That was a wonderful thing you did yesterday. I know everyone will say it was all too fast, but you are made for each other, so why let time be an issue. Both Gerry and I are so happy for you both, and I'm happy Jess will live with us as well. This beautiful home needs life, and we now have it.' She moved back to her work 'Where will you get married?'

'I think I need to consult Elizabeth about where, but for the few friends I have we could have a reception here. I'll find caterers so you and Gerry can enjoy the day.'

'Not on your life. Caterers in my kitchen, nonsense. I'll find some friends to help me prepare everything, and then they can serve when we all return from the wedding. Caterers indeed. This will be a special day for this household, and I want to make sure it's a day to remember.'

'*The end of that conversation*' he thought '*she's bossy, but she cares.*'

'Where's Elizabeth?'

'Still fast asleep when I got up. She looked so peaceful, so I left her to sleep. I'll ask Jess to call in on her when she goes up to get ready for breakfast.'

Breakfast was a noisy affair, and Gerry was late. He appeared gently carrying one of the wild orchids from the wood, handing it to Elizabeth. 'I think this appropriate for such a lovely lady.'

She nursed it in her hand. 'Thank you so much, Gerry. You've been down to the wood to pick this for me? What a wonderful thought.'

Audrey hugged her husband 'He may be a rough-and-ready farmer, but he has a heart of gold.'

They made plans for the day. Elizabeth and Jess would go home to change their clothes. Richard will collect Elizabeth around 11am to go buy rings and arrange a marriage. He will also organise office furniture for Jess. Once these tasks are complete, he will take Elizabeth to her house so both can organise themselves to move enough of their belongings to Buntins to enable them to live there.

Gerry would receive a call around Saturday lunchtime to take the van down to collect everything they packed. Elizabeth and Jess would follow in their car. They would spend Saturday afternoon unpacking in their new home. Saturday evening Audrey deemed they would all have a celebration dinner in the dining room. "Suitable attire" was her instruction.

For Jess, packing was simple. Two suitcases and three boxes are all she needs to move her entire existence, or all she wanted of it. For Elizabeth, packing was a real dilemma. This is when it really hit her; she was finally levering herself out of the past. Jess realised this, so went to her rescue, deciding for her mum what clothes to take, leaving everything remotely mumsy behind. Pack as though we're going on holiday, was her criteria, and she was brutal in ensuring her mother left the past behind.

Finally, Jess made the call to Gerry to collect what they had packed. He was there in twenty minutes. All loaded Gerry made his way back whilst they locked their house knowing they had stayed there for the last time. There were items of furniture Elizabeth would like to see if it would work in their new home, but Jess liked the idea of a clean break for both. As they left, Elizabeth took a small box from her bag, removed her new engagement ring, and put it on her finger. '*It's such a lovely ring*' she thought, as Jess smiled with joy now her mum was so happy. 'New life, here we come' she whispered to herself.

Audrey had been out shopping most of the day. She was the last to return. Jess had already finished unpacking, and Richard was showing her where to find things she might need. Audrey needed help with the shopping so enlisted both to move the shopping bags and two boxes to the kitchen. He looked at the mass of groceries on the island range. 'Was there anything left in the store after you finished?'

'Out of the kitchen, both of you. Richard could you be a dear and put the car away. Keys are in the ignition. Much to do.'

'Can I help with anything?' asked Jess.

Audrey thought about her request. 'When Richard has put the car away get him to show you where everything is in the dining room. Lay me a beautiful table.'

'Consider it done.'

When Richard had garaged the car, he joined her in the dining room. 'Would be useful if we knew what we needed' he muttered.

Jess heard this so shot back to the kitchen to find she needed two courses and dessert, red wine, champagne, port, and cognac.

Jess looked aghast at the drawers of cutlery and cupboards of crockery. 'They're beautiful, Richard, but why would I think any differently in this house. You have a good eye, and great taste.'

'Thank you, my dear. I'm glad you like it. But it would be useful if we knew the menu.'

'I sense it's a secret,' she whispered, 'so let us concentrate on the word "beautiful". What do you have in table decorations such as candelabras and napkins?'

By the time they had finished their task, the table looked quite regal; both being satisfied with their efforts. Richard made provisions for the various drinks requested. Both returned to the kitchen to find the ovens working away, but no Audrey. It was a little after 6pm. 'Why don't we grab a bottle of prosecco and adjourn to the living room?'

'Good idea. We should take three glasses in case mom finally finishes unpacking and joins us.'

Once seated and glasses charged, he asked Jess what she would wear this evening.

'I'll shock you by wearing a dress.'

'And what is so shocking about this dress?'

'That I'm wearing it.'

He liked these exchanges with her. She was quick-witted and funny. This banter was good for his well-being. He knew she would bring an extra dimension to the family.

'What are you wearing?'

'Depends what I think I can get away with. I'm trying to mould "suitable attire" into an image I can live with. Any suggestions?'

'I don't know the contents of your wardrobe, but I think jacket, shirt and slacks might work.'

'A shirt! Are you serious?' he retorted with an element of theatre. 'How preposterous.'

She laughed at him, 'This dinner has something to do with your up-coming marriage. You should consider an exception to your normal approach, as mom will no doubt put on a good show.'

'Hmmm. Hadn't thought of that. I'll bear it in mind.'

At this point Elizabeth walked through the door. He stood up. 'Hello my darling. We were just having a refresher before dinner, having completed our chores, and being kicked out of the kitchen. Would you like to join us?'

She lightly kissed him. 'A drink would be very nice. Thank you. What time is dinner?'

'Absolutely no idea. We are shunned, and Audrey has disappeared. We have prepared the table using our own imagination as to the menu and await further instructions.'

Elizabeth stood up. 'I'll go find Audrey as I need a little time to prepare for dinner.'

Audrey had been to the bungalow to get herself dressed for dinner but was now back in the kitchen. Dinner would be ready around 8pm; no help required until ready to serve.

Elizabeth elected to take a bath. Richard and Jess chilled with their drinks until the last minute. As Elizabeth had not touched her drink, he suggested Jess take it into the kitchen for Audrey and then quickly retreat. Audrey appreciated the thought. *'Nice having Jess here'* she thought.

At 7:30 both Richard and Jess decided it was time to don "suitable attire" ready for dinner.

Elizabeth was out of the bath preparing her makeup.

'Did you enjoy your bath, my darling?'

'Very nice. It was good to relax after such a whirlwind week. Did you have a good chat with Jess?'

'She's great company. With her sharp wit she will certainly keep me on my toes. I'm very happy with my choices this week. This house will now become a proper home with the most joyous people I could hope to have around me, thanks to you.'

'My darling, it was you who swept me off my feet. But I'm so glad you did. I'm so happy, and what a wonderful home you have made for us.' She kissed him.

He was still unsure what to wear. 'I don't know what to wear to satisfy Brunhilda's instructions. Can you guide me how you think I should dress so I have your support against her potential disapproval?'

She opened his wardrobes. 'Not much to choose from in the formal wear department, my darling. What would you like to wear?'

'Free choice would be slacks, decent tee shirt, and a jacket, or slacks, collarless shirt and no jacket.'

'Does the shirt have links?'

'Yes. I have such a shirt, and I have a chain for the buttonholes of the shirt collar.'

'What about slacks, collarless shirt, and jacket with the option to discard the jacket at some appropriate time?'

He looked her in the eyes, 'Will that work for you? Will you be happy to be my companion?'

Elizabeth found his uncertainty amusing. He really had not dated in a long time. 'You'll look great. Now please get dressed and leave me to finish getting ready. We should not be late. Audrey has made a real effort. We owe her punctuality.'

He quickly showered and dressed in just ten minutes. Elizabeth had fretted about what to wear but had chosen a silk dress that clung to her figure and took years off her. She was satisfied with her choice. Her new engagement ring finished her preparation, putting a satisfied smile on her face.

'Are you ready, my darling? You look wonderful. May I escort you to dinner?'

'Come, my handsome beau, let us to the dining room.'

When they reached the dining room, he detected arrangement of the table had been finalised. Gerry was in the background, feeling awkward in a suit and tie. When he saw Richard and Elizabeth, he felt saved. 'What a lovely couple you make.' He turned to Elizabeth 'It's the first time we've seen Richard dressed for dinner. Be ready to pick Audrey up off the floor.' They both laughed.

Richard popped a bottle of champagne, poured five glasses, and handed them around. Jess appeared wearing a pinafore over her dress. 'What a pretty and delightful waitress you make my dear.'

'Richard, you do have real clothes. How handsome you are. And mother, how lovely you look tonight.'

'Thank you, my dear. You look lovely as well. I haven't seen you in a dress for some time.'

'Special occasion, mom.'

'Where's Audrey? Does she need any help?'

'We have everything under control. I'll go get her.'

Jess reappeared with Audrey, without pinafores, both looking lovely, carrying the starter. Once deposited on the table, Richard passed champagne to both. He then tapped his glass with his finger to attract attention, 'Can I welcome my darling Elizabeth and the delightful Jess to our family. I'm so grateful for their presence in this house. We now have a home. Raise your glasses to "our family"'.

'Our family' came the response.

'And a special toast to Audrey for all of her efforts to make our new family members welcome, and for this special evening.'

They all turned to Audrey and toasted her.

Audrey looked at Richard in amazement, 'Thank you dearest Richard,' she paused 'for wearing some clothes for a change. You look handsome when you're scrubbed up.'

Everyone laughed. She always had the last word.

Her gaze directed to Elizabeth, 'What a lovely ring.' She moved forward to get a closer look. 'I would like to add my personal welcome to you and Jess. I'm so happy to have you both here.'

Elizabeth kissed Audrey on the cheek. 'Thank you for everything. You and Gerry are lovely people.'

After they had finished their starter Audrey and Jess wheeled in the pièce de résistance, a whole suckling pig beautifully dressed. Richard got up from his chair to give Audrey a kiss, 'You have exceeded all expectations, Audrey. Thank you.' She humorously curtsied.

After dinner Richard announced their marriage is arranged for four weeks hence. He quipped Audrey could help Elizabeth prepare, and he and Jess would help each other as both needed help with suitable attire. Jess rose to this, 'you want me to dress you for your wedding? Bring it on. We're going shopping.'

'I look forward to it, and on your head be the result.'

Elizabeth looked on with joy at how well these two bounced off each other. *'Life will be fun with them'* she thought. What a difference she was seeing in Jess jousting with her darling Richard. She so needed this interaction.

'We'll also need to think about a guest list.'

'Mine is easy; Jim, Margaret, and Robert.'

'What about your other friends from the past?'

'The past is the past. This is my new life. I don't want any baggage. Business contacts are not friends, they're clients.'

Both Elizabeth and Jess looked at him with some surprise. Audrey and Gerry already knew his views on the past. Jess recalled her mother telling her about a darkness in his past. She suddenly felt very protective of him. She would be his friend, a true and loyal friend. She must also speak with her mum to ensure she leaves the past behind on her invitation list.

'What about your parents, my darling? Are they still alive?'

'Yes, they are. My father has Alzheimer's. There's a wonderful care home in the mountains in Switzerland where he lives with my mother who will not leave his side. I'll send them some pictures of the wedding.'

Elizabeth realised she was on sensitive ground and should quickly move on lest she spoil this evening. She picked up her glass 'I realise in all the joy this evening I have not thanked you all for the welcome offered to Jess and myself to join this lovely family. We're both overwhelmed with your kindness and generosity. Can I say thank you for both of us and raise our glasses to a joyous future together.'

Richard raised his glass 'to the future, my darling'.

'*Smart move, mom,*' thought Jess.

Audrey, who was more familiar with his history, did her busying thing getting everyone involved with cheese, chocolates, coffee, port, and cognac. The cloud quickly passed by, and joviality returned. She put Richard on port and cognac duty to get him occupied. He liked his cognac, so was fussy about how it is served.

Even Gerry had one, just for medicinal purposes, of course. He pushed his chair back and stood with his cognac. Everyone stopped to see what he was about to say. 'As the member of this family who quietly lives in the corner, with everything going on around me, I would like to come out of my corner for a moment to add a few words of my own to the momentous events of the past two weeks. When we first came here, and Richard referred to us as family, I didn't really understand what he was saying. I'm not good with words, but this evening I really feel like we are a family, and now understand what he means. Coming here, having been a farmer all my life, was a big wrench for me. But the love and joy in this wonderful home has made us both so happy we took the plunge. Therefore, I want to thank everyone for this new life we have. Cheers to you all.'

Audrey was in tears as she rose to hug and kiss her husband. The others clapped and cheered him.

It was late. Everyone had helped to clear the table and kitchen, and it was time for bed. Audrey and Gerry were off tomorrow, so the others agreed to breakfast whenever they all assembled. They all said their goodnights, having had an exhilarating evening looking to their future together. Again, Elizabeth went to bed, curled up in his arms and fell fast asleep feeling very content with her life.

Chapter 30

'Sebastian, now you've finished your exams, have you written to your father?'

He was getting ready to go out for the evening, and probably for the night. His thoughts were anywhere other than his father. 'I now have a suitable photo and know what I want to say. My exams did not go well, so I need to gently prepare him for the worse. Another year at uni is now looking likely if I'm to get a degree worth having. I'll do it tomorrow and post it on Monday.'

'You will let me see what you write before you send it?'

'Don't you trust me to compose a letter myself? I did study politics, so understand the art of rhetoric.'

'Your lack of study is closer to the truth. If you need another year studying, you need another sponsor, or get a job to fund yourself, because I will not fund you, or keep you. So you show me your letter if you want to tap daddy's bank because you urgently need an alternative source of funds.'

'Are you suggesting you'll throw me out if I don't get funds? Mother dear, how do you propose to evict me? Do you have some heavy friends to help you?'

'Sebastian dear, you're old enough to make your own way in the world. You clearly think work is below you, and this bank is dry. You need to focus on your life if you are to survive. You'll only live here if you pay your way. Otherwise, go live with your rich friends. See if they'll put up with you when you cannot keep up with them.'

'I'm leaving. Don't wait up.' He slammed the door behind him.

Chapter 31

Richard, as usual, was up early. He was so used to just five to six hours of sleep. Lying in bed did not suit his temperament. As usual, he went for a swim, made coffee, and retreated to his study. This was his quiet time to think through anything in need of resolution that day. He decided to sit back and see what Elizabeth proposed regarding their wedding. For him there was no need to get married at all as children were out of the question at her age, but he felt she wanted the security. It was to be her day, starting her new life, so is prepared to go with the flow. He looked forward to a shopping trip with Jess; probably London would be best because he knows where to go.

He would need to clear out the room he proposed for Jess as the furniture would arrive Monday. *'She can help me clear the room'* he thought. *'And she can clean it. It will give her a sense of progress towards her goal and her own space.'* He could also resolve any cabling issues before filling it with furniture. The idea of her being next to his study pleased him. He can quietly help her without appearing to have made a special effort to visit her. He wanted her to be successful, but in her own right. He can guide, but she must make the effort and experience the trials herself.

He decided just as he has his private space, her office will be her private space, a retreat when she needs it. It was the first room as you entered his workspace so did not interfere with his; just slightly reduced it. It benefited from the special air conditioning in his workspace so would be a healthy environment for the long hours he thought she would have to invest when her business goes live.

Jess ambled into his study in her jimjams. 'Good morning, Richard, Lovely dinner last night.'

He loved this picture of innocence 'Good morning, Jess. Yes, it was the perfect way to start our lives together. I must remember to get Audrey a present to thank her for such a great idea, and for the effort she committed to it. Have you seen your mother yet?'

'We had a late night. My mom needs her beauty sleep. It will be a while yet.' She paused, and then gingerly, 'can I have a chat with you to resolve some issues I have?'

'Of course, you can. Let's go sit on the sofa.'

Although there were two armchairs either side of his two-seater sofa, she sat next to him on the sofa. 'Richard, I realise I'm the appendage, the baggage in your relationship with mom. I'm very happy you let me live here, but I need to know your house rules. I want to be part of this family, but I'm a bit of a free spirit and I don't want to cause any problems.'

He smiled at her 'Jess, if you're baggage, you have just given one big vote for the pleasure of having it. But you're right, and I really appreciate your concern. We're both in unfamiliar territory, so let me propose what I think and then let's kick it around until we find common ground.'

'First, and most importantly your bedroom suite and your new office are absolutely your space. You can arrange either as you wish, and short of lighting campfires in either, they're for you to do as you please. You can even restrict access to either, as I do with my workspace. If you keep the door of your office closed, the special air conditioning keeps it surprisingly dust-free so you can either ban Audrey from cleaning, or just let her clean as and when I allow her to clean the studios. I rarely let her in here, as this is my space. Some would consider it as untidy, especially when I'm working, but I know where everything is, and that's all that matters. I let her vacuum and clean the windows about once per month – that's it. How are we doing so far?'

She planted two kisses on his cheek.

'That good? Let's move on. You already know my studios are off-limits unless I invite you in, no exceptions. You will see little red lights above the doors. If these are on, you cannot disturb me for any reason short of a major catastrophe in the household. If World War III breaks out, I don't want to know. And no matter how long I stay in there, which can be many hours, you do not offer to bring me drinks, food, or anything else. There are no telephones, mobile phones, or any other links to the outside world in those studios. You will see the devil in me if you disturb my work. Is this clear?'

'Absolutely. I sense I don't want to see the devil in you, and thus this discussion.'

'We can't resolve every eventuality today so we need a format when we can sit down together and deal with whatever confronts us. We need a symbolic situation with no distractions. Can I suggest where we are now on this sofa is the platform that symbolises we need a serious chat. If you bring me here, or I ask you to come here, we know one of us has something to say. You are a grown woman so I cannot send you to your room if you offend me but, in such circumstances, we need to sit together and find out what failed in our relationship. Likewise, if I offend you. How does this sound?'

She planted three kisses on his cheek.

'Other than this Audrey maintains general discipline around the house, as you've already seen. She can get overtly bossy sometimes, especially when she's nervous or flustered, but her heart is in the right place. I call her Brunhilda when I think she's OTT. This calms her, although I would advise against using that name with her yourself. Ultimately, I'm master of the house so I can get away with it.'

'Does this solve your issues, or do you have anything you want to add or change?'

'Just one little detail. If you're working in here, can I disturb you, even if I just need a chat?'

'If we need to talk, or you need to chat, my door is open.'

'Thanks. I feel much better. For what's it's worth, I feel very good having someone like you in my life. I need a stabiliser occasionally and I trust you to be there for me.'

'Jess, I'm very flattered you think this way, and I feel truly delighted to have you here.'

As she got up to leave, she planted another kiss. 'Let me see if mom is alive as I need some food.'

'I'll get breakfast started.'

After breakfast they cleared out the room for Jess. It was mostly boxes of papers and other media. He chose to put it into the roof void above them with the other material he had kept. 'We need to take this up to the roof void so be careful how much weight you're carrying up the stairs.'

She followed him to the end of the corridor where there was a hidden staircase up to the roof void. He opened the door, and she followed him through into a space as large as a full-size tennis court, with an arched roof, and sliding doors onto a balcony at both the front and the back. 'Wow, what an enormous space.' She put her box down and went to the glass doors at the rear. 'Look at this view.' She then wandered to the front doors. Same again. Then she looked around. There was what looked like hundreds of poster holders. 'What are these?'

'Each one of those contains the first print of every poster I've ever created.'

'Why don't you hang them on the walls? Jim's walls look fantastic with his work on display.'

'First, his are graphics, whereas mine are posters. Second, you may have noticed I collect fine art. To date, I've only hung a fraction of my collection because it takes time to identify where each picture will look its best. Perhaps you can help me with this task.'

'Where are these pictures?'

'When we go down the stairs, you'll see a storage room on the other side of the corridor.'

'Can I have a nose at what you have?'

'Okay, but quickly as our primary task is to get your office ready for the furniture delivery tomorrow.'

They went into the storage room. It was crammed with artwork and other framed material. 'If you don't mind, I would like some of your work on my office wall, and even my bedroom wall.'

He looked at quizzically, 'Not very feminine for a bedroom wall. But you're welcome to have anything that is framed in here, that's my work. But if you want material Jim has created, I'm sure a request with a twinkle in your eye will be very productive. He can produce mounted prints, or he can give you the prints and I'll mount them here. His graphics are far more stunning than my posters.'

'I think a mix would be great. Can we come back when we've finished preparing the office so I can look through to see what is available?'

'On this one occasion you have permission to return to this room, but not until your office is ready to receive furniture. Good enough?'

'Thank you.'

'Can we now get on with the task in hand?'

The room was soon cleared. Jess cleaned which took longer than expected as she had to find everything she needed. Richard waited in his study until she finished as he wanted her ideas on where to put her furniture. Her first idea was to have her desk by the window until he pointed out the window faced south, so sunshine will blind her to her screen. Cabling requirements were minimal and could wait until the room was ready. They agreed to wait until the furniture arrived and then work out the best configuration. It was after 3pm before Jess went back to the storage room, and Richard went in search of Elizabeth.

He found her in the living room reading a book. 'Hi darling, are you alright?'

'Yes. I'm fine, thank you. How's it going with Jess?'

'The room is now ready for furniture. And Jess is sorting through my storage facility looking for pictures for her walls.'

'You have a storage facility for pictures?'

'Yes. I collect fine art but have only hung a few pieces. I need to find the right locations for them when I have more time. There are also some mounted posters I've created over the years that hung in my office in London. Jess is looking at these to see if she wants any of them to hang in her office.'

'I meant to ask why you don't hang your work the same way as Jim.'

'Jim's work is spectacular graphics. Mine is posters. I've suggested she flash her eyes at Jim to secure copies of some of his work for her walls.'

'What about the BAFTA's and the Oscar?'

'All Jim's work. I told you, he's a genius. I look forward to seeing what he creates for Jess. But I bet it blows her mind. I don't know if Jess realises her business will require a regular stream of new graphics as she expands her client base. I'm sure once Jim locks into her requirement, he'll provide a continuing flow of new creations for her. She'll have the best website on the planet.'

'I really appreciate your input with her. When she was building this on her own, she could get very frustrated when she needed to create artwork without the knowledge or skills. She used to see a young man who is a computer whiz in one of the consultancies near here. He did a lot for her until he realised Jess was not serious about their relationship. Jim has given her a new impetus. It has totally energised her.'

'Tomorrow she'll have an office and all the technology she needs, and Jim will bring her graphics on Wednesday. Then we'll see her level of commitment to put her business out there.'

'Changing the subject, can I take you on a tour to show you where to find things you might need before I have a hunt around the kitchen to see what options we have for dinner this evening?'

'That would be nice. But I insist on making dinner. I'm far too spoilt here. It's time for me to contribute to this family.'

'As you wish my darling.'

Jess felt as if she was in Aladdin's Cave sifting through so much wonderful artwork and his framed posters. She knew all the posters, and now she lives with the creator of these iconic pictures. But what to select? She initially wanted all of them but realised she would not have the wall space. But which ones to discard? It took her some time to select just four posters and put them in the corridor so they were safe until they installed the furniture. She felt looking at these works of art would inspire her in her business.

She bounced down the stairs to find her mum. She found her on her tour and volunteered to help her make dinner.

After dinner they all watch one of his movie collection, using his cinema projector, and then had an early night.

Chapter 32

Monday morning for Richard started much the same way as usual. Elizabeth was slowly resigning herself to the fact he was unlikely to be by her side when she woke in the morning unless she drastically reduced the hours of sleep she needed each night. Since David died, she had slipped out of early mornings only setting her alarm on tennis mornings, and then it would be 8am, some two hours after he normally arose. Now she needed to adjust to breakfast at 8am during the week. She had encountered her first downside to this new life. Or should she make that two because he was out of bed so early?

She went down to breakfast in her dressing gown to find everyone already seated and eating. 'Good morning everyone, sorry I'm late.'

'No-one is ever late,' replied Audrey, 'breakfast starts at 8am during the week, but finishes when everyone has left the table.'

'Thank you, Audrey.'

Richard was speaking with Gerry about getting the tennis court base, and drainage started. Apparently, the excavator would arrive today to remove the topsoil. He also alerted Gerry the office furniture would arrive today around lunchtime, but he was not about to let the deliverymen take this furniture up the stairs. He did not want the quality of the inside of this house being damaged or spoken of in the local hostelries. They would deal with it themselves. Jess quickly volunteered to help.

'Good morning, my darling. Did you sleep well?'

'Very well, thank you, but I must reprogram my mind to wake-up earlier. Since David died, I have not had the need, but now I feel there is good reason to savour the beginning of the day.'

'You have plenty of time to adjust to your new life. There is no urgency. With me, it's just habit.'

'What do you have planned today?'

'Much of today is about getting Jess installed in her office.'

'Would you mind if I went shopping? Jess made me leave so many of my clothes behind I need to replenish certain essentials. I also need to go to my parents to tell them our news. I will do this on my own as I need them to understand this is good for me.'

'Go have fun, my darling. Take all the time you need.'

Jess piped up, 'And leave your keys to our house here. I discarded your clothes for a reason. You must not go back there. I want to see all new clothes that match this new life.'

'My dear, would you prefer to go shopping for me?'

'No mom. But think what will please the new man in your life, and you will buy well.'

Elizabeth threw her napkin at Jess, and everyone enjoyed the fun in this exchange. She turned to Richard, 'Is this your influence on my daughter? Now telling me how to shop.'

He smiled at her. 'I'm sure you will choose well, my darling. You looked exquisite for dinner, so more of the same, please.'

'Help, Audrey.'

'Take no notice of them. What do they know about dressing a beautiful woman?'

'Thank you, Audrey.'

Richard thought it time to escape. 'Come Jess, get yourself dressed, and let's to work. I need to check the markings for the site of the tennis court with Gerry to ensure it's in the right place but will be right back.'

With that, they were gone, leaving Audrey and Elizabeth in the kitchen to gossip.

The furniture arrived around noon, and the deliverymen were told to leave it by the front door. Richard had already appraised Jess where he kept stationery supplies, had found her a printer she could use in her office, and how to connect to the network printers available for higher quality requirements. He had also explained how the server was configured and allocated her 2TB of hard drive space for her use.

They unpacked the furniture outside. When Jess saw the quality of the furniture, she felt the best sign of appreciation was her now established kiss on the cheek. Between them, this act said more than words.

They carefully moved it all up to her office, and after several trial layouts, finally found a suitable home for everything. Gerry went to clear the packaging before joining them for lunch.

After lunch Richard selected the cabling she needed and helped her to connect everything, including to the server. She sat in her executive chair and surveyed her new domain.

'Are you okay now to get yourself settled?'

'Thank you so much Richard. This is fantastic. I don't know what to say.'

'When you don't know what to say, use a kiss.'

She bounced up and gave him a barrage of kisses.

He left to allow her to get herself organised. She went along the corridor to collect each of the four posters and then decided on the right space for each. She would need Richard to hang them.

Audrey came upstairs with a vase of flowers and put them on her desk. Jess gave her a big hug and dissolved into tears. She was so overwhelmed with the generosity of her new family. Audrey stayed with her for a while until she calmed enough to get focussed on the task in hand.

Chapter 33

Tuesday morning tennis was a very different affair. Elizabeth made no overt reference to her new situation, but they arrived together, and she was sporting her new engagement ring. Arriving together did not arouse any particular interest, but as soon as one person spotted her ring, word went around like a chain reaction. Richard stood back as the female members of the club engulfed Elizabeth with interest and questions. Peter commented to Richard they thought the partnership was as tennis players, but clearly more to it. Congratulations all round leaving a shortfall in the sets played. When it came to après tennis, Richard asked one of the other male players if they could hit a few balls together, Richard feigning his backhand was somewhat sloppy today. He wanted no part in the inquisition Elizabeth will surely face.

Driving home she was full of the joys of spring. Her secret is out, but she is more than happy to be formally associated with her man. It was a load lifted for her as she adjusted from her old life to this new, exciting adventure. The next dilemma would be which members to invite to the wedding without offence to others. Not so easy as Richard is clearly not into more than a select few.

Chapter 34

Jim arrived mid-morning with the graphics he had created for Jess. He first went to Richard and quietly handed him a letter. 'This arrived from Sebastian. I suggest you bin it. You have what you need. The past is the past.'

'Thanks, Jim. If you think I should bin it, why bring it to me? You could have returned it.'

'I'm not good with these things. But I smell trouble. My address is not common knowledge; only the people we deal with. And no-one knows you have moved here because I wanted to give you time to finish this place. Sarah must know about this letter.'

Jim went to see Jess, who was eagerly waiting for him. Richard sat in his chair looking at the letter, wondering why such a letter now. Coincidence or trouble?

To read it, or not. He could always ignore it or write back to say the timing is wrong. He opened the envelope to find three pages, handwritten, and a photograph. It read in a tone of reconciliation, describing his teenage years, and his current situation at university. He wanted to meet. '*What to do?*' he thought, '*I could meet him in London. Certainly not here until I know his motive for contact. He will be consumed in his finals, and I'm busy with my wedding.*' He pondered on when and where. For now, he would keep this to himself.

He was already at lunch with the others when Jess came hand-in-hand with Jim, guiding him to the bench seat and sat next to him. In just a short time she had become very protective of this troll-like person whose genius was an endorsement of the proverb you should never judge a book by its cover. Once lunch was in progress Jim turned to Richard 'Do you think those rusty fingers of yours could get back to your keyboards and generate a sixteen-bar loop to sit under our website welcome screen?'

He looked at Jim somewhat bemused, 'What have you generated that requires music?'

'It's a multi-language welcome screen which draws people into the site in eight languages depending on where the IP address is located. My graphics for the site should give buyers the sense of comfort they would feel going to their local store. The producers represented by Jess are not major names, just as your local store is likely to be a family business – small but reliable. When people enter the site, it will respond to them in their local language and present images they can relate to in their daily life. The music needs to be neutral and comforting, to give a sense of safety and well-being.'

'Jim, who is writing the software needed to identify the location of IP addresses, and to attach the appropriate welcome screens?'

'We have it on our new website. We can easily adapt it for Jess.'

'We have a new website. Since when?'

'I've been working on it for months. I've engaged a web designer techy to write all the software we need, and most of the software I want to use with Jess's business is already tested.'

'And what are we calling our new business with this new website?'

'I've registered totten-buntins.biz to build the platform. But we can change this later to whatever we choose.'

Richard laughed, 'At least the name is ridiculous enough for a media company. When did you intend to tell me about this?'

'When you've finished this place to where you have the time to fully engage in business again. I have nothing to do, so I thought it a good idea to get our platform organised. It's good fun building interactive graphics for the web.'

Jess joined the conversation 'The graphics Jim has designed for me are amazing. They are visually brilliant. They unconsciously guide the visitor to where they want to go and encourages them to go there.'

'Okay, okay. It's my fault for encouraging Jess to ask you to help her, so I should have expected something extraordinary. What you're saying is we're going to spend the afternoon in the music studio creating a soundtrack to your graphics. And when do we discuss our project?'

Jim looked at Richard in his natural innocent way 'I've nothing else in my diary for today.'

Richard turned to Elizabeth, 'You've just witnessed why I don't keep a diary. This is the real world when I'm working – Jim, using a one simple statement request, commits us to a task that will take hours to fulfil. If you want to back out of our marriage, now's the time.'

Everyone laughed.

Jess piped in, 'Can I watch you at work? I would love to witness the creation of my soundtrack.'

Jim reached for her arm 'Jess, you would have to be invisible. You cannot speak or make any noise. When we're working, "Do Not Disturb" means exactly that. Can you do this?'

'If I fail to comply throw me out.'

Richard turned to Elizabeth 'Perhaps my darling Elizabeth should compose something for you. I understand you can play a piano.'

'Yes, my darling, I play – but only other composer's music. This task sounds like it needs an expert composer, and you're the best.'

Yet more laughter.

'Well, eat up you two. We have work to do. Jess, if you need a pit-stop now is the time as this task could take anything from a couple of hours to as long as it takes.'

It took all afternoon to generate what Jim needed. Before they could start Richard reflected he had not seriously used this studio since installation and thus it took time to fully configure and commission the active components before he could look at what Jim had generated, and how he wanted it to work.

Once Richard started to compose, Jess observed his fingers worked the keyboard automatically from the images on the screen. Then he would use the computer composer to refine the music until he had a sound complimenting the graphics by creating the required mood. Having achieved a suitable Western-style version, Jim then added the need for an adapted version for the Far East in scales typical of that region. Richard quickly realised Jim wanted a sixteen-bar loop that can be adapted to the style of music appropriate to the language. He was creating eight different music loops, rather than the one requested. Having seen the fantastic graphics Jim had created, he resigned himself to the task. Jess sat there amazed at the creativity she was witnessing. She felt so privileged to be a fly-on-the-wall with these two incredible people. *'No wonder they're in such demand'* she thought.

It was almost time for dinner when they finished. They had not stopped for anything, not even a drink. Richard switched on the main studio lights to see Jess still looking enthralled at what she was witnessing. Somewhat surprised 'Jess, you're still here. Congratulations on staying the term without us noticing your presence. Was it worth it?'

'Incredible. I wouldn't want to miss watching the two of you at work for anything. It's truly amazing to observe such creativity in motion. Thank you so much for allowing me to be here. I've seen Jim create fabulous graphics from an idea and now watched as your fingers convert his graphics into sound. Truly amazing.'

'Let's go see what's for dinner. Then, Jim, you and I need to go bury our heads and discuss your potential project.'

Jim told Jess he would come back tomorrow with his computer whiz and integrate the graphics and the sound into her system.

Chapter 35

Jim was back the following day with Tom, his website techy, who looked at what Jess was trying to create. First, he suggested her laptop could not stand the loading of such graphics for more than a few users at the same time. She needed much more processor power. Jim, seeing her face drop at the prospect of having to buy a larger machine, piped in he had a spare machine she could use. Little did she know, later, Jim asked Tom to go purchase what he thought she needed and put it on his account.

Over the coming week Tom configured her website, set up the shop accounts she needed for safe payments on both Amazon and PayPal, and loaded the first five producer accounts she had from local businesses. He also created the software such she did not have to intervene in the order process. Purchases would flow through her system directly to the producer who would then process the order and ship the goods. It subtracted her commission from the payment to the producer, so both were secure as to payment, thus maximising cash flow to both her business and the producer business.

After a day of testing the process with the co-operation of one of the producer businesses, her website went live. That evening there was a family celebration of the launch of her business including Jim and Tom. Jim had instructed Tom to monitor the system remotely, and directly, if necessary, to ensure she had a stable platform to the outside world.

All Jess needed now was more producers to sign up. Although potential producers could sign up online to be part of her website, she knew she would have to promote herself and her business. For this she needed transport. She used her mother's car but knew she would have to consider the needs of her mother. Richard spotted this constraint. He could see Jess was committed to finding more small producers. He announced he would buy Elizabeth a new car for her wedding present. Elizabeth gave her car to Jess.

Her dream was now a reality. She had processed her first orders. Tom ensured her website featured highly in the search engines. He was now waiting for advertisers to take an interest in her business as he knew the amazing graphics would appeal to them. This would generate additional income for Jess. In fact, Tom had taken quite a shine to Jess, although he kept his contact purely on a business footing. He did not want any problems with Jim, who he saw as a long-term client, and who was footing the bills for Jess without her knowledge. He decided to let Jess know of his interest but let her take the first step if she wanted to extend their relationship.

For each new producer, Jim would create new graphics. Jess could agree higher commissions with such producers as they were getting superior graphics for their products as part of the deal. She was in business.

She wanted to thank Jim for all his efforts on her behalf. She asked Richard what she could get for him. He told her he could not think of anything physical he needed, but he would appreciate a day out somewhere. But where? Richard remembered the annual International Technology Show would be staged at the ExCel Exhibition Centre in London in a couple of weeks. He knew Jim would love to go. But he warned her he would want to be first there, and last to leave, so be prepared for a long day.

Chapter 36

Both Richard and Jess were up early for their shopping trip to London. They wanted to catch the 8am train from Melton Mowbray to St Pancras International getting them into London around 9:30. As they were travelling first class, they would have breakfast on the train.

Richard had chosen Knightsbridge as his preferred start with Harrods as the first store to visit. He knew this area well so he would not have to go searching for clothes. Shopping for clothes for himself was not his idea of fun, but he is intrigued to know what Jess would choose for herself. He wanted to spoil her today so told her if she sees something she likes, and he likes her in it, there is a good chance she'll get it. She needed clothes for visiting her clients as well as for the wedding. He also knew she had little money of her own, having been saddled with sizeable university debts. He made a mental note to get his accountant to quietly look at the options to lift this yoke from around her neck, especially as she was now in business and loan repayments would kick in once she drew an income.

When they entered Harrods, he suggested they each go to their parts of the store for clothes, hunt around for one hour, and then link up at the coffee shop to compare notes. He knew he would finish in about fifteen minutes, but he wanted something for Audrey. Her efforts to welcome Elizabeth and Jess were way beyond the call of duty, and he wanted her to know this. He went to the Cartier jewellery counter and spent some time deliberating what he might buy. Buying for a woman was in the far distant past, especially someone Audrey's age, so he was thankful one lady serving on this counter was in the same age range as Audrey. He profiled Audrey to her and, using his data, she chose a very simple but elegant gold necklace. He liked her choice. This purchase was safely completed.

He had another fifteen minutes before he needed to meet Jess. He realised he might need accessories such as cufflinks for his wedding day, so had a wonder around the various counters to see what he liked.

He linked with Jess, and they ordered coffee. Jess saw he had a package. Her natural nosiness wanted to know what he had purchased. He softly but firmly made her aware it was nothing to do with their shopping and thus would remain a secret. It then occurred to him Jess might need/like some jewellery for the wedding. Opportunity lost; but he would try to recover this situation during the day, especially now he could put it in the same bag as the necklace, and thus deflect prying eyes.

For the first time he saw Jess confused and unsure. She had not thought to ask her mother if she was to be a bridesmaid, or a maid of honour. What is her mother going to wear?

'Phone her and ask,' he suggested.

Her mother was not wearing white, and Jess could wear as she pleased. Calm was restored.

She wanted to see what he had selected before taking him to view her selections. When they scanned his potential options, she liked most of his choices, but not for a wedding. He clearly did not want a conventional suit and tie package, and certainly not black or white. His choices were more middle-aged rock star, elegant but a mix of semi-formal and casual. She agreed with his argument to buy something to wear only once made little sense. But what about her mother? She will expect a degree of formality. This would not be easy.

She helped him to choose various items from his selection, which he then purchased. Then they went to the lady's department.

Selecting for Jess was easy. She was beautiful, had a good eye for what suited her, and any of several outfits she chose would be good for the wedding. He agreed to two outfits for the wedding, and additional clothes suitable for visiting clients.

It was now lunchtime. He went to one of his favoured restaurants very close to Harrods, leading Jess down a narrow lane known as Pavilion Road and entered Sal E Pepe. The maître de instantly recognised him, suitable greetings exchanged, and after praise for his beautiful escort, they were shown to a well-positioned table for two.

Lunch ordered he asked her if she was having fun.

'Finding what we need for you will be interesting.'

'How did you get on with Jim at the Technology Exhibition?'

'Incredible. You were right about the long day, but I learned so much. Boy, does he know his technology. He wanted to know about all the new media devices in minute detail and how they worked. He was like a kid in a toy shop.'

'Just before lunch we went to the Sony stand where he wanted specific information about their new media products. The guy we spoke to was polite; but not particularly attentive until he asked Jim who he was. Then it was like royalty had arrived. This guy went to get someone more senior who greeted Jim like he was the President. Once they realised Jim is returning to the media world, they provided everything he wanted to know. The senior guy even took us to lunch.'

'Some stands either gave him their products or committed to send them to him. It surprised me how many people knew him – never by sight, but certainly by name. Some asked him if he was interested in producing work for them. He agreed to have you speak with a couple of them.'

He smiled at her, 'I thought it would be a good day out for both of you. Jim is very special. He doesn't get out much, and if you saw him on the street, you would never dream of his capability. But his graphics speak volumes to the people in that business. It will be interesting to know which companies he wants me to speak with.'

'Whenever you want to reward Jim, just take him out for the day. Alton Towers would be another place, except keep him off the tough rides for the time being. A more sedate outing could be musical theatre. He loves to see the stage productions for new ideas.'

'Considering what I already owe him, I would need many outings to remotely repay him. But it's a good idea. If going out for the day is what he likes, then I'm happy to take him wherever he wants to go. I'll speak to him to see if we can set up a regular date.'

'Just having such a beautiful woman on his arm is reward enough for him. Perhaps you should take him shopping for his wedding suit as he won't know what to buy.'

'As mom doesn't want me to attend to her, I could be his escort for the wedding.'

'That really would be great as everyone else has a partner. Good thinking.'

Lunch arrived.

After lunch, they scanned the other men's clothing shops around Knightsbridge. This was not productive. She could see he was becoming bored with the entire process. She was thinking they would not be successful. Then she had a brainwave idea. *'If you want to dress a man, take him to Saville Row'*, she thought. 'Okay mister, follow me.'

He was very amused when she turned the corner into Saville Row. She had a quick scan of the various tailors to see if she could see anything remotely obscure enough to suggest the shop would have something out of the ordinary. She selected the first shop she thought might help. The assistant thought her quest amusing to dress an aging rock-star for his wedding to a more conventional lady – her mum. No suits, no stuffy shirts. Unconventional and unorthodox, with a hint of normality to placate his bride.

'Well sir, it would appear we have a challenge on our hands. But we will certainly attempt to fulfil the wishes of this lovely lady.'

After much searching, and rejection, the assistant came from another room with a jacket which looked like a cross between a frock coat and an Indian Sherwani coat with a high stiff collar. Jess instantly loved it. It was so rock 'n roll, elegant, and perfect for him. He looked at it with a very uncertain expression. But when he looked at her, she was beaming a big approving smile. He tried it for size. Other than the sleeves were a little too long, it was made for him. She took him to a mirror, turned him one way, and then the other. She said nothing out loud but was screaming at him from inside to like it.

He looked at her, 'What do you think?'

'I love it. You look fabulous. But we need trousers and a suitable shirt.'

The assistant quickly decided this was a sale so went to find suitable trousers, and a silk shirt with an upright collar to match the jacket. Richard changed into the full rig and reappeared to the applause of Jess. 'Even I would marry you dressed like this.'

'And you think your mother will accept me dressed like this?'

'I'll make sure her dress compliments your suit. I love it.'

The assistant agreed to shorten the sleeves of the jacket and courier it to him.

They were finished. Their quest now completed. They could go home, mission accomplished.

On the train returning home Richard had been thinking about Jim and getting him out more. For years Jim had gone nowhere for pleasure as he had no-one to go with. 'Jess, would you consider going with Jim on city breaks, say to Paris, Munich, Leipzig, Vienna, and St Petersburg. All your costs will be covered. But he has been nowhere for years. It would be good for him.'

'I would love to, business demands permitting. Of the cities you mentioned, I have only seen Paris and Vienna.'

'Could Tom and your mother oversee your business while you're away?'

'From a systems point of view Tom already fulfils this task. I guess I could get my mom to check to see if any admin tasks need attention, so it's possible.'

'Can you mention it to Jim and don't take no for an answer? I need another three to four months to complete the build at home before considering any major media projects, so he has time on his hands. He needs to get out, but he won't do it alone.'

'Since finishing university I've not been anywhere either as I've focussed on starting my business. It would be nice to see some of these cities, especially through the eyes of Jim.'

'That would be really great, and thanks.'

'No problem. You really care for Jim, and I'm happy to help.'

He thought to himself, '*This lady will transform his life. What a great asset she is.*'

When they eventually arrived home, it was after 8pm. They decided their purchases would be secret, and she would keep his wedding clothes in her room until the wedding day. She would also intercept the parcel with his jacket and hang it for him. As they had such a pleasant lunch, a light supper was all they needed. Audrey and Gerry had already left for the day, and Elizabeth had eaten with them.

As they finished a nice glass of wine, they congratulated each other on mission accomplished. She agreed to contact Jim the following morning to organise his shopping trip, probably to Stamford, and inform him of his escort for the wedding.

Chapter 37

The sun is shining; the air is warm, even at 7am in the morning. Occupants of Buntin's Place are waking to the reality today Richard and Elizabeth will marry. The wedding is set for 11am at the Registry Office in Stamford. Audrey has planned the day with military precision. The first orders of the day are for everyone to be at breakfast at 8am sharp as her team of helpers would arrive at 9am at which time breakfast must be finished and cleared away.

Gerry had spent the entire afternoon the previous day cleaning and polishing both the Range Rover and Bentley, inside and outside. They sparkled. They would all go together with Gerry driving, and Audrey riding shotgun. Richard had made his Range Rover available to Robert to bring Jim, Jess and Margaret as Jim did not have a car of his own, not being a driver, and the car he provided for Margaret and Robert was more functional than prestige.

Richard had just arrived in his study as he heard her skipping along the corridor. 'Good morning, Richard. Lovely day for a wedding. I want to wish you a lovely day. I know all this fuss is no more your bag than it is mine, but today is about mom, welcoming her into a new life with her wonderful new husband – that's you. I hope you'll enjoy the day, and if I see you looking forlorn, I'll come and smile at you. All your wedding clothes are hanging in my wardrobe when you need them.' She gave him a big kiss and was off.

He felt better already. After just five weeks, he could no longer imagine this house without her. Her early morning visits were exactly the medicine he needed to kick-start the day. He felt loved, and he enjoyed being needed.

He had prepared a checklist of things he must do, including not forgetting the rings. Now all he had to do was to quietly get ready whilst not getting involved with all the activity. His role is only to be there.

All assembled in the living room. Elizabeth commented on how splendid he looked in his unusual, but attractive attire. She looked lovely in a saffron dress.

Richard was carrying two boxes. He put both on the coffee table. 'Audrey. You're missing something. Could you come here and see if we can resolve this matter?'

She went to him somewhat bemused as he picked up one of the boxes.

'Please turn around and look outside.' He took the necklace from the case and put it around her neck.

She looked shocked as she went to a mirror. 'Richard, it's beautiful. But what have I done to deserve such a fabulous present?'

'Your services, beyond the call of duty, in helping me to make this house a joyous family home. This is a token of my thanks to you.'

For once she was speechless. She settled for a hug and kiss 'Thank you.' Both Elizabeth and Jess went to admire this beautiful addition to her attire.

Jess moved to Richard, 'Now I know what was in the package at Harrods. What a lovely man you are.'

'I have something for you as well', as he picked up the second box.

She opened it to find a beautiful necklace and earrings. She gasped, with tears welling in her eyes 'Richard. What a fabulous gift. What did I do to deserve this?'

'Will you wear them today?'

'Of course, I will. Will you put the necklace on for me?'

After he had clasped the necklace, she replaced her earrings. 'Wow. You know what works for me.' She planted a big kiss on each of his cheeks.

'Now we are all dressed for the occasion shall we make our way to Stamford.'

The wedding was a simple affair. They had limited the total number of guests to the twenty places available at the dining table should the weather not be suitable for an outdoor reception. Thus Elizabeth, with much prodding by Jess, had whittled down her guest list to just twelve people, including her mother and father. Jim looked decidedly human in the clothes Jess had selected for him during their shopping trip, his trip to Richard's preferred hairdresser, and rounding off his demeanour with the broadest of smiles throughout the day.

Richard and Elizabeth made their vows and declared man and wife. After the photographer had taken the requisite pictures, they made their way back to the house. It was nice enough to be outdoors, and Audrey's helpers had outshone themselves with the decoration of the quadrangle with flower arrangements that arrived whilst the wedding party was in Stamford.

The most troublesome part of the day for Richard was listening to her parents trying to make amends for their judgement of him. They tried to dilute their embarrassment by lavish compliments about the house. But he had no time for people who tried to interfere in his life. Elizabeth was not a youngster at the start of her journey into a marriage. He was gracious for the sake of Elizabeth but did not envisage having much contact with them in the future.

It also occurred to him the secrets of his home would now be the exposed to the community knowing the tennis club members, and other friends invited by Elizabeth, would dine out on this knowledge for weeks. His anonymity was about to be exposed. He had insisted on no guided tours, and everyone confined to the ground floor. As the weather was very sympathetic to an outdoor reception, this provided people the opportunity to ramble around the grounds. He was very uneasy about this amount of exposure to his world.

After everyone except for Jim, Margaret and Robert had left they all settled for a peaceful time together reflecting on how many lives had changed for the better in such a brief space of time.

Eventually it was time to retire. As they reached for each other in bed that evening, it seemed natural to consummate their marriage before blissfully finding sleep.

Chapter 38

Richard decided, on this special day, the first day of his new life with his new wife, to stay in bed and wait for her to awaken. She was so happy to see him there, still lying next to her. 'Good morning, my wonderful husband. So lovely to see you when I wake.' She moved into his arms for a good morning kiss.

'Good morning, Mrs Lyons, my lovely wife. I hope you enjoyed your day yesterday, and I look forward to our life together.'

'It was truly a wonderful day, thank you.' She smiled to herself, 'I will always remember the never-ending smile on Jim's face with Jess on his arm. It's the first time I've seen him stand to his full height. And you must give praise to my daughter, not wearing heals, so she did not dwarf him. Have you ever seen him so happy?'

'That delightful daughter of yours shines a light on everything around here. I'm so happy she's taken an interest in him. I hope she can change his perspective on life and even encourage him to find a wife of his own. He has given so much to so many. Now he needs to find happiness away from his studio. If you ever have any ideas about someone to love and care for him amongst your friends, please do not be afraid to try to bring some love to his life.'

'I'll give it some thought. The way you look out for him does you credit. Between us all, we'll find a way to achieve your desires for him.'

'Are you disappointed I don't have time for a honeymoon for a while?'

'Goodness no. Can you please advise me of a nicer place on this earth to be than here? And look at the lovely people we have around us. We have all we need here, my darling. I understand why you want this place finished before the autumn. And how wonderful it will be when you have finally realised your dream home. A honeymoon symbolises getting away for a while to be alone together. In this house it's easy to be alone together if that's what we need. And the bonus is no travelling. Fear not my darling, I'm so happy where I am, here with you.'

She added, 'If my memory is working well, I recall we have the house to ourselves this weekend. Jess and Jim leave on Thursday afternoon to the airport for their early flight on Friday morning. Audrey and Gerry leave to see her mother after lunch on Friday and have the weekend off. No builders either. I'm sure we can have some fun together for a few days.'

'Thank you, my darling. Shall we start by taking a shower together before breakfast?'

'What a lovely start to our honeymoon.' She kissed him tenderly. 'I'll go get the shower warm.'

After breakfast Richard made his way to his study, detecting he was being followed. Those footsteps were instantly recognisable. As he reached his study door, he turned to see her bounding up the last few steps of the staircase and head towards him. As she arrived, she took his hand and led him to their sofa.

'I have a request. Instead of presenting arguments, I'll ask you directly. If you want my reasons, then I'm happy to share them with you. Is this okay with you?'

'Of course. Fire away.'

'Yesterday my mom became your wife. Today I would like to adopt you as my dad. For all intents and purpose, you already play this role so I would like to compliment you by referring to you as my dad or daddy. Probably "my dad" to others, and "daddy" to you. Would you allow me to do this?'

'I would be truly honoured, but what does your mother think?'

'She's happy if you are.'

'Can I refer to you as my daughter when I feel the need?'

'Of course, you can, and it would honour me to be your daughter.'

'Well then, my daughter, your request is granted.' They hugged, and she was very generous with her kisses.

'As I'm now your adopted daughter, and Jim is practically your brother, do you think he will mind if I call him "Uncle Jim" because that's how he treats me.'

'I think it will be the best present he's ever had. He's coming for lunch as we have a new project prospect to discuss. You can ask him yourself. But expect endless tears of joy because he has no-one else but me.'

Excitedly changing the subject, 'what can you tell me about your new project? Is it a major brand?'

'My projects' are secret. And it's only a potential project, small, and with acceptable deadlines, and is a result from your trip to the Technology Exhibition. Your Uncle Jim has got the bit between his teeth now he has you as a client and wants more work. But we must go slowly with him. I can't risk him having another heart attack, not least because he's not yet strong enough. It will interest me to see how he copes with your city break to Paris this weekend. Do you have enough cash as I have a pile of Euros in my safe?'

'Jim has given me a credit card on his account to take care of the proposed trips, and he has purchased for me another pre-paid Euro card with Euro 10,000 already loaded. I have no idea what he thinks we're going to purchase. Maybe a few Euros in cash would be useful, but otherwise we're good to go.'

'I'm so glad he agreed to these trips. I noticed how much he enjoyed yesterday with his beautiful escort, so I'm looking forward to some real changes in him.'

'He can be real fun. He has a naughty schoolboy side to him. I think our weekend will be interesting. And we've already applied for our visas for Russia. St Petersburg is next. Can't wait.'

'Good. And now my daughter, if you're finished, I have work to do to prepare for my meeting with your uncle Jim, so be on your way.'

'Thank you so much daddy. I'll make you proud of your daughter.'

As she skipped away, he thought to himself, *'I'm already so proud to know you, so being my daughter can only swell my pride.'*

Audrey and Elizabeth spent the morning clearing the quadrangle, having moved the abundance of flower arrangements to various locations in the house. When Jim arrived, Robert went directly to help Gerry move the tables and chairs away, ready to be collected. Jess was in her office, and Richard still in his study. Jim made his way to the study. After they had exchanged greetings, he was informed Jess was in her office and needed a quick word before lunch. When he emerged, he was hand-in-hand with her, tears streaming down his face. Richard stood smiling at them.

'You knew about this, didn't you? Are you trying to give me another heart attack?'

'I knew about it a couple of hours ago. But thought you may be happy with the idea of being an uncle.' They both laughed.

'Come. Let's go get some lunch.'

Richard led the way with Jim and Jess behind, still hand-in-hand. When they got to the kitchen, the others were already assembled. Before they sat, Jess made an animated announcement.

'As we are in a period of transition, I would like to make an announcement regarding my new role in this wonderful home. This is now my Uncle Jim, and I've adopted Richard as my dad.'

Everyone applauded her and cheered. Jim increased his tear flow as his chest swelled with pride. His social skills were lacking, but he knew this new role made him feel very happy. Although he is always treated as family in this house, he felt an outsider. With this new role he is now comfortable he is an integral part of this lovely family.

Chapter 39

When they arrived for tennis, they are welcomed as celebrities with many congratulations on their marriage. The few attendees to the wedding had already spread the word about the house, and the wedding festivities. Elizabeth enjoyed the attention, albeit she knew Richard would like to be somewhere else. But these are her friends. She could not invite them all to her wedding, so wants to share a little of her joy with them.

A few of the male players were more interested in him now they knew he was the owner of the large new house on Buntins Lane. Some of them clearly wanted to rub shoulders with wealth. Richard was polite, but not interested. He kept after tennis socialising as short as possible.

Their tennis was now much better. She was settled with her new partner, and familiar with his tactics. They were now considered the pair to beat.

Chapter 40

The week rolled by. Jess and Jim left after lunch on Thursday for their overnight stay at Stansted Airport hotel prior to their early morning flight to Paris on Friday. After lunch on Friday, Audrey and Gerry left to visit her mother.

'Alone at last, my darling husband. We have the whole place to ourselves. What shall we do to amuse ourselves?'

'Now we are completely on our own for the first time since you moved here, I have something I would like to discuss with you. I noticed the garden at your house is very ordered and cared for. Did you maintain your garden, or did you have a gardener?'

'I did it. I enjoy gardening. Why?'

'There is one remaining task to complete this house – the garden. Gardening is beyond my skill set. I'm happy to let Gerry loose on the walled garden because he's a farmer. But he doesn't have the skills and eye needed for a garden fitting for this house. Would you be interested in designing and oversee the gardens here?'

'Of course, I would. I would love to add my piece to this wonderful home.'

'Can we spend some time this afternoon walking the grounds so I can tell you the areas available so we can start to prepare the ground, and hopefully plant before the Autumn? I have a plan you can use to make any notes.'

'Thank you for making me feel useful. Don't think me silly, but I've felt a little like a lodger for the past few weeks. Putting me to work on such a significant project will give me a sense of really belonging here.'

'While Jess is not here, I have a request for you. As you know, I've put my house on the market. But I've not been back there since we left to come here. I need to dispose of all the things Jess wouldn't let me bring here. There are a few pieces of furniture I would like your opinion whether we can use them. And I need to clear out the office files. I don't want to go there alone. Would you come with me and help me decide what to do with everything?'

'My darling Elizabeth. I've been wondering what you intended to do about your house. And I completely understand why you don't want to be there alone. Why don't we take the van tomorrow morning, loaded with packing crates, so we can bring back what you want to keep, or dispose of? Then we can organise professional clearers to complete the task before we have it cleaned. We will then dispatch this issue from our list.'

'Looks like we're in for a busy time. We better get started.'

Although planning the formal gardens was not the romantic idea she had for their time alone together, it put a spring into her step. Everyone was busy except for her. Now she felt a part of the success of this home, as this task would require some three acres of planning – a significant project. And to get it finished in just three months would involve real effort. She was happy and excited as he showed her the various plots she needed to consider. She also wanted to add a visit to a major garden centre nearby on Saturday afternoon, both to get ideas, and to find out his preferences.

When they returned to the house he wanted to go for a swim, but she found a notebook, sat at the kitchen table, and wrote some thoughts whilst they were fresh in her mind. He noticed a change in her. She had quickly locked into her new project, showing a commitment he had not witnessed before. She was so happy with her assignment. He knew he could consider this task as done.

After nearly an hour she was content she had grasped the magnitude of the requirement and ready for a swim. 'Thank you for waiting darling but I had some thoughts as we were walking. I needed to write them down. But now we can have a little fun before a nice dinner for two this evening.'

Chapter 41

Although his routine would have him out of bed soon after awaking, he thought this weekend he would make the effort to be there when she wakes. This required compromise. But he needed an excuse to wake her sooner than she would normally awake. He went to the kitchen to prepare coffee for himself, and tea for her. He carried both back to their bedroom. The action of putting her tea on her bedside cabinet did the trick.

'What a lovely thought, my darling. Tea in bed. Thank you.'

'Did you sleep well?'

'Very well. What a romantic evening we had. Candle lit dinner for two for the first time.' She thought for a moment. 'Darling, it's so lovely to wake with you by my side can I suggest a compromise regarding my need for sleep and your ability to cope with very little. Could I ask that at least one day a week we plan to wake such that we're together? Being woken up as you did this morning is perfect for me.'

'I have thought about this. Over twenty years of early rising is difficult to break. As we spend all of Thursday morning together, what about if we extend this to waking and preparing together as a starting point?'

'Sounds like we may miss a few matches, but what a pleasant way to be distracted.' She snuggled in and kissed him. 'Shall we have a practice at preparing together before breakfast?'

When they finished with breakfast, he went to the basement to retrieve a pile of packing crates and loaded them into the van before driving to the kitchen entrance ready for their trip to her house.

The first task was to get the front door open as mail had piled up blocking entry. They quickly extracted relevant mail.

He noted a real mood change as she walked into the living room. The room was as they had left it, but it now looked

125

discarded and forgotten. She sat on the sofa surveying the magnitude of the task to clear her history from this house. This would be a daunting trial of courage.

'Richard, I don't know where to start. Can you help me, please?'

'My darling, can I suggest we start with personal effects. Don't sort them now. Just pack them and you can sort them at your leisure. Then show me what items of furniture you want me to consider. We can deal with the rest another day.'

'I have clothes I was told to leave behind. Perhaps they should go to a charity shop.'

'Good start. Put everything you want to send to a charity shop in one crate and I'll get Gerry to deliver it for you. I'll bring the crates in, and you can get started.'

He unloaded the crates from the van, having given her the first one so she could get started. He knew the sooner he could get her out of here, the better.

'What about the papers in the office?'

'The only files remaining are those we really need to keep for another five years for tax purposes.'

'While you deal with your personal effects, do you mind if I pack the business files?'

'Of course not. You know where the office is located. There is also a computer. We should remove the hard drive as it has much sensitive data on it.'

Within the hour the charity shop items, another crate of personal effects to be kept, and all business files were crated and on the van. Then she selected pictures, photographs, and other artefacts she wanted.

She had clearly had enough of this task. There were too many memories.

'Elizabeth, is there anything else of significance you want to retrieve as I think you need to get out of here.'

'I can't think of anything. I've decided against the furniture.'

'What about if I send Audrey and Gerry here to put things in order before organising removal? Indeed, you could ask your estate agent if they would like it left furnished for selling purposes.'

'Yes. That will be fine. I might come back with Audrey.'

'Then let's put a smile back on your face.'

When they got back to Buntins, he drove the van directly into the garage without unloading. There was no hurry. What was more important was to wash away her sadness, and what better way than a playful swim.

The afternoon trip to the garden centre proved daunting for him. It was very large, with so many varieties of plants. She noted his expressions. This brought a smile to her face, and she occasionally laughed out loud. He laboured on as she pointed to various significant plants, explaining to him where she would put them. When she noticed he had lost the will to live, she took him by the hand and led him out of there. She had what she needed to start planning.

Chapter 42

Sunday morning was a more romantic affair. They were out of bed, not bothering with robes as they strolled to the pool for a playful swim, after which they returned to their bedroom for more serous playtime before taking a shower together. Sparsely dressed, they arrived in the kitchen after 10pm where they agreed breakfast would become brunch with a bottle of champagne to wash it down.

Richard wanted to inject a little more adventure into their day while they had the place to themselves. 'Darling, you expressed an interest in driving one of my tractors. Would you like me to show you how to drive a tractor and then we can have a race around the fields.'

'Are you serious? You will let me play with one of your boy's toys. What about if I break it?'

'It will hurt you long before you can hurt it. There're built for rough handling so unlikely even a woman can break them.'

He quickly side-stepped the elbow aimed at his ribs. 'There are women farmers around here who could no doubt show you a thing or two about tractors.'

'No doubt my darling. But they're experienced drivers. You have never sat in one before, let alone driven one if I remember correctly. Come on. Get dressed. The place is ours, so no-one will see you. No need for self-consciousness. Let your free spirit loose and have fun.'

'You're on. Let's go.'

Once she understood the controls, she had fun, especially when she realised the faster you go in an undulating field, the harder it is to stay in your seat.

Chapter 43

Back to normal. Jess was back. He had missed their early morning greetings.

'How was Paris?'

'Beautiful, but hot. Uncle Jim had put together a very full and exhausting itinerary. He wanted to go everywhere. But don't worry, I reined him in if I thought we were overdoing things. Sometimes you just need to stop, take in the views, and absorb the atmosphere. In this way I could ensure we had regular breaks. But he was up for it. No sign of fatigue or strain. We had a lovely dinner on Saturday evening at an outdoor bistro on the Seine, viewing the attractions and watching Paris night life go by. I would say the weekend was a great success. We even did a little shopping.'

'And how did the two of you get along?'

'Absolutely great. There's much interesting knowledge in that head of his, and he's fun with it. We discussed anything and everything. Despite his cave-dweller lifestyle, he has a good understanding of life.'

'Think you could draft a profile for a dating agency for him?'

She laughed, 'I think we would do better putting him into the right place at the right time. Any woman who can get past the visual will find a lovely guy.'

'Thanks for the effort. Where to next?'

'We've talked about this. We want to go to St Petersburg before it starts to get cold, so we hope to receive our visas this coming week. Maybe we need to go to the Russian Embassy if we want them quickly, but I'll check online and go from there.'

Taking a saucy tone, 'How did you and mom enjoy your weekend together in this big house all on your own?'

'You're too young. On your way. See you at breakfast.'

As Elizabeth was at her parent's home for her regular visit, he paid a visit to Jim to hear his side of the Paris trip. When he arrived at Totten's, he found Jim already planning his itinerary for St Petersburg. 'So, you enjoyed your weekend with my princess?'

'It was great. And Jess is such lovely company. We have such plans for future trips. Can't wait.'

After a little thought, 'the only issue I have is they're not long enough. So much to see, but so little time. Would you consider the idea the four of us go on holiday somewhere which has both a historic interest, and a place where we can relax? I realise I will be limited on my exploration activities, but if we could have a break every couple of days, that would be fine. What do you think?'

'I think it's a great idea. I could do with a break, and we still need a honeymoon. Why don't you research some options that include a beach, tennis, and guaranteed sunshine for October or November so the four of us can decide which we all prefer?'

'It will also be a celebration of you finishing your castle. Your life has taken quite a turn this year, so you deserve a break. I'll report back within the week.'

Chapter 44

He could hear her approaching along the corridor, but the sound was different. As she entered his study, he noticed something very different about her. She is dressed. 'To what do I owe such a turnout? Are we going somewhere?'

'Good morning daddy' and kiss. 'I'm taking Uncle Jim to Battersea Dogs Home to see if we can get him a dog.'

He looked at her in astonishment, 'You and Jim are going to get a dog? What brought this on?'

We discussed it in Paris. My thinking is Jim needs someone around him who will provide unconditional love and requires him to look after them. He needs regular exercise and fresh air if he's to fully recover. A dog doesn't care what he looks like, or the hours he keeps. A dog is man's best friend and requires walkies at least twice every day. I've discussed this with Margaret and Robin, and they both agree and will insist he takes care of the dog.'

'I've spoken with Battersea Dogs Home and explained the situation. They have a four-month-old Yorkshire Terrier should fit the bill perfectly. Today Jim will come with me to see how they get on together.'

'My lovely daughter, you never cease to amaze me. Whatever next?'

'To teach him how to drive.' With that, she was gone.

When he arrived at breakfast, everyone was there except for Jess. 'Good morning, ladies. Good morning, Gerry. Has Jess already left?'

Audrey responded 'Ages ago. A slice of toast, a yoghurt, and gone. Where's she going?'

'To London with Jim.'

Elizabeth joined in, 'Is this another city break?'

'No. They're going to Battersea Dogs Home to get Jim a dog.'

They just looked at him bewildered 'what? Whose idea was that?'

'Our lovely princess has decided Jim needs someone to love. Can't fault the logic. Can't wait to see how it works out.'

'And when did this idea first take root?'

'Apparently whilst in Paris. Jess then consulted with Battersea explaining the situation, and they have a suitable dog. Now they need to see how Jim and the dog get along.'

'Does Margaret know about this?'

'Oh yes. And in full support.'

'Does she have any other crazy ideas for Jim?'

'She is going to teach him how to drive. This one I must see. Jim has fantastic hand-eye co-ordination, but his feet do their own thing. He had three driving lessons and one crash before he decided three pedals and two feet do not compute with him.'

'She has really taken him under her wing.'

After a little thought he pondered, 'I'm interested to know how this affects her business. She appears to have taken her eye off the ball.'

Elizabeth responded, 'I think her eye is right on the ball. She has you and Jim designing her website. Tom is taking care of all the technical side to keep her site active. Tom has now built an on-line producer subscription application, so producers are now coming to her. And Tom has also built a wholesale request application because the demand is there. I think he fancies her, but he's not brave enough to expose his feeling. And I've been assigned the tasks of administrator and bookkeeper. She only needs to see potential producers. She has a current turnover over £50,000 in just a few weeks. I think she is quietly managing all of us very well.'

He thought about what Elizabeth had said. 'This is my fault, isn't it? It was my idea to give her this help. She really has us under her management. Cheeky girl. But if she can bring Jim to life and give him a better future, then she has my gratitude. Jim is far more important than a little shady management.'

Elizabeth touched his hand in appreciation.

Jess arrived home, having pre-advised Audrey she would be home for dinner. Everyone was already seated when she bounced in with a big smile on her face.

Elizabeth greeted her with a kiss, 'Good trip dear?'

'Fabulous, and so much fun.' She dropped her bag on the island counter and joined them at the table.

'And how is Jim?'

'Like a kid with the most fabulous toy in the world. I have pictures and a video on my phone. It was so lovely to see how this little dog immediately bonded with him. It was difficult to see who was the most excited.'

'You brought it back with you!' Elizabeth asked.

'It was a marriage made in heaven. Once he had this dog in his arms, there was no way he would give her back.'

Audrey, now getting interested 'Show us the pictures.'

She found the pictures on her phone and passed it around the table.

Looking at the pictures Audrey asked, 'What type of dog is it?'

She is essentially a beautiful Yorkshire Terrier who was the runt of a litter of pups born at Battersea to a rescue dog. She's fully trained. Even litter box trained. He has named her Brandy because of her colour. She's so cute.'

Richard joined in, 'Is Jim prepared at home for a dog?'

'We went to the Battersea shop. He bought three baskets, a travel cage, litter boxes and litter, blankets, leads, toys, food, and anything else he could find. My car was full. They chipped the dog and even engraved her name tag on her collar. That dog will be spoilt rotten. She sat on his lap all the way home.'

They were passing her phone around and making comments about how they looked together.

Richard looked at Jess, 'where did you get this idea?'

'From you. Remember telling me on our shopping trip he needed a companion to get him out more and give him another interest. The unconditional love of man's best friend is a perfect solution.'

'So what you're saying is this was your idea if all goes well, and my fault if it goes wrong.'

'Daddy, when you see them together, you'll see how great your idea. As they are a little short of two miles from here, I've told Uncle Jim I expect him to walk here with Brandy on nice days. It will be so good for his health and well-being. And she'll get him out of his studio for at least two walkies every day.'

'This I must see. But I applaud you for your initiative. How come you didn't bring a dog for me?'

'Daddy, you have your hands full with me.'

Everyone fell about with laughter.

Chapter 45

When she arrived at his study, he wasn't there. 'Ha, its Thursday. Late sleep in before tennis.' She went for a swim.

She strolled into the kitchen, now back in her jimjams. Audrey was busy with breakfast. 'Good morning, Audrey.'

'Good morning, my dear.' She stopped what she was doing, 'That was a lovely thing you did yesterday, and a brilliant idea. I've been thinking about a companion for Gerry when he's working. In here there's always someone around, but out there he spends long periods on his own. Do you think

Battersea might have a suitable dog for him? Can't be a puppy or else he would spend half of his day trying to find it. But a dog used to the country would be good.'

'I can ask them to look out for one. But there are rescue centres around here. They are more likely to have dogs trained for the country. I'll do a little research and see what I can find. Most of these centres will accept a request for a specific type of dog and let you know when they have one. I went to Battersea for Jim because he has very special needs and they were very good at identifying a good fit for him. But Gerry is a much easier case.'

'Thank you dear. Let me know if you find anything.'

Richard came into the kitchen dressed for tennis. Good morning, ladies. He exchanged kisses with Jess. 'Your mother and I are going to see Jim after lunch to see if your exploits yesterday have resulted in chaos and another heart attack. Can't wait to see this new Jim.'

'Have you spoken to him this morning?'

'No. Margaret answered. Jim is out walking Brandy.'

'Can I come with you?'

'As the dog already knows you, I would suggest you keep your distance for a while. Let her completely bond with Jim. I have a little experience with dogs from my youth. They need one master, pack leader, whatever you want to call it. I want to be sure Margaret also understands this, so there is only one person who'll be pestered for walks.'

'Battersea told us something to this effect, so I agree to keep away for a while. I'll miss her. She's so cute.'

'Why didn't you get one for yourself if you feel that way?'

'I would never do such a thing without consulting you first.' She clung to his waist and looked at him with a cute smile, 'I have you if I want to go walkies or pester.'

He laughed at her and held her close.

When they arrived at Totten Place, the first thing they heard after ringing the doorbell was the yapping of a dog. Jim opened the door with Brandy tucked under his arm. Richard desperately wanted a picture of the vision standing before him. What a greeting. What a change.

Once the door was closed, Jim put Brandy on the floor. She stood at his feet, wagging her tail. Elizabeth knelt to stroke her, 'You really are very cute.'

Margaret appeared. 'Hello Richard. Hello Elizabeth. Have you ever seen anything like it? He's besotted with this dog. He's only entered the studio to show her and to install a basket for her. Unbelievable.'

'And how do you feel about it, Margaret?'

'Its wonderful therapy.' Turning to Elizabeth. 'You have a wonderful daughter. She knew more than any of us how to get Jim out of his studio.'

'Thank you, Margaret. Since Richard and Jess came together, she has really blossomed. And she thinks the world of Jim. I'm very proud of her.'

'Come through to the lounge and I'll get some tea.'

Jim sat with Brandy on his lap, still wagging her tail and looking attentively at these new people. Elizabeth sat next to him, playing with the dog.

Richard looked at Jim 'I understand you bought half of Battersea yesterday.'

'And I would have bought more if Jess had a bigger car. She had to stop me. I would sooner reward Battersea for such a super present than the supermarket.'

'Why do you need three baskets? Dogs usually get attached to one basket.'

'That's why I took three identical baskets and blankets. She has one basket in here,' pointing to it, 'another in my bedroom, and the other in my studio.'

'You are going to allow your dog into your studio when you're working?'

'You wouldn't let me keep Jess as my assistant, so Brandy is my new assistant.'

They all laughed as they visualised this idea.

Margaret reappeared with a tray. 'Fat good having a basket in his bedroom. When I went in this morning with his tea, he was asleep, and she was asleep on the bed next to him.'

'Why didn't you bring Jess with you?'

'I think it better she leaves you to bond with Brandy. Same goes for you, Margaret. A dog should only have one master.'

'It's okay, Richard. Jess and I spoke about this before. The rules are clear. Come rain or shine, if Jim is here, he's on walks duty. When he's away, then we'll take turns.'

'Well Jim, it looks like you have a real project on your hands.'

'No Richard. I have a friend and companion who needs me to take care of her.'

Richard was touched by what he had said. *'Jess you're a saint,'* he thought, *'you're due a reward when you need something.'*

'While you're here, I've found us a potential holiday in October. It's in Mexico, on the Yucatán Peninsula, at a place called ClubMed. It has everything we could possibly need and perfectly located for me to explore the Mayan civilisation. There are seven guided tours, so I think fourteen nights will be enough for me to take each tour with breaks. Also, Jess doesn't need to escort me on every excursion if she would prefer the beach. What do you think?'

He turned to Elizabeth 'Darling, what do you think about taking our honeymoon in Mexico, albeit Jim and Jess will also be with us.'

'I know ClubMed so I'm thrilled there will be lots to do, and excellent food, so yes.'

'Okay, we're on, and I'll probably want to see some of the Mayan sites myself.'

Jim smiled, pleased with himself, 'I'll get Jess to book everything for us. This will be my wedding present to you both.'

He quickly objected, 'But you've already given us a wedding present.'

'That was just a token until I could think of something more appropriate. What do you give the man who has everything? I think a delightful holiday away without the worry of what I might be up to is as good as it gets.'

Richard laughed 'okay, you're on. Shall I inform Jess to go ahead as I sense she already knows about it?'

'We have discussed it, so tell her.'

Richard turned to Margaret, 'Can you find out every jab he could need and make sure he has them. His immune system is probably fragile, so let's not take any chances. Talk to our GP, if in any doubt. Also spend a few weeks getting him acclimatised to sunshine and ensure he has appropriate clothing – long-sleeve and brimmed hat for exploring.'

When they returned home, Jess was eager to know how it went with Jim. Elizabeth hugged her, 'You have made Jim very happy. You should be very proud of yourself.'

Richard looked at her sternly, 'I understand you've been secretly collaborating with Jim about a holiday.'

'I was consulted, as with all our trips.'

'Well then, my message to you is book it.'

'Oh wow. Great. Consider it done, and thanks.'

Chapter 46

Jess came dancing into the kitchen for lunch. Everyone else was already assembled. She sat next to Richard. 'Okay daddy I've booked everything for Mexico, including a limo to, and from Gatwick. The upgrades on the flights were mind-blowing. I don't know what limit uncle Jim has on his credit card, but I sat there scared I'll break the card limit, but it always works.'

'How much did it cost?'

'Nearly £30,000 with flight upgrades but they only took £10,000 deposit now with the remainder due 45 days before we go. But I also put the Russia trip on his card, and that was nearly £4,000.'

'What? £4,000 for a weekend in St Petersburg. What have you booked?'

'Uncle Jim likes to travel in style, staying in excellent hotels. But breakfast is included, and we need to stay in a hotel at Heathrow the night before we leave.'

Chapter 47

It was a bright August morning. Elizabeth was away for a few days looking after her sick mother. By 7am Richard had completed his morning ritual and was sitting in his study planning the more boring aspects of running such a household. Jess came bounding into his study, wished him good morning, grabbed his hand, and led him to the sofa.

'I have an issue I urgently need to discuss with you. It's complex, so I need you to listen to the entire issue before formulating any opinion. I've been analysing and researching this problem for over six weeks, and we now have the opportunity to optimise a solution. Is this okay with you?'

'Of course. I can tell by your voice its important.'

'But please Richard, let me explain my whole thinking before any comment or interruption as it's the bottom line that counts, not the process.'

'*She called me Richard. This must be serious*' he thought. 'You have my full attention, and my silence until you are ready for me to respond.'

'Thank you.'

'A comment mom made to me just after your wedding triggered this issue. Her regret was she could not give you a child. She's also concerned I'm not dating, let alone have a relationship that could produce grandchildren for her. I'm so happy with my current situation and the opportunity to develop my business to bother about such things, although I would like a child sooner, rather than later. In any event, I'm currently in a rest period with my contraceptive pill, so need to be careful.'

'My mom is very important to me. I'll do anything to give her whatever she needs for her continued happiness.'

'My initial thoughts were to surrogate for her. I did the research about how this works, and the process needed for insemination; not pretty. Then I had to consider who would sire this child. I nearly came to you then, but decided I didn't have enough data, or argument for a considered debate. I continued to consider the options. Now I have a comprehensive solution to put to you for your opinion.'

'The parameters of this solution are that my mom would like a child between you. She would also like a grandchild, and I would like a child. We could solve all these parameters in one simple solution. I could use your sperm to fertilise me, ensuring the resulting child would contain the DNA of all three of us. It would be our collective baby.'

'The only remaining practicality is how to inseminate me with your sperm. We could go to an IVF clinic. This would require me undertaking hormone therapy. You provide the sperm, an egg extracting from me to be fertilised and then reinserting into my womb. All timely, painful, and lacking in any dignity. Alternatively, you could inseminate me yourself – short, sweet, and safer for me. Thus, to my request. Would you consider siring my baby to satisfy the needs of my mom and myself?'

'Jess, Jess, Jess, what are you asking me to do? Have you considered if I want a child in this house? Are you seriously asking me to betray your mother because this is certainly out of the question? I can see your logic, but logic rarely counts in emotional relationships. And if I'm reading between the lines correctly, you want me to have sex with you for insemination. You are walking into a minefield of problems and asking me to go with you. I love you dearly, Jess, but what you ask is a nightmare scenario for me.'

She expected this response. 'What about if I convinced mom this is good for all of us?'

'And you think you can achieve this?'

'One hundred percent sure. I know my mom. Her conservative side will initially resist. But just as we both knew you two would be good for each other whilst she was stuck between conservative past and radical future, a little push by me, and a bigger push by you, achieved a quick result. She's now so happy. That she expressed to me her sadness she cannot give you a child, and her constant desire for a grandchild, will win the day. Added to this, the fact this child will have our collective DNA will make her feel an integral part of the process, rather than a bystander. Richard, this will work for all of us.'

'And what about the impact on your own marriage prospects?'

'You have taught me not to sacrifice opportunity today for something that may or may not happen in the future. Package deals today are commonplace, I'm part of one. If a man loves me enough, he'll take the package. If not, I have a fantastic home here with a very special family for myself and my child. What more could I want?'

'And what makes you think I want another child at my age?'

'I sense you feel you let Sebastian down. You made time for him for the first ten years of his life, and only him, whilst you built your business. I think you would make a great father, grandfather, whatever you prefer. And I think you would enjoy the opportunity to do it differently this time, especially now the business demands on your time no longer exist. What else are you going to do with your life? What legacy do you have within the family? I feel privileged to act as a daughter to you, but I'm not your biological daughter. You help me with this solution, and we'll have a biological connection in our child.'

'When do you propose to put this to your mother?'

'When I know I'm pregnant. It will be much easier to get her on board with the certainty of a child, rather than her contemplating the messy issue of insemination between us without the certainty of a result.'

'And how will we deal with the delicate question of exactly how this insemination occurred?'

'We only need to say you donated sperm, no more. Her head will be way past that point once she realises a baby is imminent.'

'How much time do I have to consider this?'

'Richard, you have a quick mind. Extensive deliberation is not part of your thinking. The reason I came bounding in here this morning is this'. She took a testing stick out of her pocket. 'This tests if I'm ovulating. I've been watching my menstrual cycle now for six weeks. This morning it's positive. We're the only people here for the next two days. The sun shines on us to do this now. It will only take a few minutes and, to be sure of success, my research suggests I ask for four attempts with at least four hours recovery for you in between. I propose three attempts today, and one tomorrow morning.'

'You forget I need to achieve an erection.'

'*He's running out of objections*' she thought to herself. 'I'm no virgin – far from it. I realise I may need to help you, but much more fun than the alternative. And we see each other naked practically every day.'

'My dear Jess. What to do. I cannot fault your thinking, and certainly direct insemination is safer than the IVF process. But if your mother feels betrayed, you destroy everything we have, something I so want to avoid.'

'I have absolutely no desire to hurt my mom, or you. The two of you have given me so much in the past months. What have I contributed? This gives me a way to contribute something special to the two people I most dearly love in this world, but I need your help.'

'I feel I'm left with only two choices; concede to your request or go lock myself in my studio for two days.'

She laughed and then gave him a big hug and a kiss. 'Thank you. It will all be good, I promise.'

'But if this proves embarrassing for me, I'll stop immediately.'

'Don't worry, we'll have fun.'

They went to her bedroom to start the first insemination. She was as good as her word as she adeptly coaxed him to full erection and encouraged him to ejaculation. She held him close and whispered in his ear, 'Thank you. It was good. This is destined to work.' and gave him his customary kiss on the cheek.

He told her to lie still for a while, and he'd go to start breakfast.

She came dancing into the kitchen with a broader smile than usual. How could he possibly refuse to help this bundle of fun with her heart's desire. She brings so much joy to the family, and now she wants to add the next generation, as much to satisfy his darling Elizabeth as herself.

As they enjoyed breakfast together, she continued to call him by his name rather than her requested "daddy".

'Can I ask why you've reverted to my name rather than your preferred daddy?'

'For the purposes of what we are doing I have purposely reverted to the actual situation to help you help me.'

'I must congratulate you for the detail of your proposal. It was the only reason I was prepared to take the risk of the consequences. But you get any part of this wrong and you will destroy everything we hold dear.'

'Don't worry. And I'll revert to my preferred relationship with you after our last session tomorrow morning. You need to understand I've spent more time with you in the past few months than I did with my father for the last five years of his life. Don't get me wrong, I loved my father, but he became so busy with his work he never had time for me. The only reason mom saw him was because he depended on her to run the business administration. That's a detail I omitted this morning. Once I know I'm pregnant, I'll teach mom how to keep my business going when I'm too busy giving birth.'

'But back to my point, you're a proper father to me. You love me like a daughter, you make time for me, you're there for me when I need you. You can't put a price on the well-being I feel knowing this.'

'I also know the position I put you in with my request regarding the outside world. Your so-called conventional thinkers won't get past incest, although this is blatantly not true, and they will ask why mom is prepared to accept this situation. I must protect mom against this ignorance, but she has overcome so much convention over the past few months. By the time I give birth, I think we will tune her into our way of thinking.'

She pondered for a few seconds, 'It might help you understand this situation if I tell you what happened to mom when Dad died. I was in my final year at university so I couldn't spend much time with her. My dad only made time to mix with people who were likely clients. My mom lost touch with most of her childhood friends. After he died, the invitations to dinner practically evaporated as she was a single woman with no intention to continue with the business. She only had two friends who would invite her, and then rarely.

The only social interaction she had left was the tennis club. You have already seen partnerships are well established. Finding a partner was difficult, again, because she was single and a potential threat to someone else's husband. When I finished university, I could see she was so lonely. She offered to fund me for a year to help me start my business. But what she really wanted was for me to help her complete the process of closing dad's business – she couldn't face this on her own. Then you came to our rescue and completely liberated both of us. You came up in conversation for some weeks before she found the courage to ask you to be her partner, and I knew she was daring to contemplate more than a tennis partner relationship. She was already well on her way to overcoming her conservative inhibitions the first morning you played together. She was positively buzzing when she came home, not least because you had won all four sets. And the story with the club champions was hilarious. When she told me she was in your pool with you naked, I was initially shocked. But then I realised this was a do-or-die decision by my mom. Thank goodness she had the courage. That one act of courage liberated both of us. Look how quickly she advanced your relationship. But brazen hussy? Absolutely not. She had spent weeks fantasising a life with you, fighting her conventional instincts. Once she saw how you lived, and we would get along, there was no holding her back. You have given both of us a new life. I have everything I need here in this wonderful family, and I have absolutely no intentions to leave here anytime soon. But I would like to contribute something I know my mum would wish for both of us.'

'Jess, if it's any consolation, I cannot imagine this house without you. You fulfil a need in me to nurture, and you are a wonderful daughter to have around. You say you don't contribute. Every morning when you bounce in here for breakfast in your jimjams with your beaming smile, it makes my day. You're 23 going on 18 and it's lovely. And what you've done with Jim is beyond value.'

She hugged and kissed him.

'There is one question I'd like to ask you, but I feel reticent about possibly prying into your private affairs.'

She could see his anxiety so put her arm through his 'You're my dad. No. Wait. You're my fantastic dad. I feel I can share with you my deepest thoughts, secret anxieties, and talk to you about absolutely anything. And now you discard all normal boundaries to help me have a baby. I know deep down you'll always be there for me, no matter what. You can ask me anything you like.' She looked at him with a twinkle in her eyes, 'you may not always approve of the answer, but I'll never deny you the question.'

He kissed her on the forehead. He felt himself welling up inside as he gazed at her thinking *'what have I missed all these years?'*

She gave him a moment with his thoughts. 'What did you want to ask me?'

He gathered himself back to the moment. 'I'm intrigued to know why such a wonderful lady is not dating. There must be guys around here queuing for your favour.'

'Think about it. I went through school, then to university, where I had more than my fair share of fun. After leaving university a little over a year ago, my focus was to have some worldly fun after years of study, and start my business, before thinking of settling down. I now have a wonderful life here, and not in any hurry to change it. Our efforts this weekend will remove any anxiety about the female time bomb, so I'm not in need of anything else at present.'

'Your mother mentioned some computer guy you were dating.'

'Peter? Not dating as such. He's a computer whiz who works for a consultancy in Stamford. He was helping me with my website. Being nerdy, he has difficulty attracting women. I couldn't afford to pay him, so paid him in kind, which suited both of us. This worked until my doctor suggested I should take a break from the pill, and we even discussed using a coil. We had to resort to condoms. No matter how the media dress up using a condom, the timeout needed to put it on was a real passion killer for both of us. His proposed solution to this was to formalise our relationship, get married, and let the kids flow. But not for me. I had no feelings for him in that way. That was the end of that relationship; just a few weeks before you came onto the scene. And now I'm glad I didn't have a coil fitted.'

'Your mother thinks Tom has an interest in you.'

'I know. He left his calling card. He's a nice guy, but I'm not ready to make any other changes to my life, and he doesn't have the magic to change my mind. I think the fear of losing his business with Uncle Jim will keep him at bay.'

'Surely your desire to have a baby will defeat your aim of worldly fun, as you call it.'

'Got that covered. When I've finished using my body for motherly duties, I can get my shape back, and have fun knowing I have two doting people here who will fight for the opportunity to care for our baby.'

'I assume you mean your mother and Audrey.'

'They will so want to be part of the care of our baby, and I won't deprive them of their desire after everything they've done for me. And, coincidentally, this allows me time to have some fun.'

'You really have got your bases covered. I applaud your thinking.'

She nudged him in fun and looked at him with her mischievous grin, 'Maybe Michael, Audrey's son, will come back. I could bring his bloodline into the family with another child. We had a fling before I went to university. This is how I know Audrey so well, and why she will welcome our child.'

'For what it's worth I think you're the daughter Audrey yearned, but never had. She treats you like a daughter, and I agree she will support your quest. Gerry is a different story. I'm not sure how he'll respond to me being the father.'

'I think Gerry will think it odd but keep his peace when he sees the reaction of Audrey. The maternal way she feels for me has not escaped his notice.'

'Come lady, get yourself dressed. We have shopping to do if we want to eat.'

This was the first time they had the house to themselves, so they spent this valuable time at each other's side for the entire weekend. After shopping, they had a light lunch before engaging in the second round of insemination.

Later that afternoon they sat together in the living room to talk about her desire for a photoshoot. He explained to her a photoshoot has an objective, or theme. But he would not consider a glamour shoot as this was not for him. She could create a storyboard, find the props she needed to tell the story, and he would try to shoot it for her. Alternatively, she could try to model for him using some of his ideas for creative art. She couldn't think of a story she wanted to tell as an individual, so offered to model so she could understand the process. They agreed to have an initial test shoot the following afternoon to see if her skin tones would work without makeup, or would they need to deploy Mandy, his makeup artist of choice.

For the remainder of the day they talked and talked. Jess described her childhood, her time at university, her dreams, and aspirations. He reciprocated with the story of his life from as far back as he could remember. They were bonding closer and closer together. A call from Elizabeth briefly interrupted them to say her mother was now much better so she would return in time for dinner tomorrow.

Just before they went to their respective beds, they concluded the final insemination of the day. He could see she would sleep with a big smile on her face. She so wanted this to be successful.

Once in bed himself, he reflected on the day, and her extraordinary request. He was still very anxious about how Elizabeth would receive the news of his involvement in this pregnancy, but Jess was right, they had to lead Elizabeth where she knew she wanted to be, but still lacked the courage to step out of her conservative background. Then there was the potential confusion of his role with this child. Would he be the father, or the grandfather? Is Jess carrying this baby as a surrogate for her mother or will she be the mother? All these issues would need to be resolved within this convoluted structure. But they only become issues once there is a pregnancy.

He thought she had overlooked his potency. After all, he had not used it for some years. Maybe his body had decided he had no further use for it and switched it off. Only time will tell as he drifted off to sleep.

Chapter 48

As soon as he awoke, he went to Jess to finish his task. He wanted his daughter back. She was still asleep as he stroked her hair to gently wake her. As soon as she saw him, her beaming smile greeted him. She knew why he was there so lifted her duvet to encourage him in to finish his task. Afterwards he held her for a while as she drifted back to sleep. He left her with a very satisfied smile on her face. As he gently closed her door, he whispered a prayer for her success.

When she finally awoke, she donned her jimjams and went bouncing down the corridor to his study, full of the joys of spring. 'Good morning daddy, what a lovely day' as she kissed his cheek.

She was back. This was the Jess who made him feel so good about life.

'Before I forget daddy, thank you for believing in me. It will all be good, I promise you.'

On balance, he believed she would honour her commitment to convince her mother they had solved an issue for all of them. In any event, the deed is done, so no regrets.

'Ready for some breakfast?'

After breakfast they went for a walk around the grounds as he needed to think through the works schedule for the following week. This had been a lonely task throughout much of the build program. But now Jess was with him, complimenting his plans, making valid suggestions for a tweak here or there, or even encouraging him to think again about certain aspects. What mattered to him was they did this together. He wasn't alone. He could share his vision and plan with a daughter he loved, and she responded.

When they finally returned to the house, he suggested a very light lunch if they were going into a photoshoot. He also asked her to don her jimjams for lunch as he did not want to wait while lines on her body left by tight clothing waned away. A model goes through makeup without clothes, thus allowing these lines to disappear.

When they entered the studio and lights were activated, he asked her if she was sure she wanted to do this as she should not feel pressured to do anything. She expressed her desire to understand the process and what he was trying to achieve with her.

'Okay lady, get rid of the jimjams and go stand on that spot so I can find the right lighting angles for you.'

After adjusting various lights, he asked her to sit down so he could balance the light for low shots.

Once he was happy with the lighting, he wanted to explain what he proposed this afternoon.

'I want to find the natural shapes your body can produce, see the way your muscles contract for each shape, and thus find the most elegant and graceful positions for your body type. What I propose is we go through the alphabet with you attempting to pose each letter. It does not matter if you use the capital letter version, or lowercase. Also, it does not matter if the letter is not in the correct upright position. I am not looking for the letters, but the way your body shapes them. But first let me take shots of you in the upright position. The first will be straight on. Then you turn 90 degrees, and so on until I have the four sides of you. Stand upright, but not to attention. When I say "go" breath in, filling your chest cavity, not your abdomen. Keep your breathing natural, but hold for the count of two when you finish breathing in. Ready? Go.'

He soon had the four sides of her in his camera memory. 'Now let us try the letters. I will shout a letter. Think of the best way you can deliver the letter. You can sit or lie, whatever is easier. Mould yourself into the letter shape as best you can. Once settled, breathe in and hold for a count of 2.'

They went through the alphabet. He helped her formulate a few letters, but for most of them she was adept at finding a suitable pose. Having reached the letter "Z" which she performed kneeling, he told her he had finished. She relaxed, stood up, and he caught the very shot he really wanted.

'Put on your jimjams and we'll take these shots through to the edit suite and see what we have.'

She felt honoured he would invite her into his inner sanctum, prepared to show her how he weaved his magic on her pictures. She sat next to him while he activated his edit suite and loaded the memory module from the camera. He went through the first four pictures, which revealed she spent more time sunbathing on her back than she did on the front. There were also texture changes, some not discernible to the untrained eye to parts not normally exposed to the sun. Then he explained how a good makeup artist could blend these areas so they would not affect the texture variances captured by the camera. She found the intricacy and complexity totally absorbing. It somehow did not occur to her they were discussing her naked body in some detail.

He moved on to the letter shapes. For each one he could tell her which muscle groups were comfortable, and which were stressed. Using different letters, he could explain the difference in artistic shape between a muscle group comfortably contracted, or stressed, and why this was important when trying to compose an art piece.

Finally, he came to the last shot. He looked at it. 'Now that's the Jess I see every day. Relaxed, with your beaming smile. I would have this on my desk, but I don't think your mother would be pleased, so it will stay in here.'

He experimented with the texture, adding a little background. It stunned her what he could quickly change, and the difference it made to the overall picture. Then he activated the big screen at the centre of the wall. He applied colour filters which made her look like an Andy Warhol picture. He sent the first to the top left quarter of the big screen. Then he changed the colour filters again to get a different version which he sent to the top right of the big screen. He continued until he had the four traditional colour washes made famous with Marilyn Monroe as the model.

Jess was truly amazed. 'That looks fantastic. I would readily put that on my bedroom wall.'

'Would you like me to finish it and printed it for you?'

'I would love it.'

'But what would your mother think?'

'The colour filters wash much of the intimate detail so why would she say anything. I can imagine you'll further refine these images, so why should she see it as anything other than a piece of art. If I'm prepared to display it in my room, who else should be concerned?'

'Okay, I'll finish it over the next few days and let you have it in appreciation of you being my lovely model.'

She asked him what he was looking for in his quest for a work of art he could hang in a gallery. He told her about one idea he had about the unification of contrasting races, referred to this project as 'Love Is All Around Us' using the underlying premise love is a universal human emotion where race, colour, and creed should play no part. He would need two near identical models, one being white, and the other being a chocolate colour, but not black as this would impose demands on his photographic lighting skills not yet mastered for a colour picture. He could then use these models together in mirror image poses which should reveal their differences are only skin colour and nothing else.

'So you need a chocolate coloured me, and me.'

'If you wanted to take part then that's exactly what I need.'

They had been working in the studio for over two hours before emerging back into the fading daylight. 'We had better think about dinner as your mother should arrive soon.'

'Let me get out of my jimjams and I'll see you in the kitchen. And thanks for a wonderful afternoon. I can now see how serious you are about your work. I feel privileged you let me have a glimpse of your artistic dream.'

Chapter 49

Sarah was waiting for Sebastian to get home. He had indicated he would be home for dinner around 7:30 but it was now after 10:30, his dinner assigned to the bin. But she was not going to bed until she knew the contents of a letter that had arrived for him today. The postmark was Stamford. This must be from his father.

He pushed the door closed with his usual excessive force. 'I know I'm late, but I got talking with some mates. Time just rolled by. I suppose I'm too late for dinner.'

'I don't know why I bother cooking for you. Since you finished university, you never arrive home when you say you will.'

'Just chilling after my exams. No law against it to my knowledge.'

'You have a letter from your father,' handing it to him.

'Took his time didn't he. I sent him my letter weeks ago.'

'If you open it, you might have an explanation for the delay.'

'What you mean is you want to know what he has written. It's addressed to me, not you. Perhaps I should read it first and then decide if I'll let you read it.'

'Sebastian, open it and let me see what it says. This is my idea, and you need my guidance if you are to raid Daddy's bank.'

He threw it at her, 'you open it.'

She read it to herself first. 'It's short and to the point. He says he waited until your exams were over and wishes you success. Quite surprised to hear from you. He has stopped all business and moved to the country with Jim because Jim had a severe heart attack two years ago and is only now getting his strength back.'

She looked up 'well that explains why they sold up. Without Jim, your father could not compete. Why didn't someone tell me? Jim was like family.'

She returned to the letter 'he wants to meet you, but for lunch in London. He has provided a mobile telephone number to contact him to arrange a date. That's it.'

'Well mother, my charm offensive has opened the door, so we are one step closer to our goal.'

'Don't you get cocky. This is a cautious letter. He's going to take a good look at you before he lets you anywhere near his new life. He has said nothing about what he's doing other than taking care of Jim. I suggest you need to call him mid-morning when you're sober. Just arrange your lunch. Do not engage in lengthy conversation on the phone. He'll be listening for any clue why you're so interested to make contact. You're better face-to-face than on the phone. And one more thing. He only uses mobile phones for his convenience. Unless he has changed his lifestyle, the chances are he'll not answer because he rarely carries his phone with him. Just leave a quick message when it's convenient to call you back and make sure his number is in your phone directory so his name shows on your phone when he calls so you can compose yourself before answering. If you're not in a suitable place to speak to him, let the call go to message, quickly move to somewhere convenient, and phone him back within minutes. Do you understand?'

'Are you sure we need all this stage management? You make him sound like some psychoanalyst.'

'He understands people very well. That's what makes him so good at what he does. He knew how to press the right buttons in people to encourage them to buy the goods he advertised. You cannot afford to make any mistakes. You must manage your guard very well if you're to succeed. Heed me well.'

'Okay. I'll call him tomorrow, and I'll try to aspire to your teachings.'

'Sarcasm will not work, only careful wit. It would be helpful if you knew some of his work. He has produced so many iconic posters. Even after we divorced, I could walk past a hoarding, or see an advertisement in a magazine, and instinctively know if your father produced the image. If you can afford the time in your busy schedule with your friends, I'll tell you about his work. A little flattery will not harm your cause.'

Chapter 50

Richard was sitting in his study reviewing the plans for the walled garden as specified by Gerry. The depth of the footings was close to one metre, and even the step into the garden was a single stone piece with a close-fitting solid door. Nothing at ground level, or even up to one metre sub-ground was going to penetrate these proposed fortifications, no moles, rabbits, or badgers. The topsoil inside the area was being removed to enable walling structures to be built to allow growing areas of different pH levels. He even included a water storage facility using the rainwater from the bungalow roof; and to his amazement, included beehives. He wondered if Kew Gardens was remotely as elaborate.

He was contemplating the cost of the excessive nature of this design, not least because birds will still fly over the seven feet high wall and deposit seeds from their excrement. His mobile phone came to life. He glanced at the number display. He did not recognise the caller.

'Hello'

'Hello dad, it's Sebastian. Thanks for responding to my letter.'

'It was quite a surprise to hear from you, son. How did your exams go?'

'Okay. I got my degree, but I'm considering resitting next year to see if I can get a better grade. You mentioned meeting for lunch. I'm flexible, so tell me where and when.'

'How does next Wednesday at Sal E Pepe in Knightsbridge at 12:30 sound? If you don't know where it is, ask your mother.'

'Sounds good to me. I look forward to seeing you.'

'I'm very interested to meet you after all this time. If you get there before me, just tell the maître de you are with me, and he'll take care of you.'

'How's Uncle Jim?'

'He gets stronger every day, but he still needs to be careful.'

'Can you give him my best wishes?'

'Certainly.'

'Okay, I'll see you next Wednesday. Bye.'

At lunch he decided it was time to disclose his contact with his son, primarily to Elizabeth.

'My darling, there is something I need to tell you. A few weeks ago, my son, Sebastian, made contact through Jim. I responded, much against the advice of Jim. Today we spoke on the telephone, and I've agreed to meet with him next Wednesday in London.'

'This is good news. Why didn't you mention it before?'

'The letter arrived the day after our wedding. I couldn't decide whether to respond as the timing is suspicious. And he could only have obtained Jim's address through Sarah. I only sent the briefest of responses, inviting him to meet me in London. He knows nothing of my new life here, or even of this house. He thinks I still live with Jim. Having only now assembled a wonderful family around me, I'm not sure I want any disruption at this time.'

'But he's your son. Surely you must at least give him the opportunity to meet you. You can then determine if you want to establish regular contact. You said yourself you had a good relationship with him for ten years before your divorce. Sarah may have alienated him after your divorce, but he's a grown man now with his own mind.'

'It's the Sarah connection that gives me cause for concern. But you're right. I should at least meet with him.'

Chapter 51

It was Friday morning. He could hear Jess skipping to his study. Usual morning greetings over, she took him to their sofa. 'I think I've found a chocolate coloured me, and she's prepared to test.'

'Have you told her in detail what this shoot is about?'

'I've told her she'll be naked with me in your studio for an art shoot. I've made it clear to her this is not about glamour, but art. She's done nothing like it before, but as we went through school together as good friends, she would like to at least be considered.'

'Who is she, how old is she, and what is her ethnic origin?'

'She's my friend, Famida. She's my age, and she's of Iranian decent.'

'Jess, no self-respecting Muslim is going to pose naked for me.'

'Her parents escaped from Iran as young students with their families when the Shar was deposed because they were Christian. She's no different to me except for her gorgeous Arabesque skin colour.'

'Is she prepared to let me take skin tone test shots of you both to see if you work together?'

'She's coming here after she finishes work today to see your fabulous picture of me. Tell me what you want us to do, I'll tell her, and then see if she's comfortable with the idea. Perhaps you can test us this evening.'

'All I would need today is the equivalent of the test shots I did with you, but both of you together. A full frontal, then back-to-back, then your backs, and finally, face to face. You both need to have the same skin temperature, no makeup, and no clothing marks. The easiest way to achieve this would be to get out of your clothes into loose robes as soon as she agrees to take the test, then remove all makeup. Let me know you're prepared to go ahead so I can ready the studio, and then go to the pool and stand in the water up to shoulder depth, but only until you are both acclimatised to the water temperature. Don't get your hair wet. Then quickly get out of the pool, dry off, robes on but not tied, come straight to the studio, robes off and stand facing the camera on the mark I'll lay down. While you are in the pool, show her how to stand and breathe. Any questions?'

'All crystal. Thanks.'

'After you've both dressed bring her to the video edit studio and I'll tell you what I think. If I can balance your skin tones, I'll explain to you both how the shoot will work so I'm sure you both know what I want from you. Either of you can back out before going to the expense of getting Mandy here.'

'You'll have a makeup artist here for the shoot?'

'Certainly. Mandy works with the very best and will quickly know what I need. There will be bikini patches that need to be removed, and other sundry blemishes I would like to avoid. It's also good practice to have someone as experienced as her present for a shoot, so there is never an issue with what takes place. But she doesn't come cheap, and I'll need her for half a day.'

'Would you be prepared to take a few art shots of Famida that she can keep?'

'I could do a few after the shoot I want to do so long as it's clear I retain all rights to any pictures I take. She will have to sign a consent and release form, so you should sign one as well to keep everything balanced.'

'Okay daddy. See you at breakfast.'

Famida arrived late afternoon. Jess took her for a quick tour, and then to her room to show her the picture of her created by Richard. She loved it and agreed to a test shoot. Jess took her to meet Richard and to tell him they would be ready in forty-five minutes for a test shoot. He had spent the afternoon installing his turntable into the studio, as this might give him more options without needing to change lighting.

By the time they arrived in the studio, the temperature had increased to a comfortable level with the heat from the lights, and Jess could see the mark on the turntable denoting where he wanted them. They were quickly out of their robes and on to the platform.

'Okay ladies. Could you please stand full height, arms and fingers fully extended by your side. Try to breathe at a steady tempo into your chest cavity. Breathe out. Now both breathe in, breathe out, breathe in, breathe out, breathe in, hold.' He got his first picture.

'Now turn back-to-back. Close, but not touching. Breathe out, breathe in, breathe out, breath in, hold.' Second picture in the can. He repeated this process for the remaining two turns.

'Okay, go get dressed and come back to the video studio.'

When they returned to the video studio, all four pictures were side-by-side on the big centre screen. The amount of technology in this room startled Famida. If she had any doubts as to the serious nature of this shoot, they evaporated in an instant.

He had already decided they were as close to a mirror image as is likely. Even their breasts were the same shape and aligned perfectly. This was important as the observer's eye would naturally go to the centre of the picture which would approximate to the breast-line and, therefore, should not distract from following along the remainder of the profile by lack of symmetry.

He had graphs displayed under each picture showing the variance in skin tone for each of them, explaining that minor ripples were not an issue. But where there were spikes, they would need Mandy to smooth these out. He finally turned to Famida, 'Are you comfortable with your picture sitting on this screen?'

'In here it's fine, even interesting. I'm amazed at the difference in tone across both our bodies. Your camera is obviously very sensitive.'

'Let us go to my study and I'll explain what I'm trying to achieve, and what you would both need to do to help me.'

Once seated in his study he explained his vision about producing a picture which showed the majesty of the human form, whatever colour. The eye is the worst arbiter and discriminates where there is no other difference than the colour of the skin. Love between people should not be subject to visual discrimination.

Then he explained the shoot would likely be half a day as Mandy would need at least twenty minutes on each body before the session. This is normal and allows the model to acclimatise to the studio temperature. Famida asked if she would get a picture like the one on Jess's wall.

'What I'll do after the shoot with the two of you is to take additional shots of just you and then select a suitable picture to apply the colour washes required to create what you would like. You will both have to sign consent and release forms as I will retain the rights over all pictures. Whatever I give to you is for personal use only. Is this clear?'

Both acknowledged their understanding.

'Are you both happy to go ahead with the shoot, or do you need time to consider?'

They both looked at each other, each nodding approval to the other before agreeing to proceed.

'Let me call Mandy now to see when she's free as I suspect Famida would prefer a weekend if she's working.'

She agreed it would be better for such a long session.

Mandy said she could come on Sunday morning, arriving around 10am. Everyone agreed this worked. He asked Famida to refrain from clubbing on Saturday night, and to have a light breakfast.

'Well, Famida, it's very nice to meet you, and thank you for agreeing to help me in this way.'

She responded, 'I like what you're trying to do, and Jess has nothing but praise for your work. I can't believe I'm going to model for the man who has created so many awesome iconic images using some of the best models in the world.'

He looked at her, 'And you are about to find out just how much work is involved in creating those pictures. Shoots can be long and tedious, especially when they don't go as expected. But you must look like you have only just woken up for each and every picture.'

'Are you joining us for dinner?'

'Yes. I'm spending the evening with Jess exploring this fabulous house of yours.'

'I'll see you both at dinner.'

Chapter 52

Both Mandy and Famida arrived ready for the shoot. Famida quickly went with Jess to get ready. Richard took Mandy to his video edit studio to show her the test shots. He also asked her to work with Jess first, as this would help to calm Famida. She asked for the test shots to be screened in the photo studio for reference.

'Okay Richard. Can you tell me what you are looking for during this shoot, as I did not get the feeling your last shoot with the model worked as you wished?'

'You're right. She was too familiar with specific poses, none of which gave me what I hoped to achieve. Jess and Famida have no previous experience, so I should be able to mould them around my concept.'

'What is your concept?'

'My overall study title would be love transcends colour prejudice. These girls are practically identical in physique, the only difference being the colour of their skin. I have three compositions I want to try. Even though the final pictures will be washed, I don't want any visible flaws in the skin tone of either of them as this could distract the eye from the purity of the intent. The eye discriminates between skin colour in actual life, but I want to show this as a fallacy in love.'

'So, my primary objective is to remove the spikes I saw in your test shots. What about face makeup?'

'None. This is about purity, not glamour. Hair should not be groomed. I also noticed Famida has too much pubic hair. I don't want to see any in a profile shot. Identical twins are the order of the day.'

'Interesting. I'll need some time to achieve what you ask for, but they are almost identical from what I've seen. How do you think Famida will react to me trimming her pubic hair?'

'I think if you trim Jess first then Famida will accept it as part of the requirement.'

'I suggest you vacate the studio until they're ready. I'll come get you.'

'I'll wait in my study.'

They moved to the photo studio where he ensured the test shots were on the screen, and the lighting approximated to what he needed for the shoot.

The girls arrived in their robes.

'Richard, can you get me another stool as I don't want them sitting in chairs after removing their bikini marks.'

He delivered another stool from his video studio and left them to it.

'Hello girls. I'm Mandy. I'm a professional studio makeup artist, and I've worked with Richard many times over several years. My job today is to make you look as identical as possible from head to toe and eliminate any sharp skin tone blemishes. Are you both happy for me to prepare you for this shoot?'

They both agreed.

'Shall we start with Jess? Remove your robe and stand on the platform so I can see how you reflect studio light.'

Other than they were nervously giggly as their pubic hair is manicured, they both enjoyed watching Mandy at work. How meticulous she was to every blemish needing to be addressed and even trimmed a little length from the hair of Famida to make it the same length as Jess. When Mandy had finished with both girls, Famida renamed them "Coffee" and "Cream".

'Could you both stand on the platform and turn slowly so I can see if my work has produced the required result?'

She was satisfied there were no spikes in skin tone, hair was good, and no pubic hair in profile. She completely understood this requirement as she suspected his shots will be in profile. 'Now please come away from the lights. As you are both new to this type of shoot, I'll guide you through the process so we maintain your skin temperature and makeup. If Richard gets carried away, and you start to melt, I'll call time in which case you quickly move from under the lights and cool down. You both look great, so I would like to keep you this way.'

'And just one word of advice. This type of shoot can be hard work. Just enjoy each moment and your task will be easier, and your joy will show through into the pictures. This shoot is about love, and love is joy. Are you ready to start?'

They both indicated in the positive.

'Please do not sit down or lean against anything. I'll go tell Richard you're ready.'

As soon as Richard returned, he asked them both to stand on the platform and slowly rotate as per the test shots. He adjusted his lighting.

'Now ladies, I want you to stand in profile facing each other as close as you can without touching each other. I want you to imagine you are petals of a lily and stretch your arms into the air, leaning slightly backwards.' He made further adjustments to the lighting to capture their arms. 'Okay relax but do not move your feet.'

He picked up his camera. 'Let's try a picture. I want you to believe you are petals, and your arms are an extension of the petal. Reach, but do not stretch. We need graceful. When I tell you to breathe out and then breath into your chest cavity, flatten your tummies and hold for the count of two. Ready, position, now picture your petal, breathe, hold, good. Relax.'

He quickly looked at what he had captured. He added a backlight and try again.

'Let us try the same shot again. Ready, position, now picture your petal, breathe, hold, good. Relax. Come off the platform and relax.'

He put the pictures on the remote screen so they could see the results. On each hold he captured eight shots. He picked the best frame and showed them how they could improve their posture to achieve more graceful lines. Mandy observed what he wanted from them.

'Ready to try again?'

They moved to the platform and Mandy went with them, ensuring their feet were exactly aligned, and when extended their eye line was symmetrical and shoulders square to the camera. As she moved away, he started the picture process. This time he was much happier with the result.

'Let us try another pose. Famida can you please turn so you have your back to Jess. Now shape yourself like a question mark with your arms extended as the forward curve. Jess, can you mimic her to up to your waist and then reach at an angle over her. He played with this pose for some time as he could not see what he wanted. Mandy called time, and both girls moved away from the platform. He resigned himself to leaving this idea as he had his primary visual he wanted to capture before the girls tire.

After a few minutes, they were ready. 'Ladies, please stand facing each other as close as possible without touching, square to me.' He made minor adjustments to the lighting. 'Now I want you to reach out to each other with your hands just in contact with the back of your shoulders as though greeting each other. Graceful hands please ladies. You both have lovely hands, so let me see gracefully extended fingers. Look each other in the eyes and smile.' He took a few shots.

Mandy could see what he wanted. She moved onto the platform and adjusted the lines of the girls to achieve elegant symmetry. He took another series of shots. 'Relax ladies. Come see what we have.'

He went through each shot pointing to lines that were not quite right so they, and Mandy could see what needed to change.

'Before we continue, I need to ask both of you a question. The picture I want is about love with no boundaries. How do you feel about kissing each other? I mean a genuine kiss as between lovers.'

The girls looked at each other. Jess spoke 'never really thought about it, but no objection on my part. What about you Famida?'

'Never thought about it either. But why not?'

'While I get another memory card, why don't you both practice, but don't smudge your makeup. The only contact in the picture I want will be hands and lips. Touch around the hair and neck.'

When he returned, they were feeling comfortable with the idea.

'Ready to give it a try?'

They returned to the platform and resumed their position.

'I want to try shots with hands on each other's hips, then slowly glide your hands up to shoulder blade, and then up to neck with fingers behind the ear and thumb in front. There should be passion in the kiss with Famida's head slightly turning away from me with Jess bending only her neck to engage in the kiss. Ready. Go.' He shot thirty shots. 'Relax. Come and see what we have.'

He flipped through the shots. He saw what he wanted and displayed it on the screen.

'Girls, I think we're close to what I want. Let us look at this picture in detail to see where we need to improve. Famida your quads are contracted. Please relax them. You are lovers, so no stress in your body. Coming up you are not on the breathing cycle and Jess, you need to fill your chest cavity, not your abdomen.' He pointed to the breast line 'Jess, your nipples are extended, but Famida's are not. Extended nipples enhance the concept of love. Jess, can you glance over her nipples with your thumb on the way down to her hips. Heads are a little stiff. Relax more. Imagine you are lovers enjoying each other. Then the passion will come through. Any questions?'

'How do we co-ordinate our breathing?'

Mandy piped up, 'I'll count your breathing cycles. Let me take you both through the motion as I can see what Richard is looking for.'

She took both girls back to the platform and rehearsed the full motion with both, including extending both sets of nipples.

'Thanks Mandy,' he thought 'not good for me to touch their bodies, but they seem happy with Mandy.'

They were ready. 'Remember ladies, a passionate embrace when you are ready.'

Famida and Jess looked at each other for a moment with a closeness he had not yet seen in them. Their stance was far more relaxed. They reached for each other. Mandy started calling the breathing cycles. They felt their lips touch, tasting the wetness of each other's lips. The kiss intensified as their hands glanced breasts albeit he noticed both were already extended. His camera was shooting pictures at four frames per second. The vision mesmerised him. They were not acting; they were feeling the moment. Mandy is transfixed by what she was seeing. They were all in a vortex of slow motion, with time of no consequence.

After two hundred shots, the memory was full. The camera bleeped to indicate it was no longer active. This snapped him out of his haze. The girls were still enjoying their embrace. He looked at Mandy, who had stopped counting.

'If you have a quality picture of this, I would like a copy for my album. I could feel the love projecting from these girls.'

The girls stopped and looked at Richard. 'Did you get what you wanted?'

'I hope so because both of you were spectacular. Thank you both so much.'

They walked from the platform hand-in-hand, smiling with pleasure.

He reloaded his camera. 'Famida, what about your individual shots? Jess tells me you had dance classes for some years. What standard did you reach?'

'I intended to go to dance school and passed the entry tests before realising I was not hungry enough for the hard life of a professional dancer. Why?'

'When you dance do you feel the story and rhythm in your head. Can you get lost in the dance?'

'Yes.'

'What I thought would work for you is to let you go through some dance moves with the story flowing through you. The only constraint is you cannot leave the platform. Could this work for you? I want to capture an image of your soul, which is possible if you lose yourself in the dance.'

'Can I try before you take any pictures?'

'Sure. The stage is yours.'

She went to the platform and hummed a tune. She easily dropped into a routine of elegant poses with smooth transitions.

'Was that what you want?'

'Yes, it's fine. And you can be as expressive as you want. Really go for it. Are you ready?'

She hummed again and consumed herself in motion for more than a minute.

'Did you get what you wanted?'

'For sure. You move very well. Divine.'

She turned into profile as though still dancing and held a pose. He quickly caught it.

'Famida, please stay exactly as you are.' He moved towards her. 'Mandy, can you paint a white line about 2cm wide from her head to her feet following along this line,' as he plotted the course along her body.

Mandy joined him on the platform. 'Show me that line again.'

Famida went with Mandy to have her white line painted. Jess stayed with Richard. 'What do you have in mind with this white line?'

'Jess, I saw a picture and I want to capture it.' He put the shot of her without the white line onto his screen. He looked at her still naked, speaking softly, 'you can put on your robe if you like.'

'I think it better to stay as I am while Famida is still posing.'

He understood. 'You two should get to know each other better. We could feel the passion between the two of you.'

'Are you suggesting we have lesbian tendencies?'

'Absolutely not. History is littered with relationships between women that were never considered lesbian. These women had men in their lives, but they spent so much time away fighting wars, travelling for trade, or exploration they needed alternate companionship. Women have many more erogenous zones than men so who better to have some passionate fun time with than another woman. And it's not considered adultery.'

'So you think we should sleep together?'

'Jess, all I'm saying is there is a spark between the two of you. How you use this knowledge is between you and her. When you go to get dressed, try kissing again and see where you go.'

Mandy returned with Famida. He pointed to the picture on the screen 'can you adopt this pose for me?'

She went to the platform and assumed the pose. He looked at her, but it was not what he saw. Mandy was standing by his side also looking at her, wondering what he was trying to do.

He asked her to relax and then move into the pose again. She tried harder this time.

Mandy could see it. 'Wait, I can see what you're looking for. Relax Famida while I get more makeup.'

She was soon back and refined her white line. 'Assume the pose my dear so I can get this line perfectly positioned.' She stepped back to see the result. 'Okay, my dear, when he's ready I'll direct you to the right pose. This will be fantastic if he can capture it.'

This last statement recoiled through her head. I'm the subject of a fantastic picture. 'Let's do it.'

'Famida, remember this picture is not about your body, it is about you so give me the attitude and elegance you displayed before. Set your head and let's see if we can get a magnificent picture. You might feel the platform rotate a little. Just stay as you are and hold the pose.'

She assumed the pose with far more conviction. Mandy asked her for minor adjustments until the line she knew he saw was visible. As soon as he saw the pose, he made repeated shots with two incremental rotations to get a slightly different effect.

'Great. I'm finished with you delightful models. Mandy will restore you to a natural state after which you're free to go.'

Famida asked if she could ask Mandy for advice regarding makeup for her skin colour. Mandy agreed to sit with her.

'Daddy, when do you think we can see the results?'

He thought for a moment about how much work is needed. 'Give me a week. Let's say this time next Sunday with the option to revise if necessary. Good enough?'

'Great. Thanks. Do you think you have the picture you were looking for?'

'My expectations are high. But I won't know until I see it on my screen. Perfection is difficult to capture, but the connection between you was electric, so I hope my camera caught it.'

Chapter 53

When the girls returned to Jess's bedroom, they were still buzzing with the experience.

They sat on her bed. Jess started, 'What do you think about your first photoshoot?'

'Surreal to start with. Obviously conscious of being naked at the beginning, especially when she trimmed my pube. But how cool is Mandy? Wow, what she can do with the minimum of makeup. It was fascinating to see how models prepare for a shoot. Once we started, it felt natural, even liberating. I can't wait to see the results. When can we see the pictures?'

'He told me he needs a week, so this time next weekend.'

Jess was keen to investigate what he'd said to her. She stood and threw her robe onto her bed. 'Famida, how did you feel when we were kissing each other?'

'A little weird to start with. But when we went for it, I really felt good about it. Why?'

'Would it bother you to try again now?'

'Do you want me naked as well?'

'Why not? I think that was part of the fun.'

She stood and dropped her robe onto the bed. They approached each other and started to engage in gentle kissing, each one a little more intense than the previous one. Holding each other close, their bodies connected, they sank into a passionate kiss. They naturally caressed each other. Their lips parted. Both felt the electric through their bodies stirring in their loins. They looked at each other with a satisfied smile.

Jess asked, 'What do you feel?'

'I feel strange, but good.'

'Do you fancy staying over one night and have a little fun?'

'Are you serious?'

'Yes, I am. A little fun can't do any harm.'

'Okay, let's try it. What about next Saturday as I need to be here to see our photos on Sunday?'

'Fancy a shower together before we go to lunch?' She took her hand toward the bathroom.

Chapter 54

Richard woke Elizabeth at 7am. Today was his lunch with his son, and he wanted to be on the 9:05 train from Melton Mowbray. They were soon ready, a quick breakfast, and off to the station.

Sebastian was up and dressed, ready for lunch with his father. He had made a special effort to look like he was a serious-minded person.

'Now remember, your father will want to know why you suddenly have the desire for contact. He may ask you directly, or he may just analyse you. Do not lie to him. If you need to deflect a question, ask him a question as though you are seeking information about the nature of his question. Try to steer the conversation to a question you are prepared to answer. Knowing him as I do, he'll have done some homework on us using the same channels as I used to find out about him. Keep it simple and straightforward; deflect where necessary.'

'The best form of defence is attack. Ask him lots of questions. You now know a little about his work. Use this knowledge to encourage him to fill in the detail. A little targeted flattery can only help.'

'Talk about Uncle Jim as this will also fill time. And refer to him as Uncle Jim, as this is what you used to call him. This will work in your favour as your father treats Jim like a brother. They are very close.'

'You need to have some idea about what you want to do with your life. Make it credible.'

'Talk about what you remember about your childhood with him. This will bring back good memories for him, and that you remember will warm him to you.'

'Mother, have you finished? I'm meeting my father, not going to a job interview.'

'Sebastian, believe me, all this detail is so important. I know your father, and I know what presses his buttons. He'll have bad feelings about our divorce so stay away from this subject. You were too young to understand.'

'He'll want to leave at two o'clock, no later than 2:30. Do not take this badly. The longer you spend with him at this first meeting, the more likely you'll drop your guard. Don't be late because he'll be there on time.'

'And be very easy with the wine, and no spirits. Do not let your guard down for one second – he'll see it.'

'And remove your tie. He'll not warm to you if he sees you trying too hard. He never wore a tie in all the time I knew him.'

They arrived at St Pancras International station a few minutes before 10:30. They already agreed Elizabeth would use the Victoria Line to Oxford Circus to start her shopping at the John Lewis department store. After lunch they would meet in Harrods at 2:30 or soon thereafter. Before lunch he would catch the Piccadilly Line to Knightsbridge as he had a meeting with an old friend in the business, purportedly about a project they wanted the new Jim and Richard enterprise to consider. He also knew this person was the likely source of his whereabouts to Sarah. He wanted converse information about her.

Sebastian arrived at Sal E Pepe five minutes early. He was impressed that as soon as he told the Maître De who he was; he is warmly welcome and taken to one of the better tables. *'My father hasn't lived in London for over two years, but they still know him, and treat him well'* he thought.

'And what would you like to drink while you wait for your father?'

'Just sparkling mineral water will be fine, thank you.'

He saw his father arrive. The Maître De quickly greeted him like a good friend and indicated his son was already here, pointing to his table. He noted his father looked like an aging rock star in his tee-shirt and jacket, but in good shape. He stood to greet him.

'Hello, father. So nice to see you after so many years.'

'Hello son. How grown-up you are.'

Menus were delivered, studied, and selections ordered.

'Would you like wine?'

'Yes, but only a glass. Red is preferred.'

He ordered two glasses of the house red.

He detected although his son was nervous; he was also very focussed. He needed to disturb this if possible 'Okay son, this is your call, your meet. Tell me about yourself, what you have been doing, and where you want to go from here. There is much to catch-up.'

'Before I talk about me, can I ask about Uncle Jim. It was quite a shock to mum when I told her about his heart attack. She asked me to ask how he is, and to send him her best wishes.'

'He came very close to death, and thus why we counted our blessings and got out of the business. He's still recovering, but he now has a dog so must get out, which is excellent exercise for him. He has a full-time nurse to watch over his recovery.'

'Wow. It must have been bad to still need a full-time nurse. Will he ever fully recover?'

'He gets stronger day by day, but he can never go back to his old way of life.'

'Thanks for telling me. I would love to see him again. I have memories of him spending holidays with us, especially Christmas. I still have some of his fantastic sketches. Much better than a photo.'

He thought about what Jim had said to him when delivering Sebastian's letter. No reconciliation any time soon.

'As you know we moved to Wimbledon where we still live. I went to private school for my secondary education, and then on to university which I've just finished although not as well as I hoped. I'm considering repeating my final year to get a better result. I've applied to the university to re-sit. I'm waiting for their decision. I don't know where I go from here until I know if I can return to university.'

'Where did you intend to go?'

'I studied Politics and Philosophy intending to move into politics, but not as an elected politician. I have French and German so I could move to Brussels.'

'What does your mother think of your current position?'

'She's not happy about my grades. Having supported me throughout my secondary education, she hoped I could now support myself.'

'Did she ever re-marry?'

'Until I went to university, her focus was me. She got married a few years ago, but it didn't work out, so she's divorced again. Did you get married again?'

'Yes, but only recently. In fact, the day before I got your letter. Jim has been my priority since his heart attack.'

'Congratulations. Do you still live with Uncle Jim?'

'No. I've built my own house about two miles from Jim. We've only recently moved in although there's still about three months of work to finish it completely. We still don't have a formal address.' He did not want to disclose his address, or anything about Elizabeth.

'What will you do when you finish your house?'

'Enjoy it. I have the freedom to do as I please.'

'Mum has shown me your iconic work over the years. You were one of the greats. Do you ever intend to work again?'

'Never full-time again. I've paid my dues. If something interesting comes along without the crazy deadlines we used to have imposed on us, then I'll consider it when Jim is ready. Otherwise, I need to catch up on the life I sacrificed for my work.'

'Son, I have a new life borne from a reality check two years ago. I don't know what your mother has told you about our divorce, but it was an acrimonious experience. To date, I've buried the past. For you to return to my life gives me mixed feelings of joy, and caution. Therefore, I need to understand why you've initiated this contact as your last letter to me still burns deep inside me. I'm being honest with you because I can't imagine your mother being thrilled about your contact with me.'

'Mum knows of my attempt to contact you, and she knows of this meeting. It was her who found out where you're living. I think she still feels pain about what happened between you, but that is between the two of you, not me. She knew you sold your business but was clearly distressed when I told her about Uncle Jim. Does this answer your question?

Partly. But why do you want contact after all these years, and why did you not try earlier?'

'While mother was funding my education, I felt obliged to honour her wishes. But she has known of my desire to make contact. Now she adopts the view I could probably find you without her knowledge, so better to keep our relationship open.'

'As to why I want to resume contact, I remember we had good times together when I was younger. You're my father. Why wouldn't I be interested to rationalise the past and then see if we can bury it? I was the victim of your divorce, not the cause.'

'Okay, son. Do you want anything else – desert, coffee?'

'No. I'm good.'

'Can we leave it for today? I would like to think through how we move forward. I've just seen light in my life after far too many years in the darkness, especially the past two years.

Bringing you back into my life could either enhance my situation or be another hurdle to cross, just as I thought I was free. This is not your fault, but just as you have chosen when you make an approach, I would like to time your integration into my new life. I'm very happy you want to establish contact again, but I have others to consider as well and will need to prepare them. I'll probably want to meet with you again in the next couple of weeks to discuss my thoughts on the way forward. Is this okay with you?

'Sure. I can imagine the shock of receiving my letter, but I sent it with serious intent on my part.'

'I will send you a SMS when I would like to meet again. Probably here is best as I can always get a quiet table. I don't carry my mobile as a rule, so either confirm the date I give you or suggest another. Tuesdays and Thursdays are not good for me, as I have standing commitments.'

'Mum mentioned you don't carry a mobile. Can I ask why, especially for a businessman. Mine is always by my side.'

'My mobile is for my convenience, not others. While I work, I don't like interruption. While in my studio, I have no contact with the outside world at all. Those iconic pictures required much concentration.'

'Okay dad. I'll wait for your message. And thanks for meeting with me. It's great to see you again.'

'It was interesting to see how you've grown. Let's see if we can make this work. Goodbye, son.'

He was so deep in thought as he entered Harrods he nearly walked straight past Elizabeth, who was waiting at the appointed meeting point. 'Darling' he heard, which brought him out of his thoughts as he turned to see her.

'Hello darling.' He noticed the number of bags she was carrying, 'someone had a busy morning.'

'It's been some time since I've been to a major shopping centre, so I needed to play catch-up. I even bought you a very nice tee-shirt.'

He knew she was teasing him, but she was having fun. 'Do you need to do more, or have you shopped out?'

'A woman, shopped out? You really are out of touch. As I haven't been here for years, I would like to look around if you can stand it, and then we can go home.'

'Please enjoy yourself. I'll be interested to see what you choose to buy. If I get bored, I'll wander off to the technology department and we can meet there.'

When Sebastian arrived home, his mother was sitting waiting for him. 'Good lunch?'

'Fine, thanks.' He was still thinking about lunch. He was too confused to want to debrief with his mother. They still revered his father at the restaurant. Having, for the first time and at his mother's insistence, really looked at the iconic work he had produced, he realised his father was a giant in the media business.

She cut through his thoughts, 'What's he like? Did you easily remember him?'

'An aging rock star, but in good shape.'

'And what did he have to say?'

'Uncle Jim's heart attack was terrible. He nearly died. Still needs a full-time nurse. Terrified dad.'

'Poor man. He lived in his studio, so I suppose I should not be surprised. But Jim is a lovely man once you get past his appearance. I would not wish any harm to him. He'll know of your contact with your father so I can send him a "get well" card. What else?'

'He's now in his new house although not finished, and he got married the day before he got my letter.'

'Who is she?'

'No idea. Didn't ask, and he didn't elaborate.'

'What's he doing now?'

'Enjoying life, catching up on too many years dedicated to his work. Even when Jim has fully recovered, he'll only undertake the occasional interesting project. So essentially retired.'

'How did you get on with him?'

'Fine. He's concerned you know. Clearly reticent about the past. He has a new life, and now he wants to figure out how to fit me into it.'

'But you're his son. He must take your advance seriously and fit you in.'

'Mother, he mentioned the letter you encouraged me to send to him, and it still hurts him. We need to be patient. He'll come around in his own time.'

'Son, I sense there is something you're not telling me. The only way I can help you is if you tell me all.'

Sharply, 'Mother, I need to think it through. It's not so much what he said, as what he didn't say. I also sense my timing is not good for him. Leave it out for a while. He wants to meet again in the next couple of weeks. It's crystal clear to me pushing the agenda will certainly fail. I'm out of here. I need a drink.'

During the train journey home, Elizabeth asked about both of his meetings.

'My first meet was with an old colleague who is friendly with Sarah. He wants to harness Jim and myself for special projects so, because money talks, I knew I could tap him for information about her. He told me after our divorce she had a series of liaisons, but nothing she could hold together. Apparently, Sebastian became very introvert, and this presented difficulties, especially at school. She developed a reputation of being desperate. She got married a few years ago, but this went wrong when Sebastian left public school and went to university, during which time he lived at home.

He couldn't, or would not tell me why, but I guess it had something to do with Sebastian. Perhaps they didn't get along.'

'My overall impression of meeting Sebastian is he's either very clinical, or sincere. He was nervous but very focussed at the same time. I had the sense he carefully deflected my questions when we drifted from his script. He did not do well in his finals. I would expect some excuse for this, but none was forthcoming. His only concern was funding a repeat year if the university will allow. I don't get the impression he's keen to develop a career, or ever generated any income for himself. I need to think about our conversation and then meet with him again. See if I can fill the gaps before considering introducing him to the family.'

'My darling, this is your son. Surely you have some feelings for him. You certainly have my support to develop a relationship with him.'

'Thank you. My concern is, after so many years, I'm finally part of a wonderful, loving family. I feel so good about my life, and what we have together. Do I really need to gamble my happiness for someone who, frankly, I've dispatched to the past?'

'Richard, you cannot dispatch family in this way. They're not objects you cast into the garbage. I sense you also did this with your parents, albeit not intentionally. You have an opportunity to restore these relationships. At least try it. We're strong enough to take a few knocks, but don't live your later life wishing you'd tried. I was living in the past when I met you. I tried to resist your advances and stay in my comfort zone. Look at what I would have missed if you had not swept me off my feet.'

'Okay my darling. I'll try, but I knew exactly what I was doing with you. In this situation, I'm not so comfortable.'

Chapter 55

Other than tennis on Thursday morning, and a few hours with Jim on Friday, he spent the following three days in his studio working on his pictures. He said nothing about progress, even after emerging late Saturday afternoon for a swim.

He agreed to help Elizabeth prepare dinner on Saturday evening. Although Audrey and Gerry were not on duty, they were joining the family for dinner. And Famida had arrived earlier, so they were six at the table.

Everyone is seated for dinner, enjoying spending time together.

'Daddy, I know it's only Saturday evening, but can we see your picture after dinner? The one you call "Pure Love".'

He stared at her, 'What do you know about this picture?'

'She suddenly realised she probably should know nothing and possibly spoiling his thunder for tomorrow.'

With some trepidation, 'I went to see Uncle Jim this morning. He was so excited for you I had to find out why.'

'And what did he reveal?'

'He told me you had shown him your creation because you needed a little added background. You've sent a copy to a prominent art photographer who immediately responded he wants your picture for his exhibition in London next month. You did it. You created your masterpiece and I'm so happy for you. Can't wait to see it.'

Elizabeth interrupted, holding his hand, 'why haven't you mentioned this? Such important news needs to be shared and celebrated. Let me get some champagne. My dear, can you get glasses?'

Jess sprung from the table, thankful to escape. She felt more like crawling under the table. She had spoilt his news. Not even her mother knew.

Elizabeth returned with two bottles. 'Why did you keep this news quiet? Or should I say how did you keep news of such a dream ambition realised to yourself? If Jim is so excited for you, this picture must be incredible.'

'I need another few hours to finish the picture I promised to Famida. So tomorrow I'll reveal everything, as there is more. Jim has stolen my surprise, but you will still have to wait until I'm ready to reveal all.'

Everyone except him was buzzing. He felt cheated. Why had Jim broken the most basis rule of their working relationship? He obviously has become so close to Jess he thinks she's part of the inner circle. This must be corrected. Jess saw all of this in his eyes. She felt awful.

As they moved to the lounge, he felt her grab his hand and head for the stairs 'we need to talk' was all she said.

When they were seated on their sofa, she held his hand with her head held low, 'I'm so sorry daddy. I was so excited for you I didn't think. I know I've let you down badly. I will not make excuses for my behaviour, but I'm gutted about what I've done, and pray you can forgive me.'

He lifted her head. Tears were flowing down her cheeks. He held her close. 'It's not really your fault. Jim should not have told you anything about it. Our work is secret until we decide to reveal it.'

'Come. Dry those pretty eyes of yours. You and Famida did a superb job for me, so I can't be angry with you. It's good enough you realise the hurt I feel. Let's go back and join the others. Tomorrow will be a big day in this house.'

She held him close and kissed him. 'Thank you, daddy.'

When they returned to the lounge, Elizabeth could see Jess had been crying. '*Their first tiff*' she thought 'but they're hand-in-hand so they've worked it out.'

Later that night Richard and Elizabeth were lying cuddled together in bed. 'Why didn't you tell me about such an important achievement? You can keep these things secret from others, and I certainly will not betray your secrets. But I would like to think I'm special in your life and we can share both joy and sorrow together.'

'Now I think about it, you're right. I should have let you into my news yesterday. I'm sorry. For so many years I've not had anyone so dear to me to share with, so I need to get used to my new situation.'

She held him close, 'Now I do know I'll make tomorrow a very special day of celebration for you. You've achieved another incredible milestone in your journey, and I'm so happy for you. I had my reservations about Jess and Famida posing for you. But they are both so obviously excited about being part of your creation I can't wait to see it. And to think my darling husband will have his picture on display at a major exhibition in London just fills me with pride.'

They kissed tenderly.

'There's another picture not quite finished yet. But it has the potential qualities to be special. The reason I was keeping everything quiet until tomorrow, was the need to finish the picture I promised for Famida. I have so many wonderful pictures of her it was difficult to know which to use. Her training as a dancer certainly helps her to create beautiful images.'

'How much time do you need to finish what you want for tomorrow's showing?'

'Not sure. I'll probably be in my studio when you wake up tomorrow. I hope to be finished by lunchtime.'

'Why don't we say afternoon tea at three, which should give you time to finish your pictures, relax a little, and then prepare for La Grande presentation. I'll prepare a selection of cakes, scones – the works – and champagne, rather than tea. Can I invite Audrey and Gerry?'

'Of course.'

'What about Jim?'

'On this occasion, I think not. He and I need to have a chat about confidentiality – but not tomorrow.'

'I can't say my daughter did herself proud today. What did she say to you?'

'She was very upset about hurting me, but we're okay. Jim should not have told her.'

Chapter 56

He had his swim and was in his studio before 6am. He decided which pictures to use for the Andy Warhol style collage. They were all different, but as a composition they worked very well. The girls had helped him to achieve his ambition, so he wanted only the best for them. Now he needed to decide which colour wash to apply to each picture to maximise impact.

It was noon before he switched off the red light above his studio door. He was ready, and he was very pleased with the results.

Once Audrey knew of the presentation in the afternoon, she helped Elizabeth prepare. Jess and Famida did not appear until mid-morning, and they were now busy on a grand tour of the house and grounds. Jess chose to be as scarce as possible until after lunch.

He needed something to eat before taking a shower. Audrey quickly prepared his favourite English breakfast – '*he deserves it*' she thought.

He took three presentation easels from his storage room and placed them in the living room. He left the pictures in his studio until he was ready.

The ladies had excelled at producing a range of fair for afternoon tea and which was assembled on the spacious coffee table wafting freshly baked aromas throughout the room.

They all assembled in excited anticipation of what they were about to witness. Even Gerry had appeared, although he was uncertain why all this fuss over a photograph.

Richard entered the room carrying two canvasses, both covered, and stood them on easels. He then went to retrieve the third, which stood over a metre high, and placed it on the remaining easel.

'The first picture I want to reveal is for Famida in gratitude of her agreeing to model for me. She asked for a composition similar to the one I did for Jess.' He removed the cover. It had four frames of different poses. As with the picture for Jess, the colour wash neutralised any significant potentially uncomfortable detail, but the images formed a stunning composition.

'Do you like it Famida?'

'It's fantastic. Will you sign it for me so my friends know this fabulous picture was created by a famous photographer?'

He smiled, 'But I'm not famous yet.'

'But you will be when people see your work.'

'Thank you for your confidence in me. I have some lovely pictures of you from your dance routine. When I have time, I want to work with a few of them. Your dancing lessons gave you poise, and my camera captured it.'

'Are the shots you've used here the best ones?'

'No. I tried to use the best four shots, but they didn't work as a composition. They scream to be left alone. I found four shots that sit well together for your picture.'

'Can't wait to see the others.'

'I'll let Jess know when I've worked them up into pictures.'

'The next picture is a work in progress, but I want to show it to Famida so she can understand why we painted a white line along her body from head to toe. I think it has great potential, but I haven't seen the image I want yet.' He unveiled the next picture.

'You've cut me in half. So that is what the white line was for. And you have made me darker.'

'I made you darker so the eye focusses on the abstract, rather than the detail. This picture is not about you, but an abstract form. Your body has well-proportioned flowing curves, and the separation between the two halves exactly follows your natural lines. If you remember once Mandy saw what I could see, she changed the white line to perfectly match your own curves.'

'Yes, I remember. And she encouraged me to try harder with the pose. Now I can see why. It's a stunning picture. Again, can't wait to see it finished.'

'Now to "Pure Love". I have had this picture in my mind for months but needed two models essentially identical other than the colour of their skin. When Jess told me about Famida, and I saw them together, the picture in my mind was close to reality. The essence of this picture is that love can conquer all prejudice if we close our eyes and savour it. And love is not a function of colour. All human beings can love each other regardless of race, colour, or creed.'

He lifted the cover. There were gasps. Famida placed her hands on her cheeks, 'Oh my God, wow. It's beautiful, so beautiful. It oozes love. I can't believe it. It looks like a painting.' She turned to Jess 'That's us Jess. Can you believe it?'

'Daddy, its beautiful. No wonder Jim was so excited – and with his portfolio he's hard to impress.' She jumped up to give him a kiss.

Elizabeth stood to take a closer look, 'It's truly fantastic darling but can you explain why you have brush-stroked it to blur their identities.'

'This picture is not about Jess and Famida, or any other specific individuals. It's about humanity and the love they can share if only they overcome irrelevant prejudice.'

'Then why two women?'

'Lots of traditional reasons from mother earth to what sells. We're all the same and thus the identical models. I didn't want a picture that appeals only to the high-brow elite. I want to appeal to everyone, so I used my knowledge of advertising to create a picture that will attract maximum instant attention, hoping once people look at the image, they'll be drawn into the message. I've spent over twenty years successfully capturing attention from the masses, using sensuality, and attaching them to the desire of the message. I only hope I've been successful in my art using pure love rather than sensuality.'

Elizabeth spoke. 'Famida is right. It certainly oozes love and looks like you painted it. We must have this picture in a prominent place in this house. It somehow speaks to you. I can't wait to see how it's received by the public.'

Audrey, having busied herself pouring champagne, decided she needed to contribute something. 'My dearest Richard, I've seen the beauty you incorporated into this house, and I know you as a talented, wonderful man. But this picture exceeds all of this. When I realised you were taking pictures of these girls naked, I had my reservations, as you do. But the world needs to see the beauty in your mind. I'll never question you again regarding your photographic ambitions. These girls can be very proud to be part of this picture, and the message you hope it will give to people.'

As an afterthought, 'can you do anything like this with me?'

This brought a smile to everyone. She did it again. Always the funny last word.

After the toast to Richard, he sat down on a couch only to be immediately flanked by Jess and Famida.

'Do you have more pictures in that clever mind of yours?'

'Yes. "Pure Love" is one of four images on the same subject.'

'Can we model for more?'

'If you're both willing, I would be very grateful.'

'Just let Jess know when you want us. Will the cool Mandy be here again?'

'Sure. Mandy is my preferred makeup artist.'

'Great. She's so good. I learnt so much from her.' She paused to think, 'when is the exhibition in London?'

'Not sure of the date, but I will let Jess know. Do you want to come with us to the launch evening?'

'That would be fantastic. Thank you. I'm going to make sure all my family and friends go to see it. Me in a picture in a major exhibition. How cool is that?'

Chapter 57

It has now been nearly three weeks since Jess asked Richard to help her with a child. He had gone through his normal morning ritual and was sitting in his study. He heard her skipping down the corridor. She was beaming as she entered his study, applied her customary kiss, took his hand, and led him to the sofa.

He looked at her. 'Someone is very happy today. What do you want to tell me?'

She took his hand and kissed him again, and then just sat beaming at him. 'You're pregnant. Is this what you want to tell me?'

She removed a test stick from her pocket with a smiley face on it as she nodded vigorously.

'I think I need to reverse our contact. He held her close and kissed her on both cheeks. 'Congratulation Jess. I'm so happy for you.'

'Before we go any further with this can I suggest we get confirmation from a doctor? Who is your GP?'

'We can't go to my GP. He's a good friend of mom, and a tennis club member.'

'I have a local private GP. Let me call him after breakfast.' He could not help but hug her again. 'You're some lady.'

'Until we have a proper validation, please say nothing to anyone, and please reduce your smile to your normal version. Let's avoid arousing suspicion about anything.'

She acknowledged his request, gave him another kiss, and was on her way.

He called her back 'Jess, how was Saturday with Famida?' She nodded with a smile and was on her way again.

After breakfast he made the call to his GP who agreed to see her at 4pm today. Jess was in her office working.

'Okay lady we are going shopping this afternoon, and you need to bring a fresh urine sample.' She understood.

Richard and Elizabeth attended their Tuesday morning tennis as usual. He found it difficult to get out of his mind how his beautiful wife would react to the news. She's so happy in their new life together, and he could not contemplate ruining another marriage.

After lunch he announced he and Jess needed to go shopping but would be back around 6pm.

They went shopping to authenticate their trip, but the visit to his GP was the key reason for this trip. His GP examined Jess and then called in Richard. 'Congratulations. Jess is pregnant. Very early stage and much can go wrong as it's her first pregnancy. However, she's young, fit, and healthy, so my prognosis is overall positive. I estimate late April to mid-May next year, but we can narrow this in a few weeks. If you want me to monitor her ongoing pregnancy, I'm happy to help.'

'Can you register her as your patient on my account from now on? I want you to be responsible for her throughout this pregnancy. Whatever she needs is okay by me.'

'No problem, Richard. I'll have my assistant take care of her registration, although she will still have to attend the antenatal clinic.'

Jess was very restrained in front of the GP, but as soon as she was in the car, she threw her arms around his neck in total joy. 'Daddy, we did it.'

'Young lady, you still must sell this to your mother. We say nothing today as we both need to think this through. We only have one shot, so timing and approach are important. Let's get together first thing tomorrow morning and agree a plan.'

'As you wish, daddy.'

'And try to suppress your excitement until we have executed our plan. We don't need to add covert delay to our sins.'

When they arrived home, they noisily entered through the door carrying their bags, hers containing a business suit, slacks, and tops, and two shirts for him.

Chapter 58

Jess came bounding into his study a little after 7am. She never walked for their morning greeting, and he could imagine her arriving on a skateboard if she had one. After their normal greetings, they went to their sofa.

'Okay lady, what do you have?'

'I agree with you that trying to contain my excitement could give the game away, and we should avoid delay. What I propose is to take mom for a long walk through the woods this morning so she cannot readily break away from me to come to you. I'll use argument along the lines I used with you, not least because it's the truth. I suggest you are in your study when we return because I propose to tell her you are very concerned about her response, and I want to bring her to you to express her acceptance of the situation. I think I've anticipated all her possible questions and concerns and have formulated and honed responses. I will be successful because I'm convinced this is good for all of us, and she'll sense my conviction.'

'I like the idea of the long walk, and I have faith in you to succeed. I will cross my fingers and toes for you, and I'll ensure I'm here looking suitable anxious when you return. My anxiety will not be theatre, it will be real, so be successful.'

'I will daddy. We're family, and we need each other.'

'Good luck' as he hugged her.

After breakfast Jess turned to her mother 'It's a nice day. I could use some fresh air. Mom, will you walk with me through the woods? I have something I want to discuss with you.'

'What a lovely idea. I'll go get dressed and see you back here.'

Jess waited until they were entering the woods and on their way to the place where the wild orchids grow. 'Mom, I have some exciting news for us. (pause) I'm pregnant. We're going to add a baby to our family.'

Her mother just stopped in her tracks 'but how, when, who is the father?'

Feigning a little hurt 'Mom, shouldn't you congratulate me before you ask for details? Aren't you happy for me?'

She hugged her daughter, 'I'm so sorry my dear. Of course, I'm delighted,' she moved her head back to look at Jess 'but it's such a shock as I didn't know you're dating anyone.'

'Come mom, let's sit by the orchids and I'll explain all.'

At the behest of Elizabeth, Gerry had made a small bench big enough for two and installed it where they could readily observe the orchids. They made themselves comfortable and could observe these stunning flowers shimmering in the sunlight.

'Mom. Ever since you mentioned to me you would have liked to give daddy a baby, I have been evaluating my situation, and realised what a wonderful life we now have. I have no desire to leave this anytime soon, but I would like a baby, and I know you want a grandchild. I spent weeks thinking through the possibilities, and I even considered acting as a surrogate for you. Then I had a eureka moment.

What about if I solved all these issues by asking daddy to donate his sperm for me so I could have a baby which unites all of us with a combined DNA; a baby which would be our child. I don't need another man in my life at this moment as I'm very happy where we are. I love being with the new you, and what a mentor I have in daddy. Everything is perfect. But mom, I'm the package in your relationship with daddy. I've benefitted so much but contributed nothing in return. This is my way of saying thank you for my wonderful life, my wonderful mom, and unbelievable dad. We're a triangle of love, and we have conceived this baby within our triangle, and belongs to all of us. Our triangle of love will nurture this baby with the incredible love we share together.'

'How on earth did you convince Richard to go along with his?'

'It took a lot of work. He was paranoid about hurting you. He's now sitting in his study, very concerned about how you'll react, as he doesn't want to lose you.'

'What convinced him to help you, and why did he not consult with me before now?'

'Part of my eureka moment. This baby gives him a legacy connecting all three of us. You two love each other dearly, but you met too late in life to create a direct legacy of your own. This is my gift to you both.' She let this sink in.

'He did not consult you because he didn't know if he was still fertile having not engaged in any sex for so many years. He didn't want to raise any expectations, especially with you, and then fail. You can imagine what that would have done for his manhood well-being.'

'When did you know you're pregnant?'

'Yesterday afternoon. Daddy took me for an examination.'

'My dear, I don't know what to think. Have you considered how this child will be treated in the outside world? What about your life? Finding a husband with a baby will not be easy. Your plan has many complications not only for you but also your child.'

'Mom, we will surround this child with so much love the outside world will not matter. How much have attitudes changed in your lifetime? How much have your attitudes changed in just the last few months? As for me, packages are commonplace today. If a man cannot accept my child, then he doesn't love me enough. I'm part of a package and look at the love I get from it because your husband loves both of us; me as a daughter, and thus why I compliment him by calling him my dad.'

'Please mom, I want you to be happy for me, for all of us. This baby will provide so much joy to this family and makes me feel as though I contribute. I get so much from you all. I need to give something back.' She shed a few tears to emphasize the depth of feeling she has to her cause.

Her mother comforted her. 'Your very presence in this house is contribution enough. You bring so much light to this family, and how much you've blossomed since we've been here. I can't turn the clock back on this situation, and I can't believe Richard would have agreed with you if he had any doubts about your motives. He's right to be concerned about my feelings, but I cannot doubt his love for you, and his concern for your happiness. I'm forced on such occasion to realise you're no longer my little Jess, but a grown woman with your own mind. That you're doing this for all of us makes me very proud of you. I must accept this is to be. As for Richard, he has given so much to both of us. I should be angry with him, but when I see the two of you together, it fills my heart with thanksgiving. Let's go put his anxiety to rest.'

'Mom, thank you so much. This baby will bring yet more joy to our lives, and I so want to share the entire experience with you. I want you by my side. I want this to be a family affair.'

Richard watched as they approached the house. Jess was in animated conversation with her mother. They looked in good spirit and were laughing together. '*Thank you, Jess*'.

When they finally arrived at his study door, he assumed his anxious look.

'Richard, my darling, Jess has told me her news. I was initially confused why you would do this with no consultation with me, but Jess has explained your concerns to me. We must celebrate this news and look forward to a new addition to our family.'

Richard held Elizabeth in his arms. 'Thank you so much, my darling. I would never want to do anything to hurt you. Her desire for this child was so compelling I had to help her. I think it will be good for all of us, you'll see.'

'Apparently it was a comment I made in a moment of pure love for you that triggered this idea, so I'm as much to blame as anyone else for putting such thoughts into her head.'

He invited them in, 'Let's sit for a moment because we need to consider one more aspect to this news.'

When they were all seated, 'Audrey and Gerry are family and we must inform them, and dare I suggest, the identity of the donor. I suggest we do this at lunch, but who will deliver the news?'

'You're the head of this family, my darling.'

He pondered for a moment. 'I think Jess should tell Audrey at lunch. Audrey will know we know, but she'll feel much better if her adopted daughter tells her directly. Jess you should sit with Audrey at lunch. This way we bring them into our inner circle, our family. Are we all agreed?'

Audrey was so overjoyed she could not stop crying. She hugged and kissed Jess so much. She finally looked up, 'Richard, we need to plan a nursery. My goodness, we have a lot to do.'

'Audrey, we have some months to prepare. Once Christmas is over, we'll plan to convert the living area in the guest suite into a nursery, and completely move her into the guest suite where she will have everything she needs, including a kitchenette, so all is in easy reach.'

Elizabeth looked at Richard, 'You're prepared to convert your gorgeous suite into a nursery? Are you sure you want to do this?'

'It hasn't been used to date, and I can't think of a better use for it. I want Jess to be comfortable with her baby. Jogging up and downstairs in the middle of the night is not something she should be contemplating.'

Audrey returned to her excitement, 'I'm so happy for you. A baby in the house. Wonderful.'

It was done. Her plan to have a baby was activated, and all involved were energised to bring her desire to fruition.

That night, as Richard and Elizabeth settled in bed, she felt the need to express her view of the events of the day.

'Richard, my darling, that was some shock you delivered to me today.'

'No more than the shock I felt the first time she came to me with her idea.'

'Why did you help her?'

'I could not defeat her arguments, challenge her sincerity, or her desire. She had spent weeks thinking it through, so it wasn't a whim. Under such circumstances, good parents will be supportive.'

'You really take her well-being seriously. She is your daughter in all but blood. I love to watch you two together but would like to be included. I don't like the idea my mother may have identified a potential flaw in our relationship.'

'It was difficult for me to not consult you, not least because of my desire never to lose you. But, on balance her logic to keep quiet until there was a positive result was a choice I accepted in everyone's best interest, including my own. Had this failed because I could not have provided what she needed it would have been very embarrassing for me.'

She felt his insecurity and fully understood. She wanted to be included in such decisions but did not want to cause him pain in the process. He had enough pain with his own son. She kissed him lovingly. The deed is done. Now it's time to plan for the birth of her grandchild.

Chapter 59

He was in his study, quickly going through his to do list before readying himself for tennis. One line stared at him. In all the concentration on his picture, and the pregnancy, he had forgotten about Sebastian. He picked up his mobile to send a SMS to him stating he was sorry for the delay but next Monday would be good. *'I need a few days to think this through before I meet him again.'*

Although he understood the conventional family attitude of his wife, he had never adopted the attitude that family needs to be maintained if you dislike them. His view was akin to the more realistic fact you can choose your friends, but not your blood family. He had no time for sentimentality when there was clearly no compatibility. This time he would try to get under the skin of his son to see what he was really like. But for now, his focus was to finish the house and thus his need to finalise plans for the walled garden as he would like to conclude all excavation so road and pathways can be finished. This would be his task this afternoon.

He also needed to produce a copy of his "Pure Love" picture and take it into London for the show. *'Can deliver this on Monday'* he thought. Exhibition preview is Friday of next week.

His mobile buzzed. It was a response from Sebastian 'Monday good. See you there at 12:30. Sebastian.'

'Okay. Let's see if Elizabeth is ready' he voiced to himself.

She was still dressing as he entered their bedroom. 'Are you ready for another blistering display at the club, my darling?'

'I don't know about blistering, but I feel good about our chances.'

'That's the spirit. If you're going to do it, go for it.'

She laughed. 'You're in a funny mood today. Are you getting nervous about next week?'

'To which part of next week do you refer?'

'The exhibition of your wonderful picture, my darling.'

'Why should I be nervous?'

She held him 'Because, my darling, if you weren't you wouldn't be the warm human being I know and love.'

He kissed her, 'I don't know if it's excitement or nervousness, or both. This is different to anything else I've done. It's personal.'

'And it will be a personal achievement of which you can be very proud, you'll see.'

'I hope you're right. I hate failure.'

'So, it's nerves. Just remember the response you got when you unveiled it here. That spontaneity was not partisan, it was a real emotional response, even from Audrey. No disrespect to Audrey, but she is not generally interested in art. Your message reached her, so you achieved your vision. Be assured my love, they will acclaim your picture for what it is.'

'Thank you, my darling.'

'Different subject. As our tennis court is ready, how about we select a couple this morning to come and help us christen it either tomorrow, or Saturday?'

'Do you have a pair in mind?'

'Yes, I do. They came to our wedding, but much depends who's available at such short notice. The weather forecast is good, so let's play the court before the autumn weather sets in.'

'I need some time in my studio both tomorrow and Saturday to prepare a copy of "Pure Love" for the exhibition, but a couple of hours, tomorrow afternoon or Saturday, might be a good idea to get my mind off next week.'

'Good. I'll make some discreet enquires who might be available while we're there this morning.'

As an afterthought, he added, 'Do you mind if we skip the après tennis coffee today as I have another issue I need to address today?'

'Not at all. Come on, let's go play.'

Chapter 60

Having spent much of Friday preparing a copy of *"Pure Love"* for the exhibition, he wanted to hang his original copy in a prominent position in the hallway so he could frequently observe how it appeared in the various light conditions during the day. He was unusually nervous about the presentation of this picture and could be accused of overthinking how it should be displayed. As he intended to print the copy for the exhibition on Sunday, he needed the assurance there is no more he can do to increase the quality of his creation. There was an insecurity in this process which had never dogged him during his years of poster campaigns. This was personal. The product on display was his imagination, and the message was his own.

Elizabeth interrupted him 'Simon and Jennifer will be here shortly. You need to get ready to play.'

'Sorry, my dear. I wanted to hang my picture where I can see it in different light conditions. I'll go get ready.'

'Before you go, do you want our guests to see this picture today or would you prefer to keep it from them until after the exhibition?'

'Good point. I want to leave it where it is, but I think we say nothing unless they notice it. Good enough?'

'Sure. Today is about our new tennis court so we can celebrate on the terrace afterwards.'

Simon and Jenifer were punctual. Audrey let them in, and Elizabeth went to greet them, indulging their request for a quick tour of the outside, having been carefully shepherded at the wedding.

As with all new tennis courts, it takes time to adjust to the bounce of the ball and the speed through the court. Much laughter as misjudged shots abounded throughout the game. But Richard is pleased with the quality of the surface, which is all-weather so can be played quickly after rainfall, and minutes after being swept of snow in the winter. As a full-size match play court, it was larger than the courts at the club, allowing more freedom of play.

After the match they adjourned to the terrace to enjoy the afternoon sun and pleasant conversation. Richard could detect Elizabeth missed this social interaction with her friends – something he must address when the grounds are finished. He also realised Simon, as a local Magistrate, could be trusted for his discretion, thus someone with whom he could establish a relationship. He felt the need to find local people with whom he could socialise as part of his new life in the area. Simon suggested he join the local golf club, the membership of which included several prominent members of the community. Richard has never played so not likely.

Chapter 61

Richard was ready for his trip to London, having arranged to meet the show organiser at the National Portrait Gallery to deliver his picture at 10:30. They also needed a digital thumbprint version for the various media releases, a picture of himself for the caption, and a 150-word descriptor. He had spent some hours preparing the digital version of *"Pure Love"* they needed for their brochure, and for prints to be sold in their shop, ensuring the print quality is as perfect as possible.

By 7:30 he was on his way to the station. His thoughts were to test young Sebastian on his politics, so collected three of the more serious newspapers to study what is happening in Europe. *'He has not done well in his finals, so how interested is he in his elected subject?'*

He spent a little over 30 minutes with the exhibition organiser who showed him where they intended to display his picture and providing an exhibitor pass and six guest passes for the preview evening scheduled for the coming Friday evening starting at 6:30pm. As none of the exhibition pictures were in their place, he departed for his lunch with Sebastian.

When he arrived at Sal E Pepe, Sebastian was already seated. They greeted each other as Richard sat down.

'Sorry about the delay, son. I'm submitting a picture for a major exhibition starting this Friday, so lost track of time.'

'What sort of picture?'

'It's a photographic study I did.'

'Where's the exhibition?'

'National Portrait Gallery.'

'Wow. Must be good. When can us normal people see it?'

'Next weekend. The press preview is Friday evening. If you want to come along, I'll see if I can get another ticket. Give you chance to meet the family.'

'That would be great. My dad, displaying his work in such a place. What a buzz.'

'Let's order, and then I want your views on some issues we're having with Brussels. Perhaps you can explain to me why we're in this European Union as I don't get it.'

This last comment took Sebastian by surprise. Talking about the EU was not in his script for today, and he certainly had paid little attention since his exams. He would need his charm offensive in turbo-drive today if he is to secure the funding for a repeat year.

Chapter 62

Richard and Elizabeth were sitting together enjoying a nightcap. 'How did it go with Sebastian today?'

'I'm not sure. I teased him out by asking him to explain some of the political issues today in Europe. I expected him to bore me to tears, explaining in detail what was happening. He couldn't wait to change the subject. There was no obvious enthusiasm for his chosen career.'

'What did he want to talk about?'

'Mainly to get me to talk about us, and what we're doing. He was always diverting away about what he's doing or wants to do. The only thing he wanted me to know was his university had granted him the opportunity to retake his final year, albeit no surprise to me as it provides additional funds they otherwise could not secure.'

'What do you want to do about him?'

'I'm not sure. I don't sense any sincerity in his motives. His mother has told him she cannot afford any more education for him, so he is clearly looking to me for help.'

'Why don't you give him a chance to show his true intentions. Agree to fund his year but let him know you want to see commitment from him. You could also use the year to see if you can encourage him to a fresh approach – play the father role. You've proven very successful with Jess, so why not try with him?'

'I've left it open to invite him to the exhibition on Friday. Would you like me to invite him so you can form a view?'

'I think that would be a very good first step. He'll see the success of his father, which might start the process with him. We can all take a view of him and tell you what we think. Audrey will also be good at looking at him from a different angle to us.'

Okay, my darling. I already know Gerry would prefer not to go to London, so I'll use his ticket for Sebastian.'

Chapter 63

Richard sat in his study, feeling a little anxious as Jess came bouncing in. She kissed him, took his hand, and led him to their sofa.

'Today is a very important day for this family. My fantastic dad is showing the world how brilliantly creative he is in his own right. We're all so proud of him and can't wait to see his creation on display in one of the most important galleries. Daddy, I feel so privileged to be part of this family, and your creation. So, today, we celebrate yet another important achievement in your extraordinary life, and I wanted to be the first to tell you how much I'm looking forward to this evening.' She kissed him.

He sat looking at her with tears welling in his eyes. He held her close 'thank you, my beautiful daughter. I hope the world shares your view.'

'They will, Daddy. They will.'

'See you at breakfast.' She was gone.

They had already decided to make a day of it to London, leaving mid-morning. Gerry had elected to stay back as he did not like cities, making a guest ticket available for Sebastian who would meet them at the National Portrait Gallery at 6:30pm. Famida was too excited to work today, so had taken the day off to join the party to London, having stayed with Jess overnight.

Everyone was seated at breakfast, including Jim, who was not about to miss this event.

Richard used this time to alert everyone about potential pitfalls he wanted to avoid. 'Ladies, I would like to explain how this evening will work as I want to avoid Jess and Famida being identified as the models. As they're not professional models, they would become the story. You lovely ladies may enjoy the attention for the first five minutes, but you would certainly not enjoy the following weeks of press hounding.'

Jim piped in, 'He's right. You don't want those horrid people putting you both under a microscope for weeks. They're only interested in a story, not the impact on you and your life.'

'Thanks Jim.' Looking at Jess 'The trick tonight is not to have the two of you standing together anywhere near the picture. There must always be two people between you. Jess, if you could wear flat shoes, and Famida wears heels, and different hairstyles will also help.' He had already noticed Famida was wearing slacks 'Jess, if you could also wear slacks this will help to diffuse the lines a sharp art critic would see if you were showing your legs. Do not talk to each other anywhere near the picture and please contain any excitement until we are out of there. Be a fly on the wall and observe the reaction of other people. You have already seen the picture. Your real buzz tonight will be to see the reaction of others. If I remotely detect anyone putting you two together with the picture, Jim will take Jess somewhere else as though they are on their own together, and I would like Audrey to move away in a different direction with Famida. I can then diffuse any inquisitive press attention. If I am interviewed by anyone, scatter as there will be cameras everywhere. Any questions?'

Elizabeth was first to speak 'What would you like me to do?'

'If all is calm, be my beautiful wife and companion. If we have any distractions, please ensure Sebastian is engaged and taken away if appropriate.'

And then to all of them, 'Jim is more sensitive to press people than me as he loathes them. If he spots anything, please quietly do as he asks. As we enter the gallery, I'll identify a suitable meeting point where we can reconnect. And ladies, please do not talk together about your involvement in the picture anywhere in the Gallery. Most of the people there tonight will be Press in some form or other, so they'll have eyes and ears everywhere.'

This brief lecture put a damp squib on the excitement of the day, but Jess was not about to offend her dad again over this picture. Media was his expertise, so do as he instructs.

They were soon organised and on their way to the railway station to catch their train. The discussion on the train was whether they would stay together, or the ladies go shopping whilst Richard and Jim visit with contacts with whom they would engage once they started to work again. Although this conversation lasted for over half-an-hour the outcome was inevitable as neither Audrey nor Famida had been shopping in London for some time. They agreed to have lunch, go their separate ways, and then meet at the gallery at 6:30. Richard made calls to see who they could meet with at such short notice. That Jim was with him made this task easy.

Having arrived at St Pancras Station, they quickly took a Piccadilly Line tube to Knightsbridge where Richard had already booked a table at Sal E Pepe.

After lunch, Richard and Jim left the ladies outside of Harrods before departing for their first meeting.

It was 6:30. They were all assembled on the steps of the National Portrait Gallery. The ladies had compressed their purchases into the minimum number of carrier bags they could. Richard spotted Sebastian approaching the steps. He moved down to greet him before taking him back to the others. All introductions completed they made their way into the gallery. The production of his exhibitor's pass ensured they were all politely received, had their bags deposited in the cloakroom, provided with programs, and were directed to the exhibitor's reception area where champagne was freely flowing.

As soon as they found a spot to settle, Jess quickly looked through the program to see if *"Pure Love"* was included. She found it with a thumbnail picture of her dad and a brief resume of the picture. She welled up inside with pride, but not forgetting her instructions.

Someone swiftly escorted Richard away to meet the primary exhibitor who welcomed him as if an old friend, as he introduced him to other guest contributors, and the exhibition sponsors. Photographs were taken for the Press before they dispersed back to their own groups.

'What I propose is we go through to see how my picture has been hung before the Press and other guests fill the gallery. Then we can go to see the other exhibits before quietly observing the general reaction to *"Pure Love"*. Sebastian, could I ask that any specific observations you may have regarding the picture are contained until we are somewhere else.'

Sebastian thought this an odd request, but there must be a reason.

They saw it. The same involuntary gasps as when they first observed it were audible from Jess and Famida. Seeing it hung in such a formal setting yielded a novel experience as it beamed out at them. They both remembered their instruction, but Jess was now squeezing Jim's hand so tightly he had to shake himself loose. Jess looked at him 'Sorry Uncle Jim, but I can't help how emotional I get when I see it.'

'It's okay, my dear. Let us take a few steps back to see how it looks when the entire picture is visible without scanning. She understood and followed him back about three paces. He then explained to her the different layers of visual interpretation, and why this presentation style had been chosen.

Sebastian was the next to speak. 'Dad, it's fantastic. Looks like a painting.' Then he looked closer and then turned to look at Famida. Richard noticed this, and before Sebastian could blurt out his thoughts, 'whatever your thoughts, please keep them to yourself until we are out of here.'

'But Dad…'

'No son. Whatever it is, keep it to yourself for now. There are too many Press people here for any comment, especially as you're my son. Understood?'

'Okay.'

Elizabeth noticed Richard was becoming agitated with his son for failing to follow his wishes. She moved next to Sebastian 'and what do you think of your father's work?'

'I think it's fantastic. A little confused why a photograph looks like a painting, but the picture really glows at you. I like it.'

At that moment, a reporter approaches Richard. Elizabeth took the arm of Sebastian 'time to move on to let your father do his media duties' as she led him away. Jim had already spotted this intrusion so led Jess away, with Audrey leading Famida to another room.

Once Elizabeth and Sebastian were well away from his father, she turned to him 'Well Sebastian, it's so nice to meet you. Your letter came as quite a shock to your father, but I hope the both of you can find a way forward together, and for you to be part of the family. Now you have met and talked together, what are your feelings about this reunion?'

He thought carefully before answering. He liked the welcome part but was wary of the question. 'My dad is different to what I expected, but for his age he's really cool. And his picture is spectacular. I can't help thinking Famida is in that picture, or else why is she here?'

'Sebastian, it is important to listen to your father and to accept his wishes regarding any such comments with these Press people lurking, listening for stories. As for Jess and Famida, they have been close friends since they were children. The opportunity to shop in London was high on their priority list today as you saw when you arrived.' She let this sink in. 'I hear you wish to repeat your final year at university to get a better grade.'

'Yes. Bad day at the office for my finals. I can do better so need to repeat the year. A bit of a drag really, but I need better grades if I'm to get a decent job.'

'What do you want to do when you graduate?'

'I want to get into the admin side of politics; not front-line. The process interests me, but not the battering elected politicians get. Not for me.'

'Your father tells me you would like to work in Brussels. Is this a realistic option once you graduate?'

'Should be easier than in the UK. They need political administrators with relevant language skills.'

'Ah, of course. You speak German and French. Does that make you a Franco-German anglophile?'

He smiled. 'I'm British through to my core, and always will be.'

'I would like to quietly observe the reaction of the people here to your father's picture. Could I ask you to respect your father's wishes not to discuss anything about his picture whilst we are here? He's very private about his work and has years of experience understanding how to manage media. We'll have dinner shortly at which it may be possible to express any views you have. Can you assure me you will make no further comment as I really would like to observe reaction?'

'I'm sorry if I've caused a problem. I think my overwhelming reaction to the quality of the picture blurred my thinking. I didn't intend to ignore my father's wishes. My comment was a spontaneous reaction. It won't happen again.'

'Good. Then let us go to the back of the room and spend some time observing reaction.'

Jim grabbed her arm, leading both out to the reception area with Jess following. 'They have recognised me. It would be unfortunate for me to be photographed with Jess. I have told Richard we will meet him outside in ten minutes. He has more than fulfilled his media duties, so we should get out of here. We can always return another day. Elizabeth, can you find Audrey and Famida and quietly escort them out of here?'

They all collected promotional copies of *"Pure Love"* on their way out, and Richard quickly joined them.

'Let's go to Covent Garden. I know a few restaurants there where we can avoid any more media attention.'

Once seated, Sebastian expressed confusion. 'Why is it such a big deal that Uncle Jim was recognised?'

'Son, this exhibition is about my picture, not speculation Uncle Jim and myself are back in business. It was probably a mistake for all of us to attend this evening, but I hope our abrupt exit has not detracted from the enjoyment of the event.'

'Not at all, dad. Is it true Jess and Famida are the models in your picture?'

'My picture expresses humanity. Any models I use are incidental, and their identity is intentionally obscured, so you let the picture speak to you about its meaning. I will never divulge the identity of models under such circumstances.'

Sebastian felt his powers of observation were probably correct, but he also realised his behaviour this evening was verging on the unacceptable, so withdrew from the subject. 'Whatever, father. *"Pure Love"* is clearly a fantastic work of art and I'm sure the public will most certainly connect with your message.'

All discussion regarding *"Pure Love"* ceased whilst they had a quick supper before making their way home.

Sebastian arrived home thinking more about Jess than anything else. There was something about her that occupies his mind. He would prefer her as a friend than use her as he does with most women. His mother was waiting for his report.

'Well? What are they like? How did the exhibition go?'

He threw the catalogue and the promotional picture of *"Pure Love"* at her. 'See for yourself.'

She looked at the picture. 'Wow. This is different. Does the actual picture speak to you?'

'It's fantastic. I expect it to be in the Press over the weekend judging by the amount of media interest.'

'What about your father?'

'Couldn't wait to get out of there. He doesn't like publicity. Uncle Jim was recognised, so we abruptly left.'

'He never did like the Press. Always wanted his work to speak for him. How was Uncle Jim?'

'I'd forgotten about his appearance. He still looks ill but was in good spirit until they recognised him, at which point he couldn't wait to get out of there.'

'What about his new wife and family?'

'Elizabeth, his new wife is very nice, and is certainly promoting my cause. Her daughter, who refers to father as dad, is a real live wire. I'm sure she was one of the models in that picture, but dad is refusing to reveal the identities of his models. There was also another woman, Audrey, who appears to be their housekeeper but more integrated into the family than you would expect. Everything was too chaotic this evening to get a read. But no problems envisaged.'

'What's your next step?'

'I'm expecting an invite to go there for a weekend.'

'That'll cramp your style with your party friends.'

'I need a new sponsor. Needs must.'

The journey home to Buntins was full of joy and excitement. Famida had bought tickets for Sunday. 'Can't wait to see the reaction of my folks. Me, in a major exhibition, and likely in the Press. Wow.'

Richard needed to damp her enthusiasm about her being in the picture. 'If anyone overhears you are in the picture, and they tell others, or the Press, your life will change for the worse unless you have ambitions to be a model. I love your enthusiasm for the picture but heed our words if you are identified. If I finish your other pictures, and you then decide you want to engage professionally, I will happily manage you to protect you from the ravages of professional life. But for now, be satisfied you are a part of a significant work, albeit not about you per se. Are we good?'

'You would really manage me? I'll give it some thought before discussing it with my folks. I wanted to dance, but too hard. I guess I must have an exhibitionist streak. And I don't want to work in an office, boring. I'll get back to you after I've considered my future. Thanks.'

'Modelling can be hard and brutal. If you want the opinion of Mandy, I'll see if she'll discuss it with you. If you model for me again, you can ask her yourself.'

'Can I bring my folks to meet you? I had no idea what Jess was asking me to consider before I met you and saw your work and your studios. It would be a real comfort to them if they could see how serious and brilliant you are.'

'Talk to me after you've given it some serious thought.'

They dropped Famida at her home, and Jim at Totten's before returning to Buntins. Audrey went straight to the gatehouse, and Jess to bed. Richard and Elizabeth took a nightcap to the living room.

'Well, my darling, you certainly made your mark tonight. Richard Lyons is back, with a vengeance. To the world of media, take note.'

'What was your impression of Sebastian?'

'Certainly in need of some fatherly direction, but if he had any doubts about the standing of his father, they were shredded tonight. He knows who you are and wants to be associated. He's guessed Jess and Famida are your models, but I did suggest should he disclose his thoughts to anyone, he would witness the wrath of his father. I hope he got the message. It will be interesting to get a read from Audrey, having two boys around Sebastian's age.'

Chapter 64

"Pure Love" was widely reported in the media, but Richard refused the several calls for further interviews from both the Press and other media. To him the picture was the story, not him. In all his advertising campaigns, the pictures needed to be the full story to be successful. The person behind it is irrelevant other than to the promoters.

The exhibition was a great success, with Famida reporting back through Jess her folks loved the picture, albeit they would prefer family and friends are not informed she is one of the models. They also approved of the collage he created for her, which was a great relief to him considering the nature of the content. He would now work with the other pictures he had of her, as he knew she was a natural for artistic work. Mandy requested a smaller version of "Pure Love" having heard of its success, went to the exhibition, and deciding she must have an authentic copy of this work. For her, having witnessed the genuine emotion expressed by the models, this picture resonated the true intention of her long-time friend, and new client for more exciting works.

He invited Sebastian for a weekend, albeit still not feeling good about this reunion. Sebastian crafted his response to be there around lunchtime to give him time to shed any effects of his usual Friday night out with his mates. He would stay for lunch on Sunday before returning to his "studies", another party.

He sought the opinion of Audrey, who expressed that boys of that age can be somewhat wayward. As she did not have the opportunity to talk to him, she was reserving judgement. Maybe when he comes for the weekend, she will get a better read of him.

Chapter 65

Sebastian arrived at Buntins in time for lunch, bringing flowers for Elizabeth and Jess as part of his charm offensive.

He used all his political craft to navigate lunch, after which Jess agreed to show him around including a demonstration of the fantastic graphics Uncle Jim had developed for her business website. This took much of the afternoon, allowing him to accumulate much information to consider in his quest. He also found Jess a delight to be with, something new to him with a woman.

During dinner, Sebastian voiced his compliments about Jim's amazing graphics for Jess. He turned to his father, 'How did you and Uncle Jim meet?'

He hesitated. What to do. This is a private story, but his new family probably would like to know.

'I'd finished Art College, and about five years into building my career in advertising with a major agency. Technology was still in its infancy, but integrating actual life and graphics, especially in stills, was becoming a novel way of talking to the public. For example, trying to explain how an engine works using conventional engineer design drawings does not capture the imagination. Graphic artists can bring the drawings to life, dissecting and exploding part of the engine, and showing the working parts in pictorial form. This was a fresh way of teaching and energised the imagination of the non-technical.'

'I instinctively knew this was the way forward in advertising, so started a recruitment campaign for such a graphic artist. I interviewed a variety of conventional artists who had gone through art school, showing me portfolios of their impressive ability to draw. But none could spontaneously put pen to paper and produce graphic ideas as I conceptualised a campaign. They needed a full brief, and then time to go away and think about it. I was not impressed, as the advertising business rarely provides long preparation and gestation periods, and time is money.'

He reflected 'It was a lovely spring afternoon. I was on interview duty again getting a little frustrated my idea was not really working. In came this very short, unimpressive character, almost apologetic for wasting my time before he even sat down. He was not carrying the conventional portfolio case, just a sketch book. I asked him who he was and wanted to know his background. This was before the days of extensive CV's – he responded to our advert with just a brief letter.'

'He hadn't been to art college, didn't have a great academic record, and did not have any commercial experience as a graphic artist. He was a couple of years younger than me, so very late into the game. I asked him why he'd applied for the job. He said nothing, just pushed his sketchbook in my direction. When I opened it, the content blew my mind. Page after page of incredible conceptual drawings of various products we advertised. I asked him if he could draw from a verbal brief. He said nothing, just took a pencil from his pocket and indicated he wanted his sketch pad. I had a brief prepared for these interviews, so off I went. After a few minutes, he started to draw. When he'd finished, he passed his pad back to me. I had found my graphic artist, albeit I kept my excitement to myself as I needed to know I could work with this strange man of few words.'

'I wanted to know who he was but knew the formality of the interview made him very nervous. We were sitting at a conference table, but in a room where we also had some easy chairs around a coffee table. I offered him a drink – he asked for a coke. I invited him to move to the easy chairs. He was clearly less nervous, so I decided not to question – just chat with him. I broke the ice by explaining my background to give him a clue what I wanted from him. What I'm about to tell you I have never told to anyone other than Sarah, your mother,' as he faced Sebastian. 'I would ask all of you never tell anyone else as these memories should stay buried, and especially not to Jim. I only tell you because you asked; you're family, and it would help you all to understand my special relationship with him.'

They all indicated their consent to his request.

'His background was one of the saddest stories I've ever heard. As a teenager, he was involved in a car accident in which both his parents were killed. He himself suffered serious injuries which stunted his growth. He was an only child. When he finally left hospital, he went to live with his mother's sister who had decided against having children and was not enamoured with this task, especially as the accident had resulted in him withdrawing into himself. He did not do well at school and was never going to win any academic or sporting acclaim. No-one took enough interest in him to know he could draw anything.'

'It was easy for me to empathise with his story as my father had little time for me other than constantly telling me I would never make anything of myself if I didn't follow his rules, and which advice I constantly ignored.'

Elizabeth thought to herself '*I only licked the surface of his pain when we talked of his divorce. There is much more*' remembering his reaction to inviting his parent to the wedding.

'He left school, found himself a job. As soon as he could support himself, he left home, and never went back. He has no family to call his own. He tried for years to get a job drawing but his lack of personality, looks, and character did not fit in with the norm.'

'I quickly warmed to this character, but it also occurred to me he would need to fit into our commercial environment. And he would need to handle the pressures inherent in our business. I needed to think this through. I asked him if he would give me a few days to consider how I could integrate him into our setup.'

'He thanked me but told me he did not expect to hear from me as he had heard my story before. I looked him in the eyes and told him I would contact him in two days' time if only to tell him I could not use him.'

'It was a real wrestle how to integrate him into our business because his talent was exactly what I wanted, but his character was so far away from the norm for the business. I had to change my entire philosophy to take a chance with this strange person as he had no credentials, was untested, and lacked the social skills required. But he could draw intuitively better than anyone I have ever met.'

'I called him back in, as I wanted to be sure he would be guided by me in the zoo called advertising. My career was on the line.'

'He came back, and we went directly into chat mode. He was less nervous. Later he told me I was the first person to give him a second interview. Once he opened up there was a very keen and inquisitive mind, and his academic record did not remotely reflect his intellect. I told him I wanted to integrate him into my work and asked him what salary he was hoping for. He wanted £22,000 salary. I told him this was not possible. The lowest salary in our organisation for such a position was £28,000. He nearly fell out of his chair. But, for the first time in my presence, his face lit up with that wonderful smile of his you see today.'

'After a couple of years working together, we were the team of choice for our major accounts, but Jim was never treated well because he was so different, and not socially aware. I spent much of my time protecting him from the ravages of unappreciative clowns.'

'I talked to a few clients about us forming a new agency where I could set the rules around Jim and really show what he could do. I got the support of two large accounts. The rest is history.'

Reflecting 'The only downside was I also wanted to bring him out of his shell to give him a proper life. But our order book consumed us. We lost sight of life outside of our work. We had too much success, and too little time for anything else. Jim could never refuse a challenge, and I didn't take responsibility to ensure we could balance our workload with a life. Success became an all-consuming disease; until Jim paid the price with his heart attack.'

This admission struck Sebastian. *'Was this why his mother was so embittered towards him?* But look at the money you made.'

'Son, money did not drive us. We made it; but didn't spend any other than for the business. We didn't go anywhere; or do anything where we needed money. Your mother even took our car as part of the divorce settlement. The office was in Knightsbridge, I lived in Holland Park, Jim lived mostly in the office, and otherwise with me. We didn't need a car. I never replaced it until Jim needed ferrying around after his heart attack. Think of it, I'm 57 years old, have a driving licence since I was seventeen, a clean driving record, yet only have 2 years no claims discount. My insurance premiums cost a fortune.'

They all laughed.

Jess wanted more. 'But how did you get into the movie business? How did Jim get his Oscar and BAFTA's?'

'As I have already mentioned, graphic artists came to prominence, making boring technical drawings into fabulous works of art that enthused people to want to know and understand. To do this, they had to have, at least, a basic understanding of how whatever they were drawing really worked. Thus, they accumulate vast amounts of data about everything. And much of the time they were drawing the most advanced technology available.'

'Then came along more advanced science fiction movies needing more than a few tin cans strung together trying to emulate a space craft. If you think about it, the original Star

Trek USS Enterprise is nothing more than a flying saucer with two thruster units attached. Some graphic artist who probably had drawn actual space rockets, put the then fictional concept of a flying saucer together with the knowledge of rockets to create a credible design which today is iconic.'

'I can remember the day in the early 1990s when Jim met the inventor of a working flying saucer. Jim's enthusiastic inquisition of the inventor meant he knew exactly how this craft flew. Some of you might remember a movie by Steven Spielberg where he showed we can make flying saucers, despite the science suggesting such a shape is not aerodynamically possible.'

'There was a movie struggling to find space-age designs for space craft fit for distinct functions. We were creating the promotion material. Jim heard about their problems, read the story, and designed a range of spacecraft and associated paraphernalia. They wanted more of his input. He spent months on it. The movie is the blockbuster we all know, and Jim got his Oscar. But he would not go to Hollywood to collect it in person. The Director collected it on his behalf.' He turned to Jess 'thus why when you took him to the Technology Exhibition no-one recognised him, but they all knew his name.'

'Jim can apply himself to anything graphical, as Jess knows with her website graphics. But I still desperately want to give him a life where he can enjoy his success. He's earned it, and he's such a lovely character when you know him. He's family and we need to help him find happiness.'

Elizabeth put her hand over his. What she had just heard gave her a much deeper appreciation of both his pain, and the debt of gratitude he felt towards Jim. She now shared his responsibility to make amends.

Jess still wanted more, but Audrey, realising this conversation was over as far as Richard was concerned – too much pain and regret – put her hand over the hand of Jess 'who's for dessert?'

Jess got the message. Her wonderful dad is feeling pain. Leave it be until another day.

After lunch, Sebastian considered it time to leave before wearing out his welcome. He felt good with this family, but such feelings could easily catch him out. He had what he needed. Time to consider his next step. He had secured funding to repeat his final year at university, so had his hand in Daddy's bank. How to extract more is the next task.

His charm offensive had worked with the ladies of the house, and Richard was absorbed in the reflections of his past life with Jim to consider any thoughts about his son.

Chapter 66

Sebastian's journey home was filled with contradiction. His father was supposed to be the bad guy due for a fall. But the person he witnessed was warm and compassionate – especially toward Uncle Jim. The family, as he called it, are friendly people, and made him very welcome. And Jess is a real dish. What a lady.

He was still wrestling with his thoughts as he walked through the front door. His mother was waiting for a full debrief. She noted he was contemplative.

'How was your weekend?'

'Very interesting. Why did you never tell me the story about Uncle Jim? What he went through before dad picked him up. Bit like Harry Potter with his muggle family.'

'I'm surprised he told you, as he has told no one else to my knowledge. He has always been very protective of Jim. He even lived with us when he wasn't in his studio. You only remember him being with us for major holidays because the office was closed, but he normally lived with us when they

217

started their own business; but didn't come home very much. If he did, it would be after you were asleep, and he would leave before you were awake. Did you meet him?'

'No. The weekend was concentrated around dad's new family.'

'And what are they like?'

'They're lovely people. His wife, Elizabeth, is clearly driving our reconciliation. Her husband died of asbestosis about 3 years ago. Jess, her daughter, is a real dish. Audrey and Gerry are really housekeeper and gardener, but also part of the family. It's strange; but works.'

'And what about the house?'

'Spectacularly cool. Dad designed it. It's massive with everything you could want, including 60 acres of grounds. He even has the studios he needs for his work within the house.'

'How do you think you did in nurturing a relationship?'

'Dad is clearly watching me. With the others it's mine to take; or lose. They made me very welcome.'

'Son, I sense you may have lost some of your conviction to the task at hand.'

'Mother, I wanted him to fund another year at university. He's agreed to do it. What I need to do is re-evaluate how to secure more when he'll watch me like a hawk. He'll want to see progress and conviction, which will stifle my preferred lifestyle. We need to think how to get the best of both worlds. I'm not giving up my friends just so you can get rich.'

'Listen to me, son. Most people who go through university leave yoked in debt with student loans. I could avoid this with you. And how did you repay me? You jerked around with your so-called friends instead of studying, wasted my money. Your only debt is your credit card, which must be close to maxed out, and you've enjoyed far too much of mother's bank. You owe me, big time. I have a life to live as well, so I need some pay-back. You focus on what you need to do to get me some money or find yourself somewhere else to live.'

'Maybe I'll move in with dad. He has plenty of room.'

'And you seriously believe he'll put up with your lifestyle? I know him, so the answer is most certainly NO. It's time to grow up.'

Later, as he lay in bed thinking about his weekend, he found himself confused. *'What a great lifestyle they have at Buntins – what a weird name for a house. I could go live there, but mother's right, I would have to give up my lifestyle. No way. There must be another way. Perhaps I can think of a business like the one Jess has. Low maintenance – good income. If I could hook into Jess, I would have the best of both worlds with her income, and dad's favour. Hmm, need to explore this option.'*

Chapter 67

The following weekend Jess took Uncle Jim to Vienna for another weekend break. She was starting to feel a little queasy in the mornings, albeit usually okay after some breakfast. Knowing the temperature in Vienna was likely hot, and a 4-hour flight prompted her to visit with her new private GP for some advice on how to cope so as not to spoil the trip for Uncle Jim.

Elizabeth and Gerry spent much of Sunday at the garden centre filling their needs for both the walled garden and the formal garden. Plans had been drawn and agreed. Many trees and plants to purchase. Richard considered buying shares in the garden centre in anticipation of a lucrative weekend for them.

He took the opportunity to retire to his photo studio to complete his work on the pictures of Famida he thought worthy of considerable attention. He noted she had not contacted him about further modelling but thought another photoshoot before Jess starts to look pregnant would advance his cause in his artistic ambitions. *'Must talk to Jess.'*

Chapter 68

It was now close to the end of September. Both Elizabeth and Gerry had monitored the weather forecast looking for a two-day period to plant both the garden and the walled garden.

Gerry had organised enough mature manure from one of his farmer chums to dig into all the planting areas, and this task was complete. Gerry had also laid watering lines to each area as there was no possibility of watering such a large garden manually.

They wanted to co-ordinate the delivery of plants as they would need enough plants, including the fruit trees for the walled garden, to fill a lorry. Having spent the previous Sunday at their preferred garden centre, they spent over £8,000 even with a substantial discount, but to Elizabeth's account – her contribution to her new life. She knew what she wanted; the plans were ready for each area to be planted. The garden centre would provide two people, including the driver, to help unload and position each plant. They estimated it would take two days to complete the task.

They were all sitting at dinner; the perfect time to rally the troops. She clinked her glass to gain attention. 'Gerry and I are ready to plant the gardens. Tomorrow and Friday look to be fine days so the lorry will arrive tomorrow morning around 8 o'clock. We need as much help as possible to get these plants into the ground. The garden centre is providing two people tomorrow to help as they know the plants and thus will know where to put them according to my plans. Once this task is done, they will also help to plant until 4 o'clock. Richard, Jess, any help will be appreciated. Audrey can keep us all fed and watered.'

Richard spoke first. 'What, no tennis tomorrow? How many plants are we talking about?'

'Sorry, darling. We had to find two fine days for planting. As for how many, if we can get this garden planted in two days, we will have worked hard. Saturday doesn't look so good weather-wise, so we must endeavour to finish planting on Friday.'

He turned to Gerry. 'From experience, is this task doable?'

'If everyone rolls up their sleeves and gets stuck in, we can do it. We needs to use as many daylight hours as possible, just like a farmer during planting season.'

Audrey piped in. 'Considering Jess's condition, how about Jess does the feeding and watering and I apply my farmer's wife role of helping in both the planting and harvest season. Will be good to get some fresh air for a change.'

Jess was about to protest, but Audrey covered her hand, which meant this was not open to discussion.

Richard saw Audrey's move on Jess and agreed so quickly interjected. 'Do we have enough garden implements for all of us?'

Gerry responded. 'The garden centre people will bring their own, and I bought enough for us all. No problem there.'

Richard resigned to the task. 'Has anyone thought to book masseurs for Friday evening.'

They all laughed. The next two days will be arduous but would transform this property into a beautiful home and garden. Gerry was particularly pleased with his walled garden and couldn't wait to start his winter seed planting next week.

Chapter 69

Gerry was the only one chuckling at dinner on Friday evening as he watched the others nurse their various aches and pains. But the planting was done. As with childbirth, much of the pain subsided when they viewed the result, although they expected Saturday to be painful as muscles vented their anger for being so overworked. Even Jess found it funny, but her giggles remained internal. No point in expressing anything other than a job well done. Even Audrey would need a hot bath and a large scotch to ease her pain. They celebrated with champagne but retired in pain.

At Saturday breakfast there were still groans of pain, but the landscape had changed. Richard's vision for Buntins is now complete. Time to relax and enjoy their new home.

Chapter 70

October was upon them with the realisation they were only days away from their trip to Mexico. Frantic last-minute preparations were in process with Jess also ensuring Uncle Jim was fully prepared both medically and with wardrobe. Taking him shopping was always a joy for her, albeit finding summer cloths on the verge of winter was a challenge. The benefits of online shopping became very apparent once his sizes were known.

Jim was engrossed in his studies of the Mayan civilisation to determine where, within reasonable travelling distance of Cancun, he would like to visit. His excitement level was worrying Margaret, but Brandy somehow detected any undue distress making demands upon him that turned his focus to her needs.

The limousine company thought they needed to leave Buntins at 7:30am to be sure of avoiding any problems with the heavy Monday morning commuter traffic. Jim would stay at Buntins overnight.

The long flight, even in Business class, took its toll on Jess. She had escaped the horrors of acute morning sickness but sitting on a plane for so many hours made her very uncomfortable.

They arrived at Cancun a little after 5pm local time and were quickly despatched to ClubMed where they were warmly greeted before being shown to their rooms. They agreed to enjoy a lite dinner and get an early night to overcome any jetlag issues.

Chapter 71

They assembled with a mass of other people in the lobby by 7:50 ready for their excursion to Chichén Itzá, the famous Mayan city. The sun was rising, not a cloud in the sky.

They had now been at ClubMed, Cancun for three days. Settled, refreshed from their long flight, and acclimatised, they were ready for Jim's first tour. As was usual in their projects both Richard and Jim had thoroughly studied the Mayan civilisation albeit from different perspectives. Richard was interested in the rise and fall of this civilisation and what legacy they left, whereas Jim was more interested in how they lived and communicated.

Today would be hot again. Two large buses and six minibuses were parked outside on the forecourt. Jess heard someone calling for people for Chichén Itzá. She guided everyone in the direction indicated. Before they were permitted to board the minibus, they were asked to sign a disclaimer mitigating the operator for just about every problem that might beset them, including kidnap once they left the resort. Besides their group, there was a further five people in their minibus.

As they were departing the resort, their tour guide, an aussi no less, introduced himself requesting how many languages he would need. English and French would suffice. He informed them the trip would take about two hours with a thirty-minute pit stop on the way. During the drive he explained a little about the Mayan civilisation, and how their numbers system worked. He also touted for people prepared to pay 100 pesos for a birth date certificate in Maya codec. He enticed only two people into this purchase.

Jim was amused they needed to stop at the border crossing into Yucatán Province. Papers of the driver and tour guide had to be shown, and a toll paid. There was also a one-hour time difference across the border. The tour guide explained the Yucatán region, although part of Mexico, is maintained as a historic Mayan region where the Maya language and culture are preserved. The landscape was flat, poor quality for agriculture, little or no mineral content, and because the ground was essentially limestone, there were no surface rivers. Water was subterranean, revealing itself in deep freshwater cenotes, or ponds, from which water could be drawn.

Finally, they arrived at Chichén Itzá. Jess needed to visit the bathroom. Tickets in hand, they passed through the entry gate following a guide appointed by the tour operator. They followed a pathway through a wooded area enclosed by various stalls peddling their wares of various trinkets and cloths, eventually entering a vast space at the centre of which was the impressive pyramid of Kukulkan. But this was no Egyptian pyramid built for some pharaoh, it was a temple carefully crafted around the constellations and the seasons with 365 steps scaling nine square terraces to the top platform. The guide explained Kukulkan was a serpent symbolising the divinity of the state. During the spring and Autumn equinox, the shadow cast by the sun and edges of the pyramid and the stone serpent head carvings at the base of the balustrades of the north-eastern staircase creates the illusion of a massive serpent descending the pyramid.

Richard and Elizabeth found the enormous Great Ball Court fascinating. The playing area was about the size of a soccer pitch with walls some 8m high at each end in the centre of each are stone rings set vertically surrounded by carvings of intertwined serpents. A bit like a basketball arena, but with the net set vertically rather than horizontal. The guide explained they played this game between the fittest of warriors. The downside for the scorer of the winning goal was he had the questionable honour of being sacrificed to the Gods. This sacrifice entailed removal of his heart whilst still alive and then decapitated and his skull impaled in some hall of honour. He turned to Elizabeth 'sometimes being the best has its downside' thinking of Jim's heart attack.

Jim and Jess wandered off to the Tzompanti skull platform, where Jess photographed, and Jim sketched the multi-images of impaled skulls before moving on to the Temple of Warriors where Jim found much to occupy his imagination before abruptly being moved on by the tour guide.

They had finished the tour of the Observatory, moving on to what looked like a villa adorned in a wide range of relief carvings. Jim immediately found a place to sit and started to draw the images he could see on the wall. Jess was watching his hand quickly and accurately capture each of the images. She photographed the area of interest in case he would need a recap later. A woman, slight and probably in her mid-fifties, dressed a little like an explorer, stood immediately behind Jim and slightly to his left, looking over his shoulder. She said nothing for a few minutes, merely observing the sketches as Jim quickly captured what he wanted.

It was time to move on. Jim was clearly distressed by the speed of this tour. No time to just sit and absorb the atmosphere. He snapped his sketch pad shut and reluctantly followed the tour guide.

The woman spoke. 'Excuse me, but I couldn't help observing the sketches you were making. You have very adept hands at capturing the essence of those reliefs quickly. Are you an artist?'

Jim stopped to look at her. He had seen her on the coach, so knew she was part of their group. She was only a little taller than Jim, and her somewhat frumpy appearance calmed his disquiet with the tour guide.

'Hello dear lady. My name is Jim Spencer, and if you want a conventional label for my work, I'm a graphics designer. But my interest here is as someone interested in archaeology and ancient civilisations.'

She was amused with his precise and exacting description 'My name is Katherine Blakeley, and if you want a label for me, I'm Professor of Archaeology at Cambridge, with a special interest in the social structure of ancient civilisations. I'm here in pursuit of my interest in the Mayan Empire.'

Jess was walking alongside Jim, amused by his approach.

'Very nice to meet you, Katherine' as he extended his hand to her. She reciprocated.

'And is this your daughter?' looking at Jess.

'Oh no. This beautiful princess is Jess, my chaperone, to ensure I don't get lost, exert myself, or hit this tour guide with a large rock.'

Jess was audibly chuckling at his response as she extended her hand to Katherine 'Nice to meet you, Katherine. Please excuse Uncle Jim, but he is so exasperated with the speed of this tour. He wants to sit and absorb the atmosphere as part of his sketches, but they move us along so quickly us. We come all this way but cannot have the time to feel this place.'

'I have the same disquiet with the lack of time to really feel this magnificent city. Perhaps we could express our interest to have some free time to explore; or would you be afraid of losing Jim?'

'Looking at this place through Uncle Jim's eyes will be an absolute revelation. I wouldn't miss it for anything. I can't wait to see what he does with those sketches when he has time to apply his genius to them.'

Katherine looked at Jim 'My, I appear to have met a genius. May I walk with you as I too am very interested in your sketches?'

'My dear lady, it would be a pleasure to have such an intelligent companion.'

For the rest of the visit, they chatted with Katherine, explaining to him the meaning of the symbols on the various buildings with Jim recording the shape and writing the meaning next to it. They were so immersed with each other it reminded Jess of the session in the audio studio when Richard and Jim composed her internet music with her presence quickly forgotten. Richard and Elizabeth rescued her; all three watching with pleased amusement as these two gelled with each other.

During the return coach trip to the resort, Jim sat with Katherine. She was totally fascinated by how he reworked symbols, as though modern-day tools would have been available for the carving, and then how he transposed each shape to see if there was any inherent association with the meaning of the symbol. She was amazed at how many symbols could be crudely attributed to its meaning.

Both, being totally dissatisfied with the speed of this tour, decided they would return. Richard suggested they should approach the resort reception to organise a car and driver for future excursions so they could control the timeline.

Chapter 72

Elizabeth and Jess, having enjoyed a leisurely lunch at the beach restaurant behind the tennis courts, were walking in the shallow waters of the beach towards the tip of the Cancun Peninsular at the end of the resort. Their walk back to Jade, the exclusive 5-star part of the resort, was some 500m of undeveloped shoreline with sandy beach but quickly turning to a shallow but rocky seafront and thus generally not used. The main beach was some 300m in the opposite direction close to the main village part of the resort and which was a far more extensive sandy beach but had the disadvantage the vista along the coastline was the blighted sight of the Costa del Cancun littered with hideous concrete hotel buildings. They were the only people using this baron shoreline as they walked. Normally they could use an exclusive golf cart shuttle service back to Jade but chose to walk off lunch.

Jess had booked Jade, not really understanding this exclusive area was more for what she would term 'posers' who spent their days lazing around the infinity pool wearing their expensive jewellery, sipping champagne, and nibbling caviar. The real life was in the village at the other end of the peninsula, and where they spent much of their time when within the resort. Katherine had a bungalow in the village. Jess knew for future occasions to book the village.

Richard, Jim, and Katherine had gone for the day to explore Ek'Balam, another, more recent Mayan city so a leisurely mother and daughter day.

'Mom, I have a dilemma. I desperate need your help.'

'What is it, and why so sudden?'

'I've been thinking about it for a few weeks, but it's so multi-dimensional I cannot fathom which way to go. And at its core is how you will react to it as you're a key consideration. I'm torn between your feelings on the subject and the long-term impact on your grandchild.'

'Have you spoken to Richard about it?' She had demarcations when speaking with Jess about Richard. Any reference to her father specifically meant David Sandiman, who sired her. And to use 'your dad' or 'daddy' did not easily flow off her tongue. Thus, she settled to refer to Richard in such conversations.

'No. Although he will be part of the solution, my greatest concern is how you feel about my proposal.'

'I'm listening.'

'I've been thinking about the convoluted, but wonderful life we now lead. Unconventional family structure, but very much a proper family, for which I'm truly grateful. The problem I'm struggling with is the identity of my – our – child within this structure.'

'Do you mean whether Richard is the father or grandfather?'

'No. I don't see that as a problem. I think by the time it becomes a known, attitudes will have moved on. My concern is the near-term identity of this child. I'm still known by my Sandiman surname. You've moved on to become a Lyons. Should I get married, although under this dilemma I may resist changing my surname, my surname could change. And we have the reality Richard is the biological father. How does this child identify with the family?'

'What's with a name? We're family, and we all know it.'

'But we're grownups. We understand what we have. But what about a child, say, at school where all the other kids have more conventional family structures? I see the possibility of an identity crisis. I would like to avoid this.'

'What do you have in mind?'

'My ideal solution would be to adopt your new surname so this child would bear the name Lyons, so whatever I do there is a definitive connection between my child and its grandparents. But I'm very alive to how this may offend you. By birth I'm a Sandiman, and you're my mom. I'm the remnants of your marriage to my biological father, and you may wish to retain fond memories of that period of your life through me, and now your grandchild. If that's your wish, I don't wish to take this from you.'

'Jess, Jess. Wait a minute. Aren't you making this too complicated? For someone who can incredibly see the obvious before her eyes where others can't, such as finding Brandy for Jim, you're overthinking this problem.' She held Jess's hand to face her. 'I really appreciate your thought for me. I was beginning to feel irrelevant to you now you have Richard. All that matters to me is, as your mother, you and your child think me relevant to your life. Women change their surname when they marry, but does it change who they are? If you got married and adopted the surname of your husband, does this prevent you being my precious daughter?'

Jess shook in agitation and then threw her arms around her mother. 'Mom, you are not, and never will be irrelevant in my life. And I'm sorry if you feel this way. I know I can be a little wayward, but I love you, and need you in my life.'

After both savouring their togetherness, Elizabeth pushed her to arm's length to look her in the eye. 'Tell me what you think you want to do.'

'I would like to change my name by Deed Poll to Lyons before the birth so my child will bear the name of its grandparents. This child will be the legacy of the wonderful life we have together. You and Richard are the heart of our family, and this child will not only know it belongs there, but everyone outside the family will also know this.'

'Don't you think yourself at the heart of this family?'

'Yes, and no. To the outside world, I'm the baggage from your previous relationship. I see myself, along with Audrey and Gerry, as the inner circle. Don't get me wrong, I feel the love as does Audrey, who has also adopted me as the daughter she never had. Within the household there is no confusion, but outside is a different story as you well know. I don't want to add yet another layer to this apparent confusion.'

'And what about Gerry?'

'If anyone knows what goes on inside his head, I want to meet them.' They both laughed.

Jess reflected. 'When I go to help him with his wonderful walled garden project which, by the way, is incredible with its eco credentials, we have time to chat. Richard must cringe at the cost, but we'll have probably the purest, if indeed the most expensive fruit and veg on the planet.' They both smiled. 'When we chat, I see a sadness in him. I think he's disheartened neither of his sons wanted to continue with

Blythe Farm, which I think Gerry was fourth or fifth generation?'

'Fifth, I think. Certainly, as a child, I remember his father and his grandfather as farmers.'

'And when was the last time Michael or James visited with them? Certainly not while we've been there.'

'Michael is now in Australia, making his own life. Not sure about James. Audrey doesn't say too much about them. I think you're right. They feel a little deserted.'

'I was thinking about putting the money together to send them to Australia to see Michael. Maybe this will entice him to come visit them. Maybe Michael and I can rekindle our relationship and really close the family circle.'

'I remember you and Michael had a fling together before university.'

'Yes, we did. But neither of us was ready for a relationship. I was off to university, and he wanted to find his way in life. Would be interesting to meet him again.'

Elizabeth had a eureka moment. 'Jess, you've done it again. Brilliant. I've been thinking about what to give Audrey and Gerry for Christmas. As a family, we'll send them to Australia to see Michael. What a great idea. Thank you, my dear. You're such a thoughtful daughter. Where would we be without you?'

'Do you think dad will go along with such a cost? And when will you send them? This Christmas will be the first Christmas we'll spend together as a family. I wouldn't want to miss such an occasion. Christmas is when family really come together.'

'No problem with Richard, as I'm prepared to share such cost. But I'll have to think about when. I agree we should spend Christmas together. It's summer in Australia at Christmas. Maybe January would be a good time. Need to try to communicate with Michael to see how he feels about it, but great idea. Thanks.'

'What do you think about my dilemma?'

'Have you mentioned this at all to Richard or Jim, or indeed anyone else?'

'No. I needed to know your thoughts before contemplating speaking with dad.'

'We have a first. I know about something before Richard. In that case, I'll happily discuss this with him, and when we have a considered view, we'll discuss it together as family. I like the argument my grandchild should be readily identified with its grandmother – when will you know the gender of my grandchild?'

'Thought it would be a nice Christmas present.'

They hugged. 'It would be a wonderful Christmas present, my dear.'

Chapter 73

Richard, Jim, and Katherine had left early, having hired a car with driver, to visit another ancient site expressed by Katherine as of great interest. The resort had organised packed lunches for them. Avoiding the compulsory tour 30-minute rest stops both there, and on the return trip, would further add to the time available to explore; the only constraint on time being the need to be back and ready for dinner around 7:30pm. Richard had reservations about the impact of such a long day on Jim, but prepared to see how the day played out before imposing himself. He was enjoying his new friend, and she was no athlete either.

Ek'Balam is only recently discovered, apparently by some young astronomer plotting the likely locations of more Mayan cities using the constellations as a guide. Ek'Balam means "black star jaguar" in Maya and was the capital of the ancient Talol Kingdom. To date, they have uncovered multi-storey storage and living accommodation and found a royal tomb at the top of the Acropolis. The unusual feature of this city is the compact layout and a double outer wall. This feature was the primary attraction for Jim as major cities such as Chichén Itzá are very spacious, and without fortifications.

They were gathered around a plan of the city whilst a guide was explaining what they had found to date. The guide suggested there was still much to uncover because of the unusual nature of the design of this city compared with others with much of it recaptured by nature.

Almost involuntarily, Jim spoke to Katherine. 'It's obvious why this city is designed this way. It's a fortress to protect the stores of food. As the population grew resources became scarce so rather than the open civilisation that had existed for generations the inability to harvest enough to feed everyone meant each community started to protect what it had thus deserting cities that could not be defended, building fortress style cities that could easily thwart attack from others. The Mayan civilisation were brilliant at observing the skies, even giving us the leap year, but apparently useless at understanding good farming practices and crop rotation. They starved themselves to extinction.'

Everyone heard this, including the guide. All were listening. The guide spoke. 'Interesting observation, sir, but without substantiation. We're still learning about the later period of this civilisation.'

Katherine could see Jim had registered the interest of the group of tourists being addressed and was getting agitated with this attention. She put her arm through his to let him know she was with him. 'I'll defend what he said not least because its logical, and extremely likely to be a cause, if not the primary cause of the demise of this civilisation.'

The guide responded. 'Oh. And on what basis do you think this to be the case?'

'My studies of ancient civilisations for many years.'

The guide was feeling a little perturbed he was being usurped in this way. 'And could I ask who you might be?'

With some authority no doubt defensively developed in dealing with students to offset her slight frame 'My name is Katherine Blakeley, Professor of Archaeology at Cambridge University in England, with a special interest in the social structure of ancient civilisations.'

There was a gasp from the crowd, and then a keen interest in where this conversation was going. The guide was first to speak. 'My apologies Ma'am. It's a pleasure to have such a distinguished scholar on this tour.'

Katherine detected this escalating interest was distressing Jim. It was not in her nature to be less than gracious, and she certainly didn't want to appear rude, but she had a compelling instinct to move him away from this group as quickly as possible. 'Perhaps it would help these people if you studied the latest information on the Mayan Empire. I have published both papers and a book on the subject.' Turning to Jim and taking his hand 'Come Jim, let us go explore this city by ourselves. I think we've exhausted what we can learn here.' She turned to the guide 'Please excuse us' as she led him away from the group back towards the city.

Richard observed this quietly from the back of the crowd with much amusement. *'Jim has a new friend. And she sure as hell is sensitive to his demeanour.'* Then he saw it. What a picture. He quickly primed his camera as he trekked after them. The visual was stunning. Two intrepid explorers strolling into a Mayan city hand in hand with the wide brims of their hats almost touching as they walked. He got close enough to frame them walking towards the five-storey structure to the right of the Acropolis. This made them look smaller than their actual modest heights, enhancing the quality of this image. He then dropped to his knees to shoot at a lower level. Thinking about the iconic Athena poster of the girl on a tennis court, had he just captured an iconic parody on the current interest with

Indiana Jones? He couldn't wait to get these pictures back to his studio.

He knew Jim wanted to observe the city from as high as possible to understand both the layout and the extent of its boundaries. There was a Governmental restriction on climbing the Acropolis steps, but no such restriction on climbing the steep and narrow steps of the multi-storey building known as the el Trono (the Throne) which must be close to the height of the Acropolis. They were both heading straight for the base of the stairway. What to do.

He caught up with them. 'Nice speech, Katherine; and thank you for your quick-thinking.'

'Thank you. Seeing this city through the wonderful eyes of Jim is a privilege. He's right about this city. It's so obvious. So why don't these so-called guides who I would expect to have some academic interest in the subject know these things. Why do we pay for such nonsense? Now if you don't mind, we'll slowly but surely scale these steps to the top. I can't wait to see how Jim records the vista, and whatever else he sees on these terraces.'

'Do you think that's a good idea? Jim is still recovering from a serious heart attack. This stairway is steep, and the steps narrow. You also have the heat against you.'

'I'm fully aware of Jim's condition. I'm not the fittest of people either. But we'll proceed with caution, taking our time. There's no rush. And this stairway is more suited to our height than yours. We're more the average height of a Mayan. Tall people like you with larger feet will find this climb more difficult than for Jim and myself. You may wait here for us if you find the climb taxing.'

Jim looked at Richard with a wry smile as if to say you've been told, so mind your own business. '*Not very often anyone gets the better of Richard*' he thought. Jim had an extra spring in his step as he started the climb, still hand-in-hand with Katherine.

Jim drew some fabulous sketches from various angles from the top of this building. They spent some 45 minutes at the top platform, and further time at each tier of this structure capturing as much as possible. Richard found the climb taxing but would not have missed his unofficial photoshoot of these two explorers totally engrossed in their adventure. He found the decent even more difficult. Both Katherine and Jim were seated at the bottom of the steps, amused by his discordant decent.

On the way out of the city they passed a smaller building full of skulls. Katherine explained that the Mayan people regarded death as a passing to another world, but their spirit remained. They had a festival day each year when they would feast with places laid for their ancestors with the skull on the table. During the drive back to Cancun Jim worked up a series of sketches showing what such a feast might look like. Everyone, including their driver, folded in fits of laughter as each drawing was torn from his sketchpad and passed around.

This trip fully bonded Katherine and Jim. Other than sleep together they were inseparable for the rest of the holiday, returning to Chichén Itzá privately for a whole day, and taking a further trip together to the Mayan site at Tulum, which was probably the fortified alternative to, and close by Chichén Itzá, and is the only Mayan site on the coast.

It emerged Katherine had never married. Just as she was preparing to go to university, she became pregnant. She had an abortion that went very wrong, leaving her unable to have children. This was a time before abortion was generally available. Although very attractive as a woman, her baron state made her unattractive as a mate. She had immersed herself in study and found her home in academia. Meeting Jim, and hearing his story, rekindled her interest in a companion.

They agreed to regularly meet upon their return to the UK. It would be easy for Jim to travel to Cambridge from Stamford by train. Katherine can drive. Jim was visibly disappointed when she left the resort to return home two days before he was due to leave. Jess quickly moved in to rescue him, leaving Richard and Elizabeth to spend time together to enjoy what remained of their honeymoon.

Chapter 74

The journey back to Buntins was uneventful, other than Jess did not enjoy the flight. Sleeping in a flight bed was uncomfortable for her, thus she spent much of the time on the flight walking around and sitting. She needed time to walk around the airport before getting into a limousine for the 3-hour drive home.

Jim had arranged to have Katherine visit him the following Saturday, so was buzzing to get back to make ready for her. Next to Brandy, Katherine was now his best friend outside of the family and he wanted to keep her.

Chapter 75

After breakfast, Jess went into her office with her laptop and fired up Skype. Can she find him? She had set herself the task of finding Michael in Australia without alerting Audrey, hoping he had some social media connections she could use to locate him. She searched his name, but nothing. *'If he has a Skype account, he probably uses a handle as a call sign.'*

Next stop Facebook. *'How many Michael Roswell's can there be – pages!'* What filters could she use? 'Try *Bourne Grammar School. Bingo, got ya.'* He was online. *Michael, this is Jess Madison. Can we connect on Skype as I would like to speak with you? My handle is JessMe, what's yours?*

The response was almost immediate. *Hi Jess. Lovely to hear from you. Handle is RosMick but I'll call you now.*

Her Skype app activated. She accepted the call. She could see him, knowing he could see her.

'Jess, you look fantastic. Great to hear from you. Mum told me you'd moved into Buntins. How's life with you?'

'Great. Fantastic place with fantastic family. What about you?'

'Having a ball out here. Got a good job in car sales, and about to complete on my house. Even has a pool. Why don't you come take a look?'

'It would be nice to see you again, but I'm pregnant so not into long-haul for a while. Went to Mexico a few weeks back with mom and dad. The flight was not fun.'

'Who's the father?'

'No-one I intend to marry. Just felt the need.'

'Still a wild lass. Should have kept you when I had you. What about you? How come you're still wild and free?'

'Still having fun. Haven't found anyone I want to settle with or wants to settle with me. I have a vacancy if you're free.'

'It would be interesting to see if the flames are still burning, but I have a reason for my call, which has nothing to do with sex. So listen up.'

'Oh no. My Jess is going to get boring on me. Better be good.'

'Can I ask you a personal question so I don't put my nose where it's not wanted?'

'Your nose will always be welcome so long as it's attached to your beautiful body. Shoot.'

'Is there a reason you and James have little contact with your mum and dad?'

'Can't speak for James, as we have little contact. Haven't heard from him in months. For me, I guess it's just laziness. Too much going on. But nothing sinister if that's what you mean. Why? Is something wrong with them I should know about?'

'Only that they feel deserted by both of you. There's a sadness in both I would like you and me to fix.'

'What do you have in mind?'

Mom, dad, and I would like to fund them to come visit with you in Australia as a Christmas present. They don't go on holiday, so I thought this would be a real treat for them if it works for you.'

'Jess, you humble me. You're so thoughtful. Are you sure you won't marry me?'

'Never say never, but not long distance. Perhaps when you come visit with them, we can talk. But we will be two.' She let this sink just in case he had forgotten about her pregnancy. 'We're thinking mid-January for two to three weeks. Does this work for you?'

'I'll make it work now you've put guilt and shame into the frame. What do we need to do?'

'Can you put them up or do we need to add a hotel?'

'No problem in my new house. Probably take them touring as well. A lot to see here.'

'We'll give them enough pocket money to travel around.'

'Jess, stop it. I feel guilty enough already. They're my folks, and I'll make good to them for my delinquency.'

'There you go. You really do have a heart. Come here sometime after June next year. It'll be good to see you in the flesh.'

'Naughty girl. Tempting me this way. I'll do it.'

'I'll keep you to that. We need to agree some dates in January. I'll message you my email address. Think about what will work for you and we'll organise things this end. But not a word to them. I want to see your mum's face when she opens the package with the tickets. Before I forget, give us enough time between Christmas and travel date to get their passports and visas. Probably later in January would be better. And I want you on a Skype call with them on Christmas day.'

'Now we have regimental Jess. Yes miss. Whatever you say is my command. For your info, visit the Australian Embassy to get visas. Don't do it by post. It takes forever.'

'I'll also need your address as their place of residence whilst there.'

'Whatever you say, miss. Anything else before we get back to the important subject of sex?'

She put her hand up with her fingers open so he would see it on his screen. 'Touch me.'

He put his hand so it was over hers. '*I should never have let her go,* he thought.

She was amused by his antics. 'That's your lot for today, but let's do this again. It's fun.'

'With you, lady, anytime. Lovely to hear from you. And thanks for thinking of mum and dad. I'm a thoughtless son, but with your guidance I'll make good.'

'Bye.'

She is elated. Job done plus a little tingle down her spine. She closed her laptop and went to find her mum.

Later that day, she had a call from Uncle Jim followed by an email with details. She couldn't wait to tell the others at dinner.

'Hey, guys, listen up. Uncle Jim called me today. He's going to Istanbul with Katherine. Apparently, she has a trip organised through the university to study the old town of Constantinople and invited Uncle Jim to join her. This afternoon I've upgraded their flights and hotel. University budgets do not suit Uncle Jim. They are staying in the same room. We have progress.'

Richard, with a knowing smile, 'When are these intrepid explorers leaving?'

'A week on Thursday for 4-days. And they return in the early hours of Monday morning, but I haven't asked if he needs collecting. He's taking the train to Cambridge from where Katherine will drive to the airport, but there won't be any trains from Cambridge that early in the morning. Watch this space.'

Richard, remembering he still hasn't processed the pictures of them in Mexico, 'Maybe I should go with them to record this adventure. I have some splendid pictures of them exploring Ek'Balam. Must process them as one picture I hope is fantastic.'

'Shall I ask Uncle Jim if he minds you tagging along?'

'I wouldn't want them to know I'm there. Much better pictures when they're totally immersed in what they're doing. I'll think about it.'

Elizabeth is overjoyed. 'My darling, your prayers are being answered. Your last major quest is showing good progress. I couldn't be happier. Jim is such a lovely person. He deserves an intrepid companion. Good luck to them.'

Chapter 76

Jim decided his trip to Istanbul with Katherine would not involve any support from anyone else other than his lovely princess upgrading their flights and hotel accommodation. He refused all offers by Richard and Jess to transport him anywhere. He would stand on his own feet, only needing Robert to take him to the station to catch his train to Cambridge. From there, Katherine would drive them to the airport, and upon their return would deliver Jim back to Tottens.

Their flight was uneventful but were soon thrust into the vibrant but chaotic streets of the old city. Once checked in at their hotel, conveniently located on the perimeter of the old city, they were quickly exploring. Jim found crowds daunting but Katherine was now familiar with his insecurities, so gripped his hand as she guided them through the narrow streets to visit the places she particularly wanted to explore. She ensured they found a place to sit at each location to allow Jim to work his magic in his sketchbook, knowing these pictures would both record and bring each place to life after they returned home. She so wanted to see these ancient places through his eyes. Having included some of his sketches from Mexico in a book she is about to publish on the Mayan civilisation knowing they would enhance the experience for her readers, she fully expected to include some of his drawings of Istanbul in a paper and presentation she is preparing. Her gifted companion not only brought additional dimensions to her work, but also it felt good to share such experiences. They are now inseparable, and they both are comfortable in their life together.

Chapter 77

The last day of November. As she was now into her second trimester, Jess decided today was the day to find out the gender of her child. Having survived all the potential problems of her first trimester, she was now more settled about the prospects of reaching birth, so her view had moved from a possibility to a likely reality. It was time to get fully acquainted with this person growing inside her.

Her appointment at the anti-natal clinic is scheduled for 11am. She was quickly ready for her ultrasound scan, having advised the nurse that today she wanted to know the gender of her child and would like a scan photo to take home.

The nurse did her routine scan, looking for any irregularities before turning her screen towards Jess. 'It's a boy, developing very well. Should let you know of his presence in the next couple of months.'

On the way home she was debating who to tell and when, distracting her so much she came close to driving through a hedge into a field. '*Stop this, girl. I'll tell everyone at lunch. All have their part to play, so no favouritism.*'

She arrived in the kitchen to find all assembled, but none knew of her adventure this morning, so no overt interest in her arrival. Once all were seated, she popped the ultrasound image into the middle of the table. Audrey was first to spot what it was and picked it up to take a closer look. 'It's a boy. Congratulations Jess. Is this where you went this morning?' as she handed the picture to Elizabeth.

'Yes, hot off the press. Couldn't wait till Christmas to tell everyone.'

Audrey descended into one of her flusters. 'As soon as Christmas is out of the way must start to plan. Much to do to welcome this little boy into the family.'

Everyone laughed at her theatrics.

Chapter 78

Christmas Day is cold, wet, but no snow. More gloomy than joyous Christmas vista. They deferred present opening until after breakfast. Audrey could not help laying on a breakfast fit for a family sharing its first Christmas together as a family, including champagne. Jim was beside himself with so many people in a high state of activity. He had arrived two days ago to allow Robert and Margaret a ten-day break to visit their families. It was the first family Christmas he could remember with so many people. Little Brandy was so confused she couldn't decide whether to stay in her basket away from this frenzy of activity or join in. The number of feet moving around as everyone greeted each other caused her to retreat to the sanctity of her basket, where she could view this joy at a safe distance.

Jess kept one eye on the time as she had deposited her laptop in the living room ready to receive the call from Michael. Over the previous weeks, she had communicated with him regularly to both agree on arrangements for Audrey and Gerry and to renew their relationship. She still had a sweet spot for him, and he certainly made no reservations about his feelings for her. A visit by him to Buntins was certainly on the table for next summer.

During one such call, Michael informed her his mum and dad would celebrate their 30th wedding anniversary on February 12th so they would fly, Business Class, on the 5th February for three weeks. Michael and James will collect them at Melbourne Airport. James agreed to stay with them for two weeks so they could celebrate their reunion as a complete family. Jess is very pleased with herself about this present more than any other. *'Audrey is entitled to a fabulous thank you for her incredible loyalty and contribution, and indeed welcome to this new family.'* Richard had been battling what to do to express his gratitude. Once again, Jess has risen to the task. Even Uncle Jim has contributed to make this the holiday of a lifetime for them.

Jess encouraged everyone to transfer to the living room to open presents, taking charge of distribution of presents from around the tree, ensuring the package containing the Australia trip package was foremost in front of Audrey and Gerry. It is Gerry who picks it up and opens it.

'What's this, luv. Something about Australia. Who sent us this?'

Audrey took the package to examine the label. 'To Gerry and Audrey, with much love from the family.'

Just then, the strategically located laptop came to life as they could hear the Skype ringtone. Jess answered it, expecting to see Michael. But he had also connected to James, so they were both on screen.

'Merry Christmas to everyone at Buntins. Is mum and dad there?'

Audrey had already turned to see the screen. Tears flowed freely from her eyes as she approaches the laptop still holding the travel documents and quickly followed by Gerry. 'Michael, James, so lovely to see you both. Where are you?'

'Hi mum. Hi Dad. Happy Christmas surprise. I'm in Australia and James is in Dubai. Have you opened your surprise package yet?'

Audrey looked at the package in her hand. 'Do you mean this? It says something about Australia, but I haven't worked out what it is.'

'You're coming to Australia for 3 weeks to celebrate your 30th wedding anniversary, and James will be here for two of the weeks.'

'What do you mean? How will we get there? We don't even have passports.'

'Your tickets and all the information you need to get your passports and visas are in the package you're holding. You fly on 5th February for 3-weeks.'

'Who set this up?'

'The lovely Jess. Wish she could come with you, but James and I have agreed to come to Buntins in July or August next year. But for now, you need a holiday, and we need to see you both, so get packed and on your way.'

At this point, Audrey hit fluster level. 'I don't understand. Gerry and I are coming all the way to Australia. I've never done anything like this in my life. What do we have to do?'

'Look mum. Get over the excitement and we'll call you again tomorrow morning at the same time and have a good chat about it. You'll be fine. We'll take good care of you.'

Audrey stood looking at Jess and then her sons on the laptop screen, tears in free flow. 'This is so lovely. Thank you, everyone for such a lovely surprise. She wept. Gerry comforted her.

Jess moved to the screen. 'Thanks, guys. I'll make sure they can sit and talk to you both tomorrow. And thank James for joining the act.'

'No problem Jess. So nice to see you again. And thanks for making this happen. Talk to you tomorrow.'

Michael and James signed off. Gerry spoke words never heard before, 'Bugger me. I need a drink.'

Richard went to get whisky, which he thought was more in line with the statement by Gerry than the champagne on the table. Audrey scooped Jess off her feet. 'Only you would think of such a thing. What a lovely person you are. I could gobble you up.'

Elizabeth could only sit watching this thinking *'What a lovely daughter I have. Only she would think of organising such a fabulous present.'*

The scene for the remainder of the present opening did not return to normal as Audrey was opening presents in a dream and Gerry forsaking his pile, sitting back in a daze, sipping his whiskey.

Gerry finally gathered himself and looked at the contents of their package. He found the air tickets, which, of course, had the price printed on them. 'Jesus, luv, have you seen the price of these tickets? They cost a fortune.'

Jess was quick to intercept. 'This trip is from all of us, including Uncle Jim. You deserve it so go enjoy yourselves. It's a long flight so we're sending you Business Class, so you have lovely comfortable seats which change into a bed when you need some sleep. Must have you fresh to meet your boys.'

Audrey went to Jim. 'Thank you, but what did I do for such a nice gift from you?'

Jim, sitting quietly with Brandy in his lap, didn't really know how to deal with this situation. 'You take good care of Jess, who takes care of us.'

'Thank you. But where's Katherine today?'

She'll be here around 12 o'clock, will stay for dinner, and probably the night if she drinks.'

Audrey is still in fluster mode. 'Is she staying with you?'

'Yes, why?'

'Must make sure your bathroom has the necessaries.' Off she went.

Katherine arrived, which prompted a fresh round of Christmas presents, complete with more champagne. All present recognised the familiarity Jim now enjoyed with Katherine and they thought this was the best present of all. Jim had bought Katherine a beautiful watch she had seen but priced far above her university remuneration level. They hugged and kissed to the applause of all present. Richard had quietly left for his studio, where he retrieved two pictures he had covertly worked on for some days. He returned with both covered, standing in the centre of the group, seeking their attention.

'This past year has been very special for this family, not least the addition of Katherine to our fold. I struggled hard to bring the joy to Jim has been afforded me this past year. Thank you, Katherine, for solving this problem for me. I have never witnessed Jim so comfortable and content with a relationship. I wanted to find a special present for you both that reflects how important I value this relationship. Whilst in Mexico, I saw a picture, two intrepid explorers on a new adventure to study the Mayan Empire. I hope I've captured what I saw,' as he uncovered the first picture.

There were gasps as they identified Jim and Catherine heading off to explore el Trono at Ek'Balam.

He continued. 'Having taken several pictures of our intrepid explorers during our holiday, I built a pictorial record of that trip.' He unveiled the second picture, which was a beautiful collage of pictures, mostly of Jim and Katherine interwoven with Mayan images, some drawn by Jim. 'I'm happy to prepare a second set so you both have copies. I intend to put a copy of the intrepid explorers in our gallery.'

Katherine focussed mainly on the intrepid explorer picture. 'This picture most certainly will have pride of place in my study. It's so beautiful. Thank you so much. You captured the moment perfectly.'

Christmas lunch was in the dining room commencing after the Queen's speech at 3pm. All had helped to put this feast together so not to load Audrey on this festive holiday. Gerry carved the turkey and roast pork, filling a large serving plate also containing pigs in blankets and various types of stuffing balls. Five different vegetables, roast potatoes, and luscious gravy completed the main course.

Once all plates were primed, Richard offered a brief speech and toast to welcome all to this first Christmas together as a family and offered thanks for their good fortune this past year.

After a couple of glasses of wine, Katherine related their trip to turkey. Once lubricated, she proved a capable raconteur. With Jim interjecting a little dry wit during her delivery, they kept the table amused for some time. Richard was so grateful to see Jim engage with such confidence.

Following traditional Christmas pudding and brandy sauce, they retreated to the living room where Brandy let it be known she needed walkies. The rain having subsided, they all decided it would be a good idea to brave the wintry afternoon to walk the grounds using some obscure logic it would walk off lunch. Dishwasher loaded, with a second load standing ready, they ventured outside.

Chapter 79

Traditional Boxing Day breakfast of smoked salmon and poached eggs cleared away Audrey and Gerry sat in the kitchen with Jess to engage in a less emotional Skype call, albeit Audrey was still in a state of shock.

Jim and Katherine took Brandy for a walk to Totten's to check for mail before returning for lunch.

Sebastian arrived before lunch but showing some signs of wear from a late-night party but quickly dismissed because of the festive season. It was the first time Jim spent anything other than a fleeting exchange with him, but his sense of foreboding was later supported by Katherine, whose many years in teaching had honed an acute sense regarding the attitude of her student charges. But this was not the time to air such feelings.

Lunch was again in the dining room, but far more restrained than yesterday. A full salmon Wellington trimmed, skinned, and filled with a cucumber, Dijon mustard and honey sauce accompanied by a rainbow salad, and new potatoes. Much discussion about the impending trip to Australia, including an interesting interjection by Katherine about her desire to study the Aborigine culture. Jim made a mental note to organise a trip once he has studied this ancient race.

They concluded their lunch with Richard's Italian take on bread pudding using panettoni bread soaked in grappa. Sebastian had sampled this delight at Sal E Pepe with his father, so knew the origin of such a treat. He felt at ease amongst this family and the delightful cuisine far excelled his normal diet.

After lunch, Sebastian followed Jess to her office. Jim had prepared new graphics for her system. As she loaded them, he noted the sales generations her site attracted. He had tried to look upon Jess as a sister to keep himself in check, but he knew he had actual feelings for this lovely lady, but what to do? He found her presence overwhelming and her scent intoxicating.

249

She was so different to the females he usually encountered, and mostly abused and discarded. He wanted so much to openly connect with her, not considering for a moment if she had any designs on him. This was unfamiliar territory to him.

Chapter 80

Richard and Elizabeth had discussed a dinner party with some of their tennis friends to see in the New Year but had second thoughts in favour of enjoying a full festive season together as a family. Sebastian had returned home the day after Boxing Day, feigning the need to use some of the holiday for study, but no doubt to prepare himself for some heavy partying with his friends. Jim and Katherine had visited Cambridge for a couple of day as Katherine decided she enjoyed this family and wanted to stay for New Year but did not bring enough clothes with her for a week. Audrey and Gerry had taken time out to visit with family and some of their old community friends to share their joy in their new life at Buntins.

A buffet of both hot and cold dishes had been prepared by Richard, Elizabeth and Jess and laid in the living room. Richard had prepared a stream of suitable music – more Bing Crosby than Rock'n Roll, but fully reflected the peace and calm felt at Buntins.

After toasting the chimes of Big Ben announcing the New Year, they retreated to their beds feeling blessed with their new lives and looking forward to consolidating their good fortune in the coming year.

Chapter 81

Winter in Lincolnshire can be bleak with transport systems not as advanced as other parts of the country, part of why Richard and Jim moved there. Thus, there were only two topics of focus, preparing for a birth, and the amusing mayhem organising for the trip to Australia. The nearest Passport Office was in Peterborough which, as the crow flies, is not that far away. Might as well have been in a different country with the problems of getting there in wintry conditions. The only vehicle that could readily navigate the country lanes is Richard's Range Rover, which only he drove. Gerry would frequently recall when this area was mainly farms, the farmers would keep their allotted part of the lanes clear of snow to allow traffic to flow, but most have now gone. 'Tractors can go anywhere, but there ain't no farmers anymore.'

Occasionally Richard would remind him there are two tractors in the barn with all the necessary attachments to clear the roads. 'But who's going to clear the last mile to the A1? And then there's only one lane working on the A1. Not worth the effort.'

After a lull of two days without fresh snow, it was possible for Richard to drive them to Peterborough for a two-hour process of securing their passports. Now they needed a trip to London to secure the visas they needed. Jess was allocated the task of accompanying them to London to guide them through the process described to her by Michael to secure a same day visa.

One problem for both Gerry and Audrey is understanding how it could be the middle of summer in Australia when they were in the middle of winter at home. Trying to find suitable clothing was difficult because the shops were still clearing their winter ranges in the sales. Mail order and Amazon could provide summer clothes, but Audrey needs to hold the clothes in her hands and try them before buying. She does not trust remote buying. A major exercise for Jess to gently encourage her to try. But this process provided amusing moments as packages arrived, opened and then the exultation 'I can wear that'. Jess connected her with Michael on a few occasions to lower the anxiety level, and who reminded her Australia has shops, and they sell suitable cloths for the local climate.

The bleakness of winter was certainly lightened, observing the spectacle of Audrey totally out of her comfort zone with Gerry making himself invisible. On the days poor weather conditions meant he could not work outside, after breakfast he would quickly escape to tasks in the basement and garages.

January rolled into February. The snow had cleared to be replaced by icy rain. The idea of a limousine to the airport was quickly abandoned as neither Gerry nor Audrey have navigated an airport before. Richard primed the Bentley so they could all go to see them on their way, ensuring they would have airport staff to guide them through passport control, security and to the gate – the service benefits of Business Class. Lunch at Sal e Pepe to toast the success of their venture, and a little sales shopping in Harrods made a welcome change to the isolation of Lincolnshire before the drive home.

The following three weeks revealed just how much Audrey contributed to the household, and both Richard and Elizabeth thought it fortuitous that little needed attention outside at this time of year. They all reflected that few appreciate what they have until it's gone. They were all thankful their lovely farmers would soon return to continue their important role in this family.

Once adjustments were made to roles, the 3-weeks passed quickly. As they arrived back at Heathrow early in the morning, Richard and Elizabeth drove down to London the day before for a little more retail therapy, and then staying at a hotel perfectly positioned for the airport. Jess thought the trip would be too taxing for her so elected to organise a good welcome home upon their return.

Audrey was out of Customs Control first, followed by Gerry pushing their heavily laden luggage trolley topped with a tube package some 1.5m in length. Greetings over, and Gerry quietly acting as porter, they made their way to the car. Richard fully expected their intrepid travellers to be exhausted from the long flight and likely sleep on their way home. Not Audrey. She filled the journey with all their exploits in Australia. Gerry would add the occasional 'Yes, luv', just to show he was being attentive.

Upon arrival at Buntins, Audrey spotted Jess and B-lined straight to her, wrapping her in her arms. 'Thank you for such a wonderful trip. It was so nice to see my boys again. Michael told me how you tracked him down. What a wonderful woman you are. Michael has already booked his trip here. He'll be here end of August – give you time to get over your baby duties.' She hugged Jess again. 'That's from Michael. He can't wait to see you.'

The following morning both Audrey and Gerry arrived in the kitchen for breakfast laden with presents including the long tube they had observed at the airport. Selecting the tube Audrey presented it to Jess.

'This is from Michael.'

She opened it to find a beautifully decorated Aboriginal didgeridoo some 40mm in diameter and 1.4m long. It had a hand-written note from Michael. *Hi Gorgeous. The didgeridoo provides the soundtrack to the Northern Territory and evokes all the mystery and magic of Dreamtime. The myth states that if an aboriginal woman touches or plays a didgeridoo, she'd become pregnant. You're already pregnant but if you take it to hospital with you and play it during labour it will help with the birth. See you in August. With love Michael.*

Gerry, having had lessons in Australia, attempted to demonstrate to Jess how to get sound out of this strange tube. 'Similar to the puffing you do during labour.'

Much laughter as they all attempted to achieve a tune.

Chapter 82

Spring was in the air as they approached Easter. The garden and pastures were full of colour dominated by the lovely yellows of the various varieties of daffodils, the whites and purples of crocuses, carpets of bluebells, and tulips were revealing their majesty. Fruit trees were in blossom, casting an array of colour throughout the walled garden. The plant-world was coming to life. All the work of last year was starting to yield dividends. Even Jim had resumed his walks to Buntins with Brandy. Life was looking good.

Sebastian was visiting for Easter Sunday and Monday as a short break before the final push of revision for his exams. He now felt comfortable with his place in this unusual family, albeit constantly aware of his father's scrutiny. His mindset was set to win favour with Jess. Not only did he see her as access to daddy's bank, but he also genuinely liked her. Her obvious signs of pregnancy arrested all thoughts of physical engagement with her, which probably was a good thing lest he let down his guard. But, having realised it was soon her birthday, invited her out to dinner, and would collect her at 7pm to celebrate.

His change in behaviour had not escaped his mother, enjoying the benefits of his increased attention to his studies, albeit not at the expense of his drunken nights with his rich friends. But she could see the calming influence of his father's discipline over his study routine. He would likely do well this time, which would give him options to achieve a good job, hopefully in Brussels away from his friends. He appeared focussed on his quest to attack daddy's bank, so she was satisfied with progress. The £250 per month pocket money provided by his father meant the strain on her own finances had subsided.

Chapter 83

It was 7th April, the birthday of Jess. As she was now so visibly pregnant bounding along the corridor to his study was no longer practical. She walked in a way that her flip-flops would alert him of her imminent arrival to engage in their good mornings. He stood to give her a big hug and wished her a happy birthday. He had a little present for her on his desk and had secretly organised with Gerry that the larger part of this present be placed outside the front door – not even Audrey or Elizabeth knew of it.

'I would like to give you your birthday present now as I have something to show you' as he handed her the package. She quickly opened it to find a box containing car keys.

'Daddy. What have you done?'

'Come with me.' They went down the stairs to the hallway where he opened the front door.

Sitting on the drive immediately next to the porch was a new people carrier car wrapped in a large pink bow. She gasped 'Daddy, is that for me?'

'You are soon to be two, and you need something more practical to carry a baby and all the associate paraphernalia. Do you like it?'

She responded by smothering him in hugs and kisses.

When she finished, she pressed the 'open' button on the key fob. The car issued a beep, flashed its lights, and the wing mirrors opened to tell her that her command had been received and the car was now open. She went to the driver's door and guided herself and her pregnant bulge inside. 'Daddy, its lovely' as tears rolled down her cheeks 'you spoil me far too much.'

'You spoil me every day just being here, so why can't I spoil you on your birthday?'

She got out of the car, put both arms around his neck 'You are a fabulous daddy, and I love you so much. Thank you for my lovely present.' She then gave him a real smacker of a kiss and looked at him with her beaming smile.

'Come, lets to the kitchen to see what other surprises you have.'

As they walked through the kitchen door, they were confronted with an array of party balloons, streamers, and anything else that Audrey could find. Everyone was there to sing happy birthday to her. Half of the breakfast table strewn with presents. Audrey was first to reach her for hugs and kisses, followed by her mom. Even Jim was present. He had walked there with Brandy, who was also greeting her with a vigorously wagging tail.

'This is too much. I need to sit down.'

'They quickly guided her to her seat from where she could reach her presents.

'Good morning everyone and thank you so much for this lovely surprise. I'm gob smacked.'

She opened her presents one by one, thanking the giver with a hug and kiss. The present from Uncle Jim caused her to gasp. Jim had asked Richard to take him to a good jeweller where he bought a beautiful gold necklace and earrings. 'Uncle Jim, what did I do to deserve such a wonderful present?'

'My dearest Jess, just being you. You bring so much light to my life, and now I try to bring a sparkle to your eyes.'

Having opened all of her presents she sat back looking at everyone with tears in her eyes 'You have all been so kind and generous to me. What love I feel in this family. Thank you all so much.'

Everyone cheered and clapped as they sat ready for breakfast.

After breakfast, as the table was being cleared, Jim moved in next to Richard. He put two envelopes in front of Richard. 'What do these mean and what should I do about it as I do not want to offend Katherine. As I never went to college, let alone university, I have no idea what this is about.'

Richard examined the envelopes. One was marked University of Cambridge and the other from Prof. Katherine Blakeley. He read the letter from Cambridge first. Then he read the letter from Katherine. 'Listen up, everyone. Jim has been offered an Honorary Doctorate from the University of Cambridge for exceptional services to graphics media.' He turned to Jim. 'This is a big deal, and you deserve it. And I think Katherine's offer to pay tribute to you rather than you give a speech shows she both understands your reluctance to making a speech, but more importantly, how much she wants you to accept this offer. She really cares for you, and your portfolio of work speaks for itself.'

Everyone moved back to the table to congratulate Jim. Jess wanted to read the letter from Cambridge.

'Wow, Uncle Jim. Can I come with you as your escort? The ceremony is in June so no lump anymore.'

Elizabeth piped in, 'Please don't refer to my grandson as a lump.'

Jess ignored her. 'Please, Uncle Jim. I'll hold your hand throughout.'

Jim looked befuddled. 'So you all think I should accept whatever it is?'

Richard could detect his anxiety. He put his hand over Jim's hand. A little incentive was needed. 'Jim, Katherine may have recommended you as a potential candidate, but a selection panel has rigorously scrutinised your background and work before offering you this prestigious award. They don't give these honours away. You've qualified for this award so you should graciously accept this recognition of your work.' He thought for a moment. 'Why don't we use this ceremony to launch Totten Buntin and start our work again? This would be great Press for us to let people know the dynamic duo are back.'

He looked at Richard nervously. 'Do you think we're ready?'

'Jim, you've been champing at the bit for months. Your input with Jess, and your relationship with Katherine, has kept you on the right side of sanity. And you tell me our new website is ready. All we need to do is test if we remember how to win the right mandates, and deliver campaigns, but not like before. One mandate at a time, no ridiculously tight deadlines, with a family time in between.'

'So, you all want me to do this award thing?'

There was a resounding chorus of "yes" and a cheer and clapping.

'He sat up straight. 'I'll do it then.'

Laughter all round at his theatrics.

Richard spoke again. 'You'll have Jess on one side, Katherine on the other, with Elizabeth and me as cheerleaders.'

A voice came from behind 'Gerry and I will be on baby duty.'

'Thanks. Forgot about that.'

The voice again, 'that's why I'm here.'

Jess moved over to hug Audrey. 'Thanks.'

'It's an important day for Jim and he needs you by his side. All of you need to be there.'

Chapter 84

Sebastian made more effort than usually preparing himself for his date with Jess. He knew the closer he got to her, the better his chance of access to Daddy's Bank. But it was more than this. He really liked her. For the first time in his life, he has found a woman who stirred emotions within. He had bought her a birthday present, and flowers to complete his charm offensive. But this was no act. He was really looking forward to their date, even though she was in her last weeks of pregnancy. Her baby wasn't an issue for him. She was lovely, and he enjoyed being with her.

But he is troubled. For the past few months of contact, his father has welcomed him into his new family and did not remotely display the characteristics he had learnt from his mother; quite the contrary. This family had welcomed him and treated him very well. He felt very comfortable with them all. Even Uncle Jim displayed happiness to see him reunited with his father, telling him how much his father doted on him during his early years. So why did his mother not only encourage the hate letter he sent to his father but also helped him to write it? What happened all those years ago for his mother to still seek revenge? She did well out of the divorce financially, so why didn't she just move on with her life? Why is she so hell-bent on getting more from him? He needed a drink. He had friends in North London he could meet on his way to collect Jess.

When he arrived in North London, his friends quickly noted the normally outgoing, outrageous Sebastian was subdued.

'What's with you, Seb? What's with the gloom?'

'I don't understand what the hell is happening to me. My mother tells me my father is a real bastard. But he's not like that. He keeps a very close watch on me – not surprising, I suppose – but I've tried harder this year to get better grades. But the pressure gets up my nose. He sits in his ivory tower, imposing his will on me to succeed. Then we have the beautiful, but very pregnant Jess. What's she doing to my head?'

'You need a drink, or two, or three.'

Jess was ready to go to dinner with Sebastian at 7:30 and was sitting in the kitchen waiting with the others who were having dinner. Her pregnancy was taking its toll on her. Although she had rested in the afternoon, she did not want a late night. But no Sebastian.

Dinner finished, Audrey and Gerry made their way home, Elizabeth went for a bath, leaving Jess and Richard chatting in the kitchen.

Time went by – still no Sebastian.

Around 10:30 they saw headlights at the gate. Richard opened the gates and went outside, asking Jess to stay in the kitchen as they both decided it was too late for Jess to go out tonight. Sebastian's car roared along the drive and screeched to a halt in front of Richard.

Sebastian got out of the car. Richard could see he had been drinking.

'Where have you been? You were due to collect Jess at 7:30. Why are you so late?'

With attitude, 'I stopped to meet some mates, and we had a quick drink.'

'You're drunk. Hardly a quick drink. Do you treat all your female friends this way?'

'Look old man, how I treat my women is nothing to do with you. The night's still young. Where's Jess?'

'She's inside and going nowhere with you. You've let down your guard and revealed your true character. I suggest you get out of here and don't come back.'

These words exploded in his mind. The bank of Daddy was closed. He lashed out at Richard, taking him totally by surprise. He fell to the ground. Sebastian started to violently kick him in the head and torso. 'You don't tell me what to do. You owe me, you bastard. Do you hear me? You owe me.'

Jess saw this. She ran out screaming for Sebastian to stop, trying to push him away. The effects of the alcohol made Sebastian's head swim from his exertions. He was lashing out in all directions, trying to keep her away from him. He landed an angry punch directly into her abdomen as she tried to stop him attacking her dad. She screamed out in pain and fell to the ground. He landed the blow to Richard with his foot which completed his transition into unconsciousness. He looked at her writhing on the floor. She looked at him in despair 'My baby. What have you done?'

Gerry had seen the car come into the drive from his living room window. He saw the attack on Richard and was on his feet out of his door, quickly followed by Audrey. They heard the commotion, and Jess scream out. Sebastian ran to his car and drove off, narrowly missing Gerry as he escaped the scene. Gerry noted his registration number. He ran to Jess. 'Are you okay?'

All she could say with tears in her eyes, 'My baby. He's hurt my baby.' Audrey was soon on the scene and took charge of Jess while Gerry went to Richard, who was still unconscious on the ground. Gerry dialled 911. 'Ambulance and police, please. A man and heavily pregnant woman have been badly beaten.' Having provided the address details, he then called the local police and reported a driver has just attacked Richard and Jess, who is heavily pregnant, and has driven away. Please get him and arrest him as he may have killed the baby. He gave them the car registration number. He knew the local police well, so they quickly sent messages to all cars in the county, and the highway camera surveillance room, to find Sebastian and arrest him.

The ambulance was soon there and took both Richard and Jess to hospital. Elizabeth and Audrey followed.

When Richard regained consciousness, he was in A&E. He felt awful. A nurse was attending to his wounds. The clouds in his mind were clearing, trying to recall what happened. All he could hear in his head was Jess screaming. 'Jess, how is my daughter Jess?' Tears were streaming from his eyes.' He tried to sit up, but the pain in his ribs took his breath away.

'Please, Mr Lyons, stay still. I need to get you something for your pain.'

He forced the words out of his inflamed lips, 'What has happened to my Jess?'

Audrey could hear him from outside and came running in 'Richard, Jess is okay. They have taken her to a specialist maternity unit to save the baby.'

He screamed, 'No. What have I done?' and broke down. He was distraught.

Audrey tried to comfort him. 'Come on, Richard. They're doing everything they can. She's strong, so we have every hope her baby will be okay. Elizabeth is with her.' He wasn't listening. He had descended into the depths of despair for letting this happen.

A doctor had heard his cry and sedated him. He was soon still. Tears were flowing from Audrey's eyes. She insisted she would stay with him. They told her he would have to stay in hospital overnight because of his concussion. This did not matter. She was going to stay with him. She phoned Gerry to update him, and then Elizabeth to find out about Jess. At seven weeks premature, she was in theatre having an emergency caesarean to save her baby.

Traffic cameras located Sebastian driving erratically along the A1(M) highway back towards London. He was stopped, arrested, and taken to a police station where his alcohol levels were measured. They detained him in a police cell. The duty officer recorded he was over three times the legal limit, and very belligerent. He would appear before a magistrate the following morning. The police contacted his mother to alert her of the situation.

Chapter 85

It was nearly three o'clock in the morning. Richard was still under sedation. Audrey had dozed off but abruptly awoken by her phone ringing. It was Elizabeth. 'Jess is out of theatre. The baby is alive but is in an incubator with a 50:50 chance of survival.' Audrey could hear her burst into tears. 'Jess needed additional surgery and cannot bear any more children.' Audrey broke down in tears.

Gerry took the initiative to contact Richard's private GP, Dr Robert Jeffery, who quickly mobilised to the maternity unit contacting the two best consultants in the area, and who ordinarily practiced at this specialised unit. They were the surgeons who were in theatre with Jess; one to take care of her, and the other to take care of her premature baby. He found Elizabeth to introduce himself to her and reassured her Jess was in the best hands, and he had open instructions from Richard to ensure she has everything she needs. 'Jess will be a private patient and will have the very best treatment available.' He then told her the consultants would visit with her as soon as Jess and her baby are stable. He would now go to see Richard and make private patient care available for him.

Elizabeth sat with her head in her hands, weeping. 'My darling Richard loves Jess so much. It will devastate him when he hears about her. Please God, what did we do to deserve this?'

A young woman she vaguely recognised disturbed her, but this woman clearly knew her.

'Mrs Sandiman. Sorry, Mrs Lyons, my name is Samantha Mountford. I went to the same school as Jess, and you play tennis with my father, Simon. I'm so sorry to hear about Jess. How is she?'

'She is out of surgery, but how do you know she's here?'

'Sorry, I'm half asleep, I should have introduced myself better. I'm a reporter from the Stamford Herald. Word came through there had been an incident at Buntins Place, and the police have arrested the perpetrator by the name of Sebastian Lyons who we believe is the son of your husband, Richard Lyons. We understand Jess is heavily pregnant and was seriously injured. As I know Jess, I was asked to find out what happened.'

'Word came through from where?'

'We track the police incident room. Tonight, has been very busy for them on this case. There was an area-wide search for Sebastian Lyons before they stopped and arrested him.'

'You're telling me Sebastian is in custody as we speak?'

'Yes. He'll appear before the Magistrate in Stamford later this morning. We'll be covering that hearing.'

'My God, what a night. But I have no desire to discuss this with you tonight. So please be away to your bed and get some sleep. If the police can be considerate enough to leave this until tomorrow, so can you.'

But Samantha was persistent 'Has the father of the baby been informed?'

'Away Samantha before I call your father.'

Just then two gentlemen appeared. Samantha moved away, but only as far as the coffee machine where she poured herself some water.

The taller of these gentlemen introduced himself to Elizabeth as Mr Beadman, pre-natal consultant, and then his colleague Mr Cline, paediatric consultant. Mr Beadman was clearly the spokesperson.

'Mrs Lyons, Jessica is now sleeping under light sedation, and we'll leave her this way until we return about 8am this morning. We brought her round after surgery to check she's alright, but she has been through serious trauma, so we want her to rest for a few hours. The news is mixed, but hopeful. The baby is frail, but not in any serious jeopardy. Jessica will make a full recovery. However, the damage to her reproductive system was beyond repair so, unfortunately, she cannot have any further children. We tried our hardest to avoid this situation, but there was too much blood loss for us to continue. We will monitor her every 30 minutes until I return in the morning. There is nothing you can do for now so you could go home to get some sleep, but I would like you here when we wake her. I'm so sorry we could not do more, but she's strong, and will get through this.'

'Thank you for your efforts. I'm sure you did your best for her. I'll stay with her if you don't mind.'

'Fine. There is an armchair in her room with a footstool, but we can see if the duty nurse can provide you something to sleep on if you so wish.'

'No, thank you. I'll be fine.'

'Well then, goodnight, and I'll be back in a few hours.' With that, they left.

Samantha quietly left, having overheard this conversation. She knew there was a story here and knew what she had to do if she wanted to claim it as hers. Her editor had waited months to find a story on the owner of Buntins Place after being refused an interview with Richard when he first built the house, and again when he was acclaimed for *"Pure Love"*. She needed a few hours' sleep but would be back early in the morning.

Dr Jeffrey was now at the hospital with Audrey and Richard. He had phoned ahead to get Richard moved to a private room. He had also asked for scans of the areas of injury. Richard was still sedated. He told Audrey this was probably best for him. Any swelling in his head must decrease before he hears the situation with Jess, lest his reaction puts too much pressure on his brain. He told Audrey she should go home and get some sleep, but she was not moving from his side.

The sun was rising. The doctors applied intravenous pain management into Richard and then brought him out of sedation at 8am. They could see nothing remarkable on the scans other than three broken ribs but needed to check his reactions in case of brain damage from the kicks to his head. Audrey warned them of the likely request regarding Jess, and his likely reaction. They understood and decided to only tell him Jess will be fine, and her baby was in an incubator.

Elizabeth was sitting at the bedside of Jess, who had shown no signs of consciousness during each of the checks on her vitals. After each such check, the nurse would nod approvingly at Elizabeth to indicate all is well. Her mother could only hold her hand to let her know she was there.

Mr Beadman appeared a little after 8am, scanned her monitor reports and brought Jess out of sedation to see how she reacted. Her mother was there, hoping this would keep her calm. Her baby was still alive, struggling for survival, but responding to treatment.

'Mr Beadman. I've been thinking about how to tell Jess about her long-term issues. As her mother, I would prefer if you did not tell her today. She has enough to cope with already with her baby and the beating to my husband.'

He looked at her considering how to respond, 'Your daughter is of an age where I have a duty to tell her whatever she asks. If she does not specifically raise the issue, I'll avoid the issue today, but I must tell her at some point as I have some guidance for her recovery.'

'I appreciate your understanding, thank you.'

'Shall we wake her?'

As her eyes cleared, Elizabeth was clasping her hand. Jess recognised her and started to cry. Elizabeth got up to comfort her 'It will be alright my dear. Your baby wants to survive, so you must be strong for him.'

'Can I see him?'

'You need to rest before making a journey down to the incubators. I'll ask if I can take a photo for you on my phone.'

'Thank you, mom. What about daddy?'

'He'll be okay. Audrey is with him.'

'Jess, this is Mr Beadman, your consultant. He needs to examine you and then talk to you.'

'Good morning, Jessica. How do you feel?'

'Like someone has kicked me in the stomach, weak, drowsy, and otherwise numb.'

'I'll get you something for the pain. We were able to recover your baby with no lasting damage, and my colleague, Mr Cline, your paediatrician, will be along shortly to give you a more detailed report. I'll take care of you hoping we can send you home in 4 5 days. The police wish to interview you, but I've left instructions this cannot occur until you are on fluids and have eaten something. So not before this afternoon. If you feel any distress during their visit, you should stop the interview immediately and let them wait until you're ready. Perhaps your mother should be with you to ensure they respect your wishes. Do you have any questions for me?'

'If my baby is okay, then nothing for now.'

'Good. Let me organise something for your pain. If you feel any deterioration in your condition, do not hesitate to have nurse call me.'

With this he quickly examined her wound and left to find the duty nurse to organise her pain relief.

Richard's eyes opened, but he was clearly in a daze. He looked up to see Audrey, who was holding his hand. Tears filled his eyes. Audrey soothed him. 'Hello Richard, my dear. This man wants to see if you're okay, so please concentrate.'

The doctor conducted a serious of response tests and declared him fully responsive. His own GP came to his bedside. 'Richard, Jess will be alright, and the baby is alive in an incubator. I'll keep you informed.'

Richard nodded. His GP continued, 'I'm keeping you under observation for some hours today, and maybe overnight, but you will make a full recovery.'

Richard nodded again. He had taken a kick to the mouth, so his lips were swollen, far more than when he first arrived at the hospital.

He looked at Audrey with such sad eyes. 'It's alright Richard. I'll stay right here, and Elizabeth is with Jess. We have telephone contact.' He lay back on his pillow with tears in his eyes. *'This will be a long recovery,'* she thought *'and God knows what will happen if that baby doesn't survive.'* She quietly prayed, *'come on little boy, they need you to live.'*

At 10am, Sebastian appeared before the magistrate. His mother was in the gallery, and she had instructed a solicitor to represent him. He was asked to confirm his name, date of birth, address, and occupation. The charges against him were driving under the influence of alcohol, and two counts of grievous bodily harm. They had advised Sebastian to plead guilty on the driving charge, and guilty with mitigating circumstances on the bodily harm charges as the CCTV footage from the house recorded the whole sordid assault. The magistrate ordered a two-year driving ban. When he came to the other charges, he looked sternly at Sebastian. 'Was the child being carried by the woman you so viciously attacked yours?'

Sebastian felt pangs of shame as he looked down at the floor as he answered 'No, sir'.

The Magistrate continued 'I don't know to what extent they have informed you of the current situation of the woman you struck, but I can tell you the police report indicates she has been damaged for life. Her premature baby is currently fighting for its life in an incubator. Should her baby die, you will be charged with manslaughter. You will appear before Crown Court one week from today to hear your mitigation. You will also undergo psychiatric tests and a report produced to the Court. In any event you are looking at a custodial sentence.'

'Bail is set at £1,000 and you must surrender your passport within twenty-four hours.'

Sebastian had never been kicked so hard in his life. What had he done? Why did he even go to the house so late? He saw his entire life crumbled in front of him. He is a criminal looking at a prison sentence. *'I didn't mean to strike Jess, let alone try to kill her baby.'* His anger was aimed towards his father who, according to his mother, was a monster for deserting them. *'He now has a rich life, and we don't, and it's my father's fault.'*

His mother collected him and took him home. She knew her game was over. And now she had sacrificed her son's liberty seeking her revenge.

Samantha Mountford had missed none of this. She had quietly taken photos of both Sebastian and his mother on her phone. *'If he's not the father of Jess's baby, who is?'* she thought, *'what were they fighting about?'* Her inexperienced mind was computing a multitude of variables, mostly sordid. It was time for her to confront Richard Lyons before trying again with Jess.

Samantha knocked gently on the door of Richard's room, but did not wait for any response before letting herself in. Richard was on his own. She walked to his bedside. 'Good morning, Mr Lyons. How are you feeling?'

He looked at her confused *'Who is this woman?'* he thought.

'I'm Samantha, a friend of Jess, so thought I would visit with you before I visit with her.' After a short pause, 'What happened last night? Why did your own son do this to both of you?'

He was now totally confused. How did she know about his son? He looked at her and attempted to speak 'Who are you, and what are you doing here?'

'I told you, I'm a friend of Jess and can't believe what has happened to you both.'

'How do you know about my son?'

'Because he has just appeared before the Magistrate charged with the assault on you both. He is facing a custodial sentence, especially if the baby dies.'

'Why were you in Court?'

'It's my job,' without expanding further. 'I assume you know Jess cannot have any more children.'

It was like a thunderbolt had hit him. 'What are you saying?' he demanded.

'The damage to Jess was severe, but her baby is alive. Who is the father and why isn't he with her?'

He wanted to die. What had he done to his lovely daughter? Tears filled his eyes. Samantha got her picture.

Audrey came through the door and saw her. 'Samantha, what are you doing here?' She could see Richard was distraught. 'What have you said to him?'

'Good morning, Mrs Roswell. It would appear they have not informed him of the extent of the injuries to Jess. I just wanted to know what happened last night. Why did his son do this?'

Audrey was furious 'Get out of here. How dare you interfere in this family.'

'It's my job to investigate this incident. Tell me what I need to know about last night and I'll be on my way.'

'You little madam. You get out of here now, or I'll throw you out. Go.'

Samantha knew from old this farmer's wife was not to be toyed with, so left. She had her pictures, but not enough to write the story. It was time to try to see Jess. She wanted her story in tomorrow's morning edition.

Samantha knocked and quickly entered the room but found herself confronted by Elizabeth sitting with Jess. 'I told you last night to stay out of our lives. Now get out before I have you thrown out.'

'Mrs Lyons, I have a job to do. Tell me what I need to know, and I'll be gone.'

Elizabeth was furious as she rose to her feet 'Out of here, now.'

Samantha knew there was no point in arguing her need for a story. She left, but with intent to get her story.

Later that day, his doctor decided to keep Richard in overnight to see if they could alleviate some of the swelling so he could move around and eat. Gerry came to collect Audrey, but she made it clear she would be back first thing in the morning.

Elizabeth also left for home, leaving explicit instructions Jess should not receive any visitors for any reason, committing to be back early tomorrow.

Around the kitchen table having supper with Audrey and Gerry, Elizabeth was trying to think what they needed to do. 'Who do we need to inform?'

Audrey spoke first. 'I suppose Jim needs to know. Can't think of anyone else until we have a clearer picture.'

Elizabeth quickly responded. 'No, no, we should not inform Jim. Jim and Katherine leave for Australia tomorrow morning. No need to upset them. I'll let Margaret know after they are on their way.' Pause. 'I should probably inform my parents as there is no possibility of visiting them until Richard and Jess have recovered.' She kept this call short as she needed to reconcile the situation and get some sleep before engaging with others about these terrible events.

Chapter 86

Audrey and Elizabeth were back beside their respective charges before 8am. They had given Richard drugs to help him sleep through the pain with no intention to wake him before 8:30.

Jess was awake, but an industrious nurse who had agreed to take her phone to the intensive care suite and take a photograph of her young baby had substantially improved her pain management. Although he was tiny, and shrouded in tubes and monitor cables, he was obviously alive and did not appear to be in pain. This had a remarkable uplifting effect on Jess despite her own pain, and the dreadful news she could not bear any further children.

'How's daddy?'

'I don't know. Let me call Audrey and ask her.'

'Hi Elizabeth. He's still asleep. He looks awful, but the doctor says it looks worse than it is. But he's strong, so will recover. How's Jess?'

'She's awake, with a smile on her face, holding her phone, showing a picture of her baby. Amazing how a baby dulls pain. He's fighting the fight to live, and the nurses are hopeful he will survive. So far, so good.'

'Good. I'll call you when Richard is awake. Love to Jess. Bye.'

Both the duty doctor and Dr Jeffrey appeared a little after 8:30am. They acknowledged Audrey before attending to Richard. The duty doctor gently started the process of waking him by saying his name and touching his hand. Richard opened his eyes.

'Good morning, Richard. How do you feel this morning?' Richard's response was to turn into the pillow with a look of sorrowful disdain.

Dr Jeffrey interceded 'Richard, I know the distress you must feel, but we need to know how you feel physically. Can you please point to anywhere you feel pain?'

He responded, looking at the doctors and pointed to his face and his broken ribs.

'Good. Now, using your fingers can you please tell us on a scale of one to five, where five is severe pain, how much pain you feel from your face, and then your ribs.'

He pointed to his face, and then three fingers. Then to his ribs and five fingers.

'Good. Thank you, Richard. We'll give you opiates for your pain, and then we need to get fluids and food into you. Everything will be through a straw. If for any reason you find sucking or swallowing to be a problem, then we need to know. Okay?'

Richard gave a thumb's up.

Looking straight at Richard to get his attention 'Jess sends her love, and her baby is doing well. We'll send a nurse in with your medication and your fluids.' He gave Audrey his mobile phone number and told her to call him if he needs anything. With that, they were gone.

He turned towards Audrey and reached for her hand. As he squeezed her hand in appreciation of her being there, she saw the deep sadness in his eyes as he was shaking his head in despair.

'Richard. We can get through this. It's not your fault. Jess is sitting up looking at a picture of her baby. She's strong, and so are you. I'll stay with you until we can take you home. Jess will be home in a few days.'

Audrey visited the hospital shop to get some much-needed chocolate; a secret fetish of hers in times of distress. A pile of Stamford Herald newspapers was on the counter. The headline glared at her.

Family Feud at Buntins Place
Leaves Two in Hospital and One in Custody

It horrified her as she read on.

Buntins Place, Kesteven District was the scene of a vicious family feud on Sunday night leaving Richard Lyons, the owner, and his stepdaughter, Jessica Lyons (formerly Sandiman) in hospital. The attacker was his son, Sebastian Lyons, 22, a student. Jessica was heavily pregnant. And it is believed the attack came because Sebastian Lyons realised the child was not his. Jessica underwent an emergency caesarean to save her 7-week premature child, now fighting for his life at Stamford Hospital. The severity of the attack means Jessica cannot bear more children. Sebastian Lyons was apprehended by the police escaping the scene, found to be drunk, and appeared before the Magistrate yesterday morning where he pleaded guilty to grievous bodily harm, but with mitigation, and will appear at the Crown Court in 7 days where he is expected to receive a custodial sentence. Richard Lyons is the celebrated advertising guru having his picture, "Pure Love" acclaimed at the National Picture Gallery last year, and who married the former Mrs Elizabeth Sandiman, a local resident, a year ago.

There was a picture of Richard showing his injuries and his grief – the picture covertly taken by Samantha. Audrey was mortified. 'How could she print such lies?'

Chapter 87

Elizabeth dialled a number well known to her. She heard the ringer twice before it was answered.

'Good evening Simon, it's Elizabeth.' She was tired, so this was the best she could do by way of greeting.

'Good evening, Elizabeth. I'm so sorry to hear about Richard and Jess. It must have been awful. How are they?'

'Jess will be okay, so long has her baby survives. Richard looks a mess, but he'll recover in time; at least physically. I'm not sure how long he will suffer mentally.'

'If there's anything we can do to help you through this, we're here for you all. If the story in the Stamford rag is anything to go by, Richard's son will pay the price of his actions.'

'Simon, the reason for my call is about the story in the paper. Do you know Sam wrote it?'

'Why, yes. She's very pleased with herself about getting front page.'

'Simon, did she tell you how she got her story, and how she has falsified part of it causing all of us great distress?'

'Oh, my goodness, Elizabeth. Please tell me what has happened as she's here. If she's behaving badly, I'll put this to her right now. You have enough distress without her ambition causing you more pain.'

Elizabeth related the various incidents regarding Samantha since the previous evening, and the distress caused to both Richard and Jess. She emphasised they had decided to delay informing Richard of the long-term effects on Jess until they were sure there was no pressure on his brain as this could cause serious medical problems. She also told him Sam had formulated her own conclusions as to the cause of the attack; but which were wholly fabricated and equally distressing.

'Elizabeth, I'm so sorry to hear this. Be assured I'll now speak with Sam and, if necessary, her editor. She must understand we're a close community, and we do not add to

275

the distress of our neighbours in their time of need. Please convey my apologies to both Richard and Jess, and we'll express them personally at some convenient time when they're feeling a little better. I'll also ask Jennifer to visit with Jess to see if there is anything we can do to help.'

'Thank you, Simon. I'm sorry we needed to discuss this, but we need to protect Richard from any further distress as this whole situation is my naïve fault. He'll not forgive himself for what has happened to Jess.'

'Elizabeth, please be assured of our full support in this matter. You sound so tired. Please get some rest whilst I deal with Sam.'

'Thank you, Simon. Goodnight.'

Simon went to the living room where Sam was watching TV with her mother. He grabbed the TV remote and clicked off the TV. 'Okay Sam, what have you been up to for the past couple of days, and where did you get your pictures and information for your front-page story today?'

'Just doing my job. Why?'

'That was Elizabeth on the phone giving me chapter and verse of your appalling behaviour towards them, and the fabricated nature of your story. What do you think you were doing?'

'Dad, I'm a journalist. My editor told me to cover the story, and that's what I did.'

Jennifer looked sternly at her 'What have you done Sam?'

'I realised there was a story involving the son of Richard, so went to find it. But no-one would answer my questions, so I found answers for myself. That's what we do.'

Simon interrupted, 'do you mean fabricate answers to satisfy the story you want rather than the truth?'

'I put two and two together and'

'Came up short, so falsified your account, adding to the distress of our dear friends. You should be ashamed of yourself.'

'I asked them to help me fill the gaps, but they wouldn't. If my version is not correct, then they can provide the correct version and we'll correct our story. That's how it works.'

Simon was now angry Elizabeth was right in her account, and his daughter showed no understanding or concern. 'Listen to me, young lady. If you want to be part of the gutter press, go practice somewhere else. We are respected members of this community, and there are rules of behaviour we ALL follow. Did you think for just one second about the potential impact of your thoughtlessness toward Richard when you blurted out the long-term impact on Jess, probably for effect judging by the picture you took of him. They had purposely kept that information from him until they were sure there was no pressure on his brain after the savage beating he took. The consequences of your thoughtlessness could have caused a seizure or stroke. If you think for one minute, you can hide such reprehensible behaviour behind your journalist badge, you are gravely mistaken. I'm going to speak to your editor now and tell him what you've done. If he wants to throw you out on your ear, he has my blessing. Get out of my sight.'

Sam looked at her mother for support, but it was not there.

Chapter 88

Samantha was standing before the desk of her editor, Tom Connors. 'I had a very disturbing conversation with your father last night. If what he tells me is true, you have put the integrity of this paper into disrepute. I put your story on the front page because it was factual in all respects. Tell me Sam, how much of your story is factual, and show me the evidence.'

'The only part I experienced difficulties was why his son attacked him, and the identity of the actual father of Jess's baby. No-one would talk to me about either. I had a deadline, so drew upon educated assumption, giving them the option to provide an alternative version later. They have the right of response.'

'Jesus, Sam. Where did you learn such gutter behaviour? You lied to me. I can't trust you anymore. What good are you to this paper as a journalist? This is not a gutter press national newspaper with deep pockets to fight false representation charges. We're a community paper taking a responsible attitude toward what we print. Sensational garbage does not sit with our responsibility. Get out of my sight. Go find yourself a job with the gutter press if that's where you want to be. I'll put a note on the front page of our next edition, disclaiming the assumptions of your story and noting your dismissal. Out of here.'

She knew this would damage her career prospects. She had to find the truth as her instinct told her there was a story here. She would attend the Crown Court hearing to see what would be revealed.

Chapter 89

It was now three days since Sebastian's outrage had caused so much damage. His solicitor told him Jess could not have any more children, and her baby was fighting for survival. His father, although badly beaten, would eventually make a full recovery.

He felt wretched. What made him do such a thing? His brain wanted to explode.

That evening he was fighting with his mother, blaming her for all this trouble. She had alienated him against his father, but he could now see it was all lies. She had used him. He was beside himself. She struck back, telling him his waywardness was his problem, and he needed to wake up. 'Your stupidity has thrown away your legacy, and my payback. What do you think we're going to do now?'

He was so furious with her outburst that he pushed her hard. She stumbled and then crashed her head on the mantle of the stone fireplace. She hit the floor lifeless. All Sebastian could see was dark blood pooling around her head.

He went to her. Shook her. But nothing. No sign of life at all. He screamed out in the agony of despair. He pulled himself together and dialled for an ambulance. When the paramedics arrived, they called the police and Sebastian was arrested.

Chapter 90

Sebastian underwent the required psychiatric tests in prison, but he was now totally withdrawn. He appeared before the Crown Court to hear his mitigation case. This was a sad tale of separation from his father at the age of ten during an acrimonious divorce, citing adultery by his mother. He had suffered parental alienated from his mother against his father for years. The hate mail Sebastian had written to his father was read in Court to emphasise the degree of swift alienation indoctrinated by his mother. They accepted a 10-year-old child could not have composed such a letter on his own.

Until the divorce they described him as an outgoing, bright boy. Thereafter he became more and more withdrawn, losing sight of his educational possibilities, and showing no regard for himself or anyone else. His life at university was more wayward than academic, being censured on several occasions for his poor attitude and flagrant lifestyle. They also cited him as the reason for the failure of his mother's last marriage, having assaulted his stepfather during a drunken rage.

They sentenced him to two years in a psychiatric prison for his harm to Jess and her baby, a further six months for the harm to Richard, with the trial for the manslaughter of his mother laid down for twenty-eight days hence.

Richard was in no fit state to attend Court so they had asked Gerry to be present as a witness should the defence suddenly change their stance albeit CCTV footage clearly recorded the attack on both Richard and Jess. He heard the whole sorry tale and related this to both Elizabeth and Audrey. He also noted the presence of Samantha.

Chapter 91

His days in prison gave him much time to reflect. And there were no wayward friends or alcohol to drown his sorrow. A prison psychiatrist had attempted, during several visits over those first weeks, to encourage him to confront his demons. The most painful demon to him was what he had done to Jess. He realised she was the first woman for whom he had any genuine feelings. And now her baby was fighting for survival, and he had damaged her for life. What made him behave so badly? And now his mother was dead from his need to react violently when he could not deal with his life. His life was over. He could not face another trial, having his painful life aired in public. As his belt tightened around his neck, his last thoughts were '*I'm so sorry Jess*'.

They found him hanging in his cell. He could not live with himself and his pain any longer. Having established Richard was the next of kin, the Stamford Police were notified.

Chapter 92

'Where are you lads going?'

'We've just been notified Sebastian Lyons was found hanging in his cell this morning, so we are on our way to inform his father, 'looking at his worksheet,' at Buntins Place, sir. Must be that big house that used to be Buntins Farm.'

'Oh, my God. What more can happen in this sorry tale? Okay lads, I'll go myself. Elizabeth Lyons and I go back a long way. This news needs to come from someone she knows, as I know Mr Lyons is still in a bad way, and her daughter's baby is still in hospital.'

Chief Constable Geoffrey Prior had tracked this case since it first started. He had always had a soft spot for Elizabeth at school and had hoped to catch her for himself. They had stayed good friends over the years, as he knew her departed husband, David, very well, and even attended his funeral.

Audrey saw a police car at the gate, pressed the open button, and went out to greet him. She instantly recognised the driver 'Good afternoon, Geoffrey. To what do we owe the honour of a visit from the Chief Constable?'

'Hello Audrey. I would like to say it's a long overdue visit to welcome this household to my patch, but my news is not good. Is Elizabeth around?'

'Yes. she is spending time with Richard trying to pull him out of his depression. Poor man cannot forgive himself for what happened to Jess.'

'Officially I should speak with Mr Lyons, but under the circumstances I have assumed the responsibility to speak with Elizabeth first.'

'You had better come with me. Would you like tea or coffee?'

'Coffee would be good, thanks. How are you and Gerry settling into this new life?'

'Everything was wonderful until a few weeks ago. But we'll weather this storm and make this home happy again. Jess's baby is winning the fight for survival and, God willing, be home in a few weeks. God knows what will happen if that young boy loses his fight.'

'My fingers are crossed for good news. Please give Jess my best wishes.'

'She's here. You can tell her yourself.'

'Another time, Audrey. Once Elizabeth hears what I have to say, I'll be on my way.'

'Oh my God, Geoffrey. Please, no more bad news.'

Once they were in the kitchen, 'Perhaps the living room will be best as Richard is camped in his study today.'

She guided him through the hallway and seated him. 'I'll get coffee and then find Elizabeth. Back in a mo.'

He could not help admiring the beauty and quality of this house. Having heard much gossip about this property, he could only marvel at what he was seeing for himself. He would like to view the entire house at a less painful time.

Audrey returned with a tray and put it on a small table close to him. 'Help yourself, Geoffrey. I'll go find Elizabeth.'

A few minutes later Elizabeth entered the living room. 'Geoffrey. How lovely to see you!'

He stood, and they greeted each other. 'To what do we owe the honour of a visit from our very handsome Chief Constable?'

'Elizabeth. Please sit down. I'm here in an official capacity and believe me, I wish it otherwise.'

'What's wrong?'

'Elizabeth, we go back a long way, so it pains me to bring you bad news. Officially I should tell Mr Lyons, but I'll be guided by you whether it would better come from you.'

'My God, Geoffrey, what has happened now?'

'His son, Sebastian, was found hanging in his cell this morning. They pronounced him dead at 8:30 today. I'm so sorry to have to bring you such terrible news.'

Elizabeth burst into tears. He left her to absorb this shock in the hope she would settle and compose herself. But she just looked at him through her tears. He knew his decision to deliver this news himself had been the right call. 'Elizabeth, can I get you anything?'

'Some water would be nice.'

He went back to the kitchen to find Audrey. 'Can you bring some water for Elizabeth? She has not taken my news well.'

'Geoffrey, what is the bad news? We're family here and look out for each other.'

'They found Sebastian hanged in his cell this morning.'

'Oh, no. When will this end? I'll be with you in a moment. Go back to Elizabeth. She must be devastated.'

Geoffrey returned to Elizabeth quickly followed by Audrey with water. She was still crying as Audrey sat with her to comfort her. Elizabeth looked at her, and through her tears, 'How can I tell Richard this news? He's already heartbroken enough about what happened to Jess.'

'My dear Elizabeth. We don't have to tell him today. This news can wait as there is no possibility he can, or will, attend a funeral. We should wait.'

Jess appeared but stopped abruptly once she had absorbed the scene confronting her. She had been resting, oblivious to what was happening, but she quickly registered this scene was not good. 'Mr Prior why are you here, and why is mom crying?' as she sat on the other side of her mother to help Audrey comfort her.

Elizabeth looked at her 'Sebastian is dead. He hanged himself this morning.'

'No, no, no. Daddy already has enough pain. Please, no more.'

Geoffrey decided he should exit this situation. His unsavoury deed was done. These lovely people needed to deal with his bad tidings with no further interference from officialdom. He got up and indicated to Audrey he would leave. She got up to show him out. Once outside, he told her he would pass the message back to the other relatives Mr

Lyons is in no state to get involved with the funeral. She thanked him, and he was on his way.

Gerry had noticed the police car and caught up with Audrey. 'What's happening, luv?'

'Sebastian is dead; hung himself.'

'So he should for what he did. That little bugger should go to hell for what he did to Jess.'

'Gerry do not bring such attitude into this house. We need to find a way to put all of this behind us and get Richard back from where he is. Forget Sebastian. Focus on Richard. He needs our help.'

'Who's gonna tell him about Sebastian?'

'No-one yet. No-one here will get involved in the funeral, so we have time on our side.'

'Sorry, luv, but you can't do that. No matter what yous all think, he must be told sooner rather than later. He'll not thank you for keeping it from him. He's the master of the house and must shoulder the burden, no matter how painful. Elizabeth must tell him.'

He rarely voiced his opinion, but she knew when he took the trouble to say something, he was usually right. How would she tell Elizabeth?

Chapter 93

Elizabeth broke down in tears bearing the bad tidings to Richard. She felt so wretched, especially as she encouraged him to connect with Sebastian, much against his better judgement. '*Why did I question his instinct?*'

He could only look at her as this news echoed over the perpetual voice in his head 'Sebastian, stop' and then a shrill scream of pain from his precious daughter continually rolling through his mind like a terrible song that will not go away.

That evening her mother phoned for an update on events. She explaining to her mother the news Sebastian had hung himself admitting it was her closeted conventional maternal instinct that caused these problems. She started to cry in despair. 'And now two people are dead, Jess desperately willing her son to survive with no prospect of being able to have more children, and my beloved husband, the man who rescued me, so deep in his depression that no-one can get through to him.'

Her mother responded something in the past caused the problems with Sebastian and thus nothing to do with her. She was reminded of the telephone call when her mother and father tried to dissuade her from a relationship with Richard.

She so needed to vent some anger and frustration. 'Mother, never again will I listen to anyone who questions what I do in this family. If I can get Richard back and make this family happy again, I will never question the instinct of either Richard or Jess who understood what Richard added to our lives within days of meeting him. And I will not leave his side until we can find a way to bring him back to us. Nor do I want you and dad here. Only this household can help me to put this right.' She slammed the phone down trembling with anger.

She went to bed feeling helpless, crying herself to sleep as she had done too many times over the past weeks. She had only managed to get him into bed with her a few times since that fateful night. Even then, he did not stay for more than an hour. He could not help himself bursting into tears of sadness at any time and needed to be on his own. His injuries, especially his ribs, still caused him so much pain when lying down, and he refused any form of pain management. Dr Beadman visited every few days to attend him and try to encourage him to take nourishment and something for his pain. He saw the pain as part of his punishment for the damage to Jess.

He now sat alone as the news slowly but surely registered in his mind. What had he done to cause so much pain? His mind continually tried to make some sense of what was happening to him, but it only resulted in turmoil and guilt. It was all his fault. He had driven Sarah away. She had driven Sebastian away from him in retaliation. But this was cause and effect. He caused the original problem with Sarah, everything else was effect, and thus it was his fault. He was being called to account, and now he was responsible for the pain and damage to his lovely daughter. What had she done to deserve such pain? He, and only he, should be held accountable, and should pay the price.

He was where he had spent most of his nights since returning from hospital, sitting by his swimming pool with only the pool lights. The shimmering array of colour from the pool lining danced on the water, echoing the inferno flaming in the depths of his mind. Floating in the water was more comfortable for his ribs, and he found some peace.

When Audrey arrived in the morning, she would regularly find him asleep in a robe on a sunbed stacked with three layers of cushions and would quietly leave him his coffee as her gesture she was there for him. She had not had a single day off since that fateful night. Her place was with family in times of distress.

Jess would then go to give him her usual morning greeting trying to bring him back to her before leaving for the hospital. She knew he blamed himself for everything. She tried so hard to get through to him as she so wanted him back. Although she had fantastic support from her mother, Audrey and the hospital staff, this baby was their child, and she wanted her dad with her.

The house was silent. He slipped into the water. There was now another verse to the perpetual noise in his head 'Sebastian is dead. They found him hanging in his cell.' He could not take any more. His selfish ambition had hurt so many people. How could he wallow in his successes with so many damaged lives in his wake? He must pay for his folly. He turned onto his front, hoping to end it all. He wanted to pull himself deep into the water, but the wrenching pain as he tried to exert the power needed with his arms to pull himself under was too much to bear. He could not overcome his natural buoyancy whatever he tried. As a final desperate attempt, he just lay in the water, face down, but again the pressure on his ribs was too great to give him time to exhaust the air in his lungs. He felt his failure was a metaphor for his life. He had achieved so much superficial success, but had failed as a husband and father, and even as a son. *'My son and Sarah are dead. It's my fault. My selfish desire to be successful has destroyed those around me.'* He even reflected that he also deserted his mother and father during the years before his father could no longer recognise him, leaving his mother alone to handle the tragic deterioration of his father. Blind ambition had destroyed so much. And now he had failed to destroy himself, the least he could do to make amends.

He tried again and again until exhaustion and pain forced him to stop. Lying in the water, he wondered how he could ever face life again.

Chapter 94

Samantha had her story. She had worked diligently to dig into the past of Richard Lyons, and the revelations at the Registry for Births and Deaths made her tingle with satisfaction. She asked for a meeting with Tom Connors, her former editor, to vindicate herself. She sat smiling as he read her story, knowing she could fully support every detail revealed.

'Interesting story, and I assume you can fully support all the sordid detail.'

She responded with great satisfaction, 'Every last detail.'

'Are you expecting me to print this?' as he waved it at her.

'It's a great story and shows why Richard Lyons is so keen to maintain his privacy. I was right all along. Many skeletons in his closet. He's happy to profit from the fame, but not happy to reveal the pain caused to so many along the way.'

'Sam, what evidence do you have Richard Lyons has ever sought validation by the press for his work? He refused point blank for an interview regarding *"Pure Love"* or that dream house of his. I checked to see if we were too insignificant for him. He refused all interviews, even with the big boys. He does not seek publicity and clearly has no desire to be a celebrity.'

He thought for a moment 'Sam, I refuse to print this - on compassionate grounds. I assume you know he's still in a state of deep depression – and you must bear some of the responsibility for his state with your ill-consider revelations to him. I'm not about to reveal any of this. He has committed no crimes. I have no basis to destroy a family who only desire to put their lives back together after a very outrageous and tragic attack by a dislocated son. And there is no human-interest argument in your story. If you want to write a more general feature on the unintended consequences of blind ambition, then you have the makings of a good story, or even a book. But not for this paper. We are community driven – not assassins. What if the subjects of this story were in your family? Are you so desperate you would go to print for your own selfish ambitions? Would you then be guilty of the same blind ambition? From what I see Richard Lyons has realised and now paying the price of his past. He's trying to start again, and I'm not about to use this paper to destroy him.'

'Then I'm at liberty to take this story elsewhere?'

'I can't imagine any editor taking such a story. Lyons doesn't have public celebrity status, so who cares? National papers would not risk losing big advertising accounts as Lyons could easily influence such accounts, even now. He's still regarded a giant in advertising, and I hear is preparing to resume business.'

'You have showed your tenacity to get the story. You now need the maturity and good judgement regarding the consequences of printing stories where the people involved have committed no crime other than being human. Your father encouraged me to fire you. If you cannot appreciate why your own father took this position, you seriously need to examine your own moral compass.'

As he guided her out of his office, 'I don't know what you propose to do but I should warn you against trying for any local media role. As soon as your father informed me of the libellous nature of your story, I immediately notified all the local media outlets. Only one radio station had broadcast a brief item on their news. You must seek a career elsewhere until such time as you inject responsibility into your work. Goodbye Sam.'

Chapter 95

It was now some six weeks since the emergency caesarean. Since leaving hospital Jess had gone back every day, not least to keep her breast milk flowing and to provide milk for the hospital staff to feed to her baby. He was now out of danger and putting on weight. For the past week she had been breast feeding him at the hospital to ensure she could continue to feed him at home, and to bond with this determined baby.

She returned home as usual about 1pm to find her mother and Audrey in the kitchen fretting about what to do to bring Richard out of his depression.

'I have some good news, but I want to speak with daddy first. Where is he?' as she dumped her coat and her bag. She removed a folded piece of paper from her bag before she went through to the living room to find him. Audrey and Elizabeth, sensing something was about to happen, followed her at a discrete distance.

Since the news of the suicide of Sebastian eight days ago, he had sunken deeper into the abyss of depression. His external wounds had essentially healed, his broken ribs were no longer affecting his breathing, but the scars in his mind were still fully inflamed. No one could get any response from him. He had not shaved since that fateful night when Jess lost the ability to have any more children. His personal hygiene was erratic. He hardly slept or ate. He did not speak or respond to anyone, even Jim, who having returned from Australia, visited him every day to see if he could lift him. He just found some remote corner of the house or grounds, and sat blankly looking at the floor, totally consumed in his grief.

Every day, after returning from the hospital, Jess would find him, sit by his side to tell him the daily news about their son. Once this small foetus had won the battle for survival, she thought she detected some positive response from him. But the news about Sebastian pushed him deeper.

Today he was slouched in the living room. She looked at him. There was no way she could take him to his study. Her normal ritual for what she had to say to him was not possible because he was in an armchair, both of his arms on the arms of the chair. She could only sit on his lap. He did not make any movement, just continued looking at the floor. Daddy, I have some good news for you today, and I need you to listen. She turned her back into his shoulder so she could show him the paper she had in her hand. She opened it and lifted it so they both could see it.

'Daddy, can you read what is written on this certificate. It says that David Richard Lyons was born on 8th April 2013 to Jessica Lyons, mother; that's me, and Richard Lyons, father; that's you. We have a baby who wants to come home tomorrow and I need you to come with me to bring him home.'

Both Audrey and Elizabeth were holding each other in tears as they realised what Jess was saying but sensed not to interrupt.

Jess had spoken with her mother some weeks ago about naming Richard as the father, and she was very supportive. She felt Richard needed a new focus, and his new son was a good place to start. After all, he had brought her out of her darkness, so it was now for her to bring him out of his.

'Daddy, are you listening to me? I need you. Our baby wants to come home, here with us.'

He could hear a new sound in his head 'Daddy, I need you'. It was Jess. *'She needs me. Where are you, Jess?'*

She felt him lift his head. He looked at her, and then at the Birth Certificate. Through the blur in his mind, he could just make out the words.

She felt him put his arm around her waist. She turned to look at him. Tears were streaming out of his eyes. She held his face in her hands. With tears in her eyes, 'Daddy we have a baby who wants to come home, and I need you by my side.'

He collapsed into floods of tears as she held him tight. He wept like a baby. She had broken through his despair.

Finally, he looked up at her. He was trying to smile for the first time in weeks, albeit with tears clouding his eyes. 'Is he okay now?'

'He's great. A real bundle of joy. You'll love him.'

'And you want me to come with you after all the pain I've caused you?'

She looked him straight in the eyes and held his head so he must look into hers. She spoke slowly so every word would penetrate 'Daddy, you are my rock, and you are the most important person in my life. I need you to be with me tomorrow to bring our baby home.'

He looked over at Elizabeth who was still sitting in tears thinking *'My dearest Jess has done it, we have him back with us.'*

He motioned for Elizabeth to join them. They formed their triangle of love, forehead to forehead. Jess spoke slowly and firmly, 'we are a triangle of love, we have endured, and now we need to share our love with our new baby.' They all held tightly, and then he moved his head away so he could kiss both foreheads. His tears were still rolling down his cheeks into his ragged beard.

Elizabeth could not restrain herself any longer 'Richard, my darling, we have missed you so much. Please come back to us, we need you.'

Audrey finally came across. 'Can I join in with this wonderful news.' They made space for her to join their hugs.

Once things had settled for a while, he, somewhat pathetically, asked Jess what she needed him to do. Elizabeth very nearly interceded and then checked herself as she thought '*This is Jess's play, she has his attention, let her lead.*'

'First, we need to get you looking like a real Daddy, so mom and I will bathe and shave you, and get you into some clean clothes. Then you need to eat something. Either later today or in the morning, you need to fit the crib harnesses into my car.' Then she playfully wagged her finger at him, 'And early to bed for you tonight. You have a big day tomorrow.'

Elizabeth sat back in joyful amusement at what she witnessed. She hadn't really thought about how the loss of David had affected Jess because she was away at university at the time of his death, and he had made little time for her in years. But she could see Jess needed a father figure in her life, and these two needed each other.

Finally, Elizabeth decided action was needed. 'Richard, how do you feel? Are your ribs still hurting you?'

He looked at her pitifully, 'I'm okay.'

'Then you come with me to the changing room shower. Jess, go get his shaving kit from our bathroom.'

Audrey said she would go organise his favourite food. She had read somewhere that when prisoners went on hunger strike the best way to break it was to get a superb chef to make their favourite food such that they could smell the aromas. His favourite food was a good English breakfast, and she knew how to fill the kitchen with all the right aromas.

When they got to the changing room, they stripped him of his grubby clothes before undressing themselves. This was as much an expression of love as it was a cleansing exercise, so they applied both shower heads, starting with his hair and then working down his body. When they were finished Elizabeth placed a stool under the shower, sat him on it, and then straddled his legs armed with his wet razor. She turned to Jess and asked her to go phone Susan, his hairdresser of choice, and ask her if she would come to the house this evening as he seriously needs a haircut. 'Offer her dinner, if necessary, but get her here.'

As she was adjusting herself to make space for her to shave his chin, she felt herself slipping from this lap. He cupped her bottom with his hands as though instinctively knowing her dilemma. She felt his hands steady her and smiled at him. *'He's coming back to me.'*

After every hair of his bedraggled beard had been removed, she put him back under the shower to rinse him off, dried him and herself, and dressed both in robes and Crocs.

As they entered the kitchen, the smell of smoked bacon and sausages filled their nostrils. Richard responded with instant pangs of hunger. He sat at the table salivating at what was being prepared for him. He ate heartily for the first time since that fateful night.

After he had eaten, all four of them went through to the living room to discuss the arrangements for tomorrow. The nursery had been readied for over a week, and Jess was already installed in the former guest suite. He sat in an armchair and quietly glided into a peaceful sleep. At first the women did not notice. Audrey saw him first. He had a smile on his face. She quietly suggested they regroup in the kitchen and let him sleep.

Chapter 96

After some two hours he awoke and went to the kitchen for something to drink. The women were still chatting. He asked if he could have some tea. Elizabeth got up from the table and told Audrey to defer the tea until after they had a swim. Jess got up to join them but was quickly halted when Audrey put her hand on hers. Jess looked at Audrey, who was displaying a knowing look. 'Wise old owl' she thought as she put her free hand on top of Audrey's hand to show she understood they needed some time alone together.

'Perhaps we should try to express more of your milk to add to our store if you feel ready. That little mite will soon demand more and more milk, so the more we have in store the better.'

Elizabeth took his hand and led him off to the swimming pool. 'You need to get your bag of bones moving again so you and I will have a pleasant swim.'

They dropped their robes on the diving board and walked down the steps into the water until it was up to her shoulders. 'Okay, my darling, let us see if you can remember how this works.'

He looked at her, bemused. He was feeling somewhat better. Little did she realise he had used the pool in the night during the past weeks. Little did she know, after hearing the news about Sebastian, he had tried to drown himself on two separate occasions.

He started to swim, and she stayed by his side. When she felt he was getting into his stride, she asked him to wait for her. He planted his feet on the floor of the pool and let her get close enough to put her arms around his neck. 'Next phase, my darling. Close your eyes.'

He complied as she kissed him. 'If that was nice, my darling, and you want more, you must chase me around this pool and take your reward. After each kiss, you must give me to the count of three to let me get away again.' She swam off.

He chased her around the pool until she was exhausted. She swam to the side of the pool and placed her hands on the poolside for support. She felt him draw near and put his hand around her waist, kissing her shoulder. After planting his feet on the bottom of the pool, he slowly moved his hands up to her breasts, caressing gently. She leaned back into him as a demonstration she wanted more. After a few minutes, he turned her around to face him. 'Do I get a bigger kiss for that?'

Their kiss was long and warm as they hugged each other. 'Hello my darling. It's so good to have you back.'

'It's so good to feel you close to me. I have felt so alone and desperate these past weeks. Thank you for being patient with me. I don't deserve you, any of you.'

'My darling, you have been to hell and back. But you felt our love for you, and you came back to us. It's we who need you in our lives. We all love you so much, and your love for me has transformed my whole being. You have been into the darkness of despair, now it is time to walk back into the sunshine and be our guiding light.' She kissed him again. 'Come, let us shower and get on with the rest of our lives. We have much to do, and much joy to share.'

Chapter 97

Richard was up early. He had obeyed his No.2 mistress and gone to bed around 10pm, albeit with Elizabeth in his arms. They held each other close and stroked each other until he fell asleep. She felt so good to have him back in bed with her. She had so missed the closeness they shared.

There was a dew and a sharpness in the air, but the sky was blue, and the birds were singing. When he arrived in the kitchen, Audrey was already busying herself like a headless chicken. 'What are you doing here this early in the morning?'

'Couldn't sleep. We're going to have a baby in the house. I'm so excited. I must make sure we have everything we need. I must make a list and go shopping.'

She was really flapping. 'Please Audrey, make some coffee and come and sit with me before the others arrive.'

'Audrey, I'm so sorry about the past few weeks. I must have been a real pain in the arse.'

She reached for his hand. 'Richard, my dearest Richard. I have never seen anyone in so much pain and despair in my life. If anything, you scared me. But Jess was brilliant yesterday. She loves you so much, and the beautiful bundle of joy you have given to her; to all of us. You told me when we came here we're family in this house, but we had no idea what you really meant. Now we know, and it's a privilege for both of us to be part of this family. We don't have any grandchildren yet, but I now have the equivalent with young David. I'm really looking forward to having him home. Both Gerry and I are blessed to be part of this. So be a pain in the arse occasionally if need be, but we're here for you.'

He felt himself welling up inside. '*What a wonderful family I have,*' he thought. 'Thank you, Audrey. You're a rock, and I'm so grateful you're here.'

He paused 'but I can't stop blaming myself for what happened to Jess, and even to Sarah and Sebastian. Why did I cause so much pain, and then so openly welcome that boy back before seeing his true nature?'

'Stop this, Richard. You did what any good father would have done. It was Sarah who used Sebastian to seek her revenge on you, and he was so confused after your kindness to him. From what Gerry heard in Court he got the impression both you and Sarah did not manage your marriage very well.

Had Sarah not alienated Sebastian, and you had maintained contact, you may have realised you could have possibly repaired your marriage. You didn't seek an alternative relationship, and apparently Sarah could not find a replacement for you. She chose, instead, to use Sebastian for revenge, so there was no chance of reconciliation. But that's the past, and you can do nothing about it. Now you must focus on young David – such a bonnie little boy.'

'You've seen him?'

'Yes, of course. When Jess came home, she could not drive to the hospital herself because she could not wear seat belts.' She realised this could trigger a poor response so immediately deflected him. 'This is normal for any woman after childbirth. Elizabeth and I took it in turns to take her to care for David. Jess is right. He fought for survival and is a bundle of joy. Now you need to concentrate on the future of this little baby, and the wonderful family around him. You are the man of the house. We all look to you.'

'But enough of this, Richard. We both have an important day ahead, so let's get to it. You need to fit the crib harnesses in the car. They're over there with the instructions. Go to it.'

'The more nervous she gets, the bossier she is' he thought. *'How difficult can it be to fit harnesses?'* It didn't take long to find out.

The exasperation he felt induced him to walk off his frustration through the gardens including the walled garden so lovingly nurtured by Gerry. Surrounded by new life flourishing around him calmed his troubled mind. *'Life renews and goes on relentlessly'* he thought as he returned to the kitchen seeking breakfast.

Chapter 98

Jess had agreed with the hospital to collect young David around 10am. When she came down to breakfast, she looked radiant. As was always the case in the past, her beaming smile and good morning kiss lifted his spirits. Tears filled his eyes as he recalled how proud he is of his beautiful daughter.

Elizabeth had encouraged Richard to wear slacks and a jacket, albeit he won the right to put a tee-shirt under the jacket. She had to admit it made him look younger, and it was so good to see him smiling again he could have gotten away with anything. Susan had done a wonderful job on his hair. She was happy to see he looked the part he was asked to play today.

Elizabeth elected to accompany them, so had to quickly sneak away during breakfast to call Jim to appraise him of Richard's awakening, and the imminent arrival home of young David. *'He's family'*, she thought so invited him to lunch to wet the baby's head. He was overjoyed at such wonderful news.

As their drive home was close to an hour in traffic, the nurse suggested Jess give David a good feed before starting for home. Richard watched with such pride as Jess nurtured her little bundle. Elizabeth could see his reaction. They were a complete family again, and she was so happy with life.

When they arrived home Audrey, Gerry, Jim with Brandy, Margaret, and Robert were waiting outside. For once Richard broke his rule and parked outside the front door. As soon as they released the crib from its harness, and safely in the hands of Jess, eagerly surrounded by the others, Richard went to Jim. No words were needed; they hugged each other as would long-lost brothers. The dark clouds of the past had cleared. This new life would bind this family together. *'Never again will I let the past influence my responsibility towards this wonderful family'*, he silently vowed to himself, *'nor will I ever again put work before family'*. Life would only get better for all of them.

Milton Keynes UK
Ingram Content Group UK Ltd.
UKHW020255111023
430276UK00012BA/134